Higher Ground

The spiritual quest of one of
America's Boomer Generation

Charlotte Crabaugh

authorHOUSE®

AuthorHouse™
1663 Liberty Drive
Bloomington, IN 47403
www.authorhouse.com
Phone: 1-800-839-8640

First published by AuthorHouse 07/01/2011

ISBN: 978-1-4567-3739-9 (sc)
ISBN: 978-1-4567-3738-2 (e)

Printed in the United States of America

Charles Cartwright, Cover Design

This book is printed on acid-free paper.

HIGHER GROUND

Dream - Oct. 24, 1973, Thurs. new moon, David's parents were visiting us.

David and his parents and I were all sitting outside on the road just by the dome, looking at the Milky Way. It was extremely thick and filmy looking. I exclaimed at how thick it was. Then I noticed that the stars were very large, and they began to get larger and brighter, until they were so large I could see the colors of them and their moons, and rings around some. They kept getting larger and brighter. At first the colors on them were pale and hazy. But as they got larger, the continents became visible and the colors were incredible in intensity with every hue and color imaginable. As they began to grow larger, I exclaimed that this was exactly like a dream I had once, but this was astonishing because it definitely was not a dream. I actually thought about it, and considered hard whether or not it was a dream, and was emphatically sure that it was real.

The planets came closer. The colors of their continents were astounding and vibrant. They were bright yellow, turquoise, green, maroon, purple. They were not only primary colors, but mostly what I would call off-shades, like magenta and teal and others. They were every color and the sky was blackest black.

One planet covered the entire sky and I saw that the bright yellow continent was the shape of North America. The next one was even more enormous and then I could see the surface of it. There was a large area like the surface of the moon or like a desert. There were three airplanes crashed in it. There was a wide gap like a deep canyon separating this from the next area, which was a large grassland with all kinds of animals living wild in it. They were animals almost or completely extinct now; bison, elephants, rhinos, elk and so on. The animals were unaware of the area of the airplanes or of the planes, and the planes were unaware of the animals and were unable to get to them. They had crashed when trying to discover them.

Then I saw huge cliffs with roaring water crashing at the bottom. The water was rising and crashing higher and higher. There were animals at the bottom trying to climb up the rocks, out of reach of the water. They were a little like goats, only more magnificent. (they were Dahl Sheep). I watched one and urged it on, "come on, come on up." It climbed up and it looked back at the water every time it got out of reach to see if it needed to come any further. It seemed not to want to leave the rocks below. It didn't want to come to the top of the cliffs, but every time it stopped and looked back the water crashed higher and forced it finally to the top. At some point in this struggle it began to seem that I was the goat and there were voices out in the darkness urging me up the cliff, as I had been for the goat at first. Constantly calling out, "Go on, you're almost there. Go on, you can make it."; giving me hope, keeping me going.

As the beast climbed up I looked right into his face. It was very fierce and almost human. It seemed very frightened to be coming to the top, but it was so fierce I don't know what could have hurt it.

As soon as it was to the top it changed immediately into a man. It was hairy and still resembled very much the animal, but it was human. As soon as it realized it was standing on

two feet it got down on all four, as if it would rather be an
animal and the man ran away on his hands and feet.

Wonder and awe has never been greater than when I opened my eyes and saw the sunlight on every surface in the trailer where David and I slept. My first words were incredulous. "It <u>was</u> a dream! But it was real!" Turning to David, "You will never believe what happened to me, what I've seen. It was real. It really happened !!"

I told him all of it. He listened and was amazed. He understood. He knew. It was a dream of transformation.

All through my life, for the past thirty seven years, I have pondered the meaning of this dream. It has been my constant companion, like a muse holding a lantern with a strange light. It seemed clear that the goat was the very image of struggling against something. But more than that, to get to a higher, or better place. The first thing I thought was that it was about improving my life conditions. It was just before I started back to college to finish my degree. I had the thought that it would be very difficult and I would need to persevere. Again, when I was in seminary, I had the same interpretation. These understandings were right as far as they went. But the meaning was more than just trying to improve my present life's conditions. It was about becoming all my Creator meant for me to become.

I thought of the three crashed airplanes as several endeavors I had tried and failed. Every time I had another job or career choice that didn't work out I thought of the crashed airplanes. At one point I thought they were my dream of being a teacher, my marriage, and our experiment of making a life on the north forty.

As time went on there got to be way more than three 'airplanes', or dashed dreams and unsuccessful new starts. And what did the planets and all the magnificent colors mean?

At the time of this writing my understanding of the dream has grown to this. The planets were telling me that I was leaving my old way of being in the world. My consciousness was expanding to take in things I had not been aware of. In a very real sense I was going to go to places in my mind that I had not known were there. The animals were old habits of thought, life and consciousness I was not even aware of, but which I needed to discover. The exact number of the airplanes was not important, just that there had been more than one attempt, maybe many attempts, to become more than I was.

Finally one animal, me, decided to make a run for it. It decides to go higher, no matter what it takes to get to higher ground. The rock cliff is my will that is being used to go higher. The water rising higher and crashing up on the rocks is the turbulence of the subconscious mind trying to force the animal to a greater awareness of Reality. It keeps looking back because it is hard to change and it really doesn't want to leave what is familiar, but the water keeps rising. It is either go higher or drown.

My entire journey has been about learning to listen to the voice within. It doesn't matter if I call it God, or the Holy Spirit, Universal Intelligence, Inner Self or any of a dozen other names. It is all the same. Every new venture has been for the purpose of finding my true purpose, following my dharma, or true path. That is the goat relentlessly ascending the cliff.

The end, in which the human animal returns to the beast position and dashes off on all fours, is still a mystery to me. Perhaps, as one friend suggested, it is time for a new dream, in which the human animal spreads wings and flies off into regions undreamed of.

The words of this old hymn have become the theme of my life.

Voices must have been singing it when the mountain goat was scaling that bluff in the monumental dream I had. I've thought of it many times, that animal, pressing onward, upward every time I was faced with new evidence that the Truth I want to find is there, just one more foothold higher. The beliefs I was taught as a child were only half truths, like seeing through a glass darkly. I have been rubbing at the glass, trying to see more clearly. I wanted so much to believe everything I was being told, but it never made sense. Many times I found a piece of the Truth, came a little closer. When I discovered A Course In Miracles, the words of Christ made it clear to me. It was as if then I reached the higher plane. I stand and raise my arms to heaven and rejoice.

The words of this hymn are a description of my sojourn on this earth.

HIGHER GROUND
Johnson Oatman, Jr.

I'm pressing on the upward way,
New heights I'm gaining every day-
Still praying as I'm onward bound,
"Lord, plant my feet on higher ground."

Chorus
Lord, lift me up and let me stand
By faith on heaven's tableland;
A higher plane than I have found-
Lord, plant my feet on higher ground.

My heart has no desire to stay
Where doubts arise and fears dismay;
Tho some may dwell where these abound,
My prayer, my aim, is higher ground."

I want to live above the world,
Tho fear around me swirl,
For faith has caught the joyful sound,
The song of saints on higher ground."

I want to scale the utmost height
And catch a gleam of glory bright;
But still I'll pray till heaven I've found,
"Lord, lead me on to higher ground."

DEDICATION

To Charmaine Noelle Crabaugh and David Charles Crabaugh, without whom there would be no story.

Thanks to Charles Cartwright for contributing to my wonderful cover design

To Sue Baggett-Spears and the People of Christ Church Unity, Springfield, Missouri, who have been the voices urging me on to Higher Ground.

Table of Contents

MISSOURI (Missourah)

A SENSE OF PLACE has always been very important to me. I have always loved the out of doors and since the out of doors was always my home state of Missouri I loved everything familiar about it. There is no tropical paradise that can bring joys to the heart like a day in May especially after a hard winter. On those glorious days when the sky is as blue as eternity, the sun is warm, the birds have returned from wherever they go in the winter and are filling the air with their songs of joy at being alive it is then that I realize if we had not endured the cold harshness of winter we would not be aware of the resplendence of spring.

Every season has its own particular beauty and I have always reveled in each one. I think I learned from my father's example, who only seemed to come fully alive when he was in the woods or even in the garden at our house in town. For him the noise and traffic of cities was only something to be endured. Our Dad was definitely a county boy and really wanted to be a farmer, but he didn't know how to do that and make it possible for us to live comfortably so he contented himself with being in nature whenever he could.

On the north forty we would sit and listen to the chorus of whippoorwills calling to each other at dusk. In the long hot summer afternoons the mournful sound of mourning doves could fill me with a longing I didn't understand. I learned at an early age how to imitate the cheerful call of the Bob Whites. The deer, turkeys and other wildlife were thick on Dad's little spot of ground. He was not a hunter but often he would return in the evening and tell of seeing a doe and her fawn or a ten point buck or a large gathering of turkeys. With a sparkle in his eyes, and very unlike a hunter, he would say, "I wish I'd had my camera".

Even though I've spent most of my life in towns and cities the rural scenes of Missouri have always seemed the most familiar and the most like home. The rocky red clay roads of the south part of the state, the neat well manicured farms of the north, the clear rushing streams we loved to float and the dense mystery of the Mark Twain forest are only a few of the treasures I hold dear.

In recent years a controversy has surfaced regarding the proper way to pronounce Missouri. I did not know that there was another way to say Missourah until my family moved to Springfield when I was in junior high. When I heard anyone saying it in a way that greatly resembled 'misery', I just figured they had come from somewhere else and didn't know any better. Even after all the discussion I think I may have been right about that. Missourah is the old way that rural Missourians say it. It speaks to the heart. When you listen to the sound of the words it is clear that the ahh is a soft affectionate relaxing sound. It speaks volumes about love and home. It has a comfort to it like mother and warmth on a cold night. People who love our state still call her with affection, Missourah because of the feeling it evokes. As for the argument that 'i' is not pronounced ah, well I guess you just need to change the spelling.

MY FATHER

THERE IS ONE WORD that everyone who ever knew my Father would use to describe him. Quiet. He never spoke much. But there are also plenty of other words to describe him. Gentle, hard-working, practical, honest, stable, to name a few. He was a man of integrity, a solid Presence in our lives. We all called him Daddy long into adulthood.

Daddy worked at the Missouri State Highway Dept. as a highway designer/ draftsman. When we lived in Willow Springs he came home every day at noon for lunch and took a nap before heading back to the office. He had a lot of headaches, the awful migraine kind. Mother said the office atmosphere bothered him because of the cigarette and cigar smoke and loud language from his co-workers. But I think the real reason for his headaches was that he would have really liked to spend all his days outside. Smoky air is even worse when what you really long for is the clear open air. Other peoples' language is meaningless already, but his ears welcomed the songs of birds and rustlings of the wind in grass and leaves. He wasn't a muscular man, just small and wiry, but he loved physical activity. To be moving about under the sun, in the wind or cold; building, making, planting, looking for arrowheads, of which he had a magnificent collection. That's what he lived for.

Sometime back in the 1930's, long before I was born, my father bought forty acres of rough uncivilized Ozarks land, next to my grandparents' forty acres. He always called it the 'north forty'. We would go there to cut down a spindly, fragrant cedar tree every Christmas, and pick blackberries in July and persimmons in the fall, or just go down by the pond and throw little rocks to make the bullfrogs jump. It was a place that was always there, just waiting for us whenever we had time for it. There have been times when I needed to be healed from the craziness of the world, and I went there for healing. When my parents retired they finally had time for it and went there to live. I've called many places home and had to leave them all, but the 'north forty' was always there to go home to.

He was a farm boy and had wanted to live on the 'north forty', just north of his parents' 'south forty' near Cabool. However my Mother was able to persuade him that subsistence farming just wasn't the life she had in mind for her and her daughters. As much as I, too, love the country I think my sisters and I are grateful to her for putting her foot down early on about that when I think of the poverty we could have endured. But possibly Dad was an intelligent enough man that he didn't really need that much persuading about how to best care for his family.

In spring and summer Daddy was always out in the garden every minute that he could be. One evening when I was about five I woke from sleeping in the dark house at about dusk. I must have been ill. It was silent. No one was there. I didn't know where anyone was although I think my Mother and Janie and Judy were at church and Daddy was out in the garden. I drifted into the front room from my parents room and there under the desk was crouched a dark, furry creature. I was terrified. I screamed and screamed at the top of my lungs. Daddy

4

came racing in the front door and swept me into his arms. I will never forget the safety, knowing that everything was all right; nothing was going to get me. In his own relief he had to control his amusement when he realized that I was mistaking the dark under the desk for a monster. And that was one of the very few times my Daddy ever hugged me.

Our favorite photo of Dad is one taken by Uncle Irvin, out on the north forty. Here is a small, slightly weathered old man, hands in pockets, finely chiseled features turned up and a bit to the left, in a distinctly listening pose. His attitude is one of rapt attention to something wonderful he is hearing. A grand sweep of forehead crowns the large blue eyes, focused on something out of sight, far up in the branches of one of the small oaks seen in the background. The ground all around seems to crunch back at you, completely covered with golden brown oak and hickory leaves. He's wearing a flannel shirt, a yellowed sweater, buttoned at the waist, topped with a blue denim jacket that may have originally been a woman's. The jacket is covered with paint and tears. Shabby and glorious in his refusal to listen to any other drummer than his own.

MOTHER

MOTHER WAS THE ENERGY in the family. All the time we were growing up it felt like she set the rules and all the economic, educational, artistic, moral and religious limits were set by her. But now I realize that Dad's influence was more subtle, but every bit as strong. Mom could be warm, funny, entertaining, intelligent and compassionate. And she often was, all these and more.

My Mother, Evelyn Kay, was one of a Scotts-Irish family of seven girls and two boys reared in the beautiful Ozarks hills in places that no longer exist. She told tales of a drunken father, who came home and sang "When the Roll is Called Up Yonder" while sitting at the kitchen table, drinking himself into oblivion. Her mother, Grandma Tilda, was the daughter of a preacher. All Mom seemed to remember from her childhood was hardship and deprivation. Her parents finally divorced, which was almost unheard of here in the Ozarks region in the early part of the 20th century. She always felt scarred by poverty, a drunken father and a 'broken family'.

She came away from all that with a fierce fundamental religiosity that was not shared by any of her brothers and sisters, or even by many of our Baptist friends. She was a 'hard-shell Baptist'. Alongside all her warm and endearing qualities Mother was a controlling woman. It never occurred to me as a child that my Mother could be afraid of anything. Confronted by the most fierce dragon, she would stoically glare it down without faltering. Yet it was her deep seated fears that drove her to control us with her temper and threats, usually along the lines of withholding love. She wanted us to be righteous, pure and most especially, 'good Christians'. She wanted many other things for us as life unfolded, but other things could be compromised on as long as our salvation was secure. Her belief was that to be righteous was to be safe; if not in this life, then certainly in the life to come.

The grim birth story that was told of our Mother's birth was related by our aunts as well as Mother. When the doctor was summoned to their house for the delivery he had been drinking some, enough to impair his judgment. Mother was the first of two identical twins born, but she was not breathing. The doctor laid her aside, thinking she was stillborn, and gave his attention to the birth of the second twin. However, Mom's Aunt Gertie was present. She took the baby Evelyn, and thrust her into ice water, which startled her into not just breathing, but huge gasps, I'm sure. Aunt Gertie was always considered the heroine of Mother's life and she was given her name, Gertrude, as her middle name. But can you imagine such an introduction to life on this planet? Is it any wonder Evelyn always surveyed the world with a suspicious, distrustful eye.

I learned religion at church, the Bible stories, hymns, the atmosphere of a church community, but it was Mother who taught us that God was to be feared. She rehashed the preacher's sermon at the dinner table after church, complete with shouts and table pounding. And so, she was truly the first woman preacher that I knew. It was she who taught me that God could see and knew everything I did or even thought. So I became very wary of even my own thoughts. God was out to get me. I was really grateful for Jesus, who loved me, but alas, every time I thought a 'bad' thought I drove a nail into his hands. In my mind, Mother was the personification of God. In later years the discussion of God's gender would arise. I really preferred God as 'Father'. The feminists probably thought I was just being backward again.

I believe that Mom and Dad both had the idea that it would spoil a child, to express pride in them. They didn't understand that withholding praise was at least as harmful. Mom was often demanding, but never expressed satisfaction with our performance. We didn't receive a lot of affection either.

I probably would have called her Momma forever, but my sisters started calling her Mom when they were older, so I went along with the crowd. We loved her, even when we feared her. I believe that is how she kept us so well behaved; not with just fear, but the fear of love withheld. Nothing was worse than Momma withholding her love. When Momma was upset, after the raging torrents of condemnation and threats had ceased there was silence. As far as I was concerned there was nothing to be done except to escape outdoors, which I usually did as soon after the storm began as possible, leaving it to my two older sisters to deal with. I felt that it was usually aimed at them, anyway, or at least something or someone other than me. Before we reached adolescence, whenever we had done something we shouldn't, although now I can't think of what any of those things were, Mother would send us outside to get a stick with the sharp command, "Go get a stick". That was part of the punishment, going to get the stick that you would be hit with. It had to be big enough, or you would just have to go back and then it might be twice as bad. However, I don't remember that she ever actually spanked us. It was as if just going

8

after a stick at all was punishment enough. Sometimes she would say, "Just wait until your Dad gets home". That wasn't much of a threat. I would be relieved when he got home. He might raise his voice and scold, also, and that was bad enough. Neither one of them was a strict disciplinarian in the usual sense. I remember Daddy spanking me once when my Aunt Martha and her family was there to visit, because I said, "Shit" (which Mom said all the time). I cried like a stuck pig and Mom and Aunt Marg comforted me.

In Willow Springs there was a tradition of a Fall Fiesta with a parade, and a coronation of king and queen from each grade. Each grade elected a king and queen candidate who got to ride on the class float and be in the coronation ceremony. It remains one of the great honors of my life to this day, that my class elected me the queen candidate in the fourth grade. I floated home to relay this incredible news to my mother, unable to contain my joy. To my everlasting dismay, never able to get it right, the news was greeted with groans and a torrent of complaints. She was going to have to make a costume, and be responsible for this and that. No one had asked her if she wanted her daughter to participate in all this godless folly. I ducked out the back door while she was still going. Nothing could change the fact that my class had actually voted for me! I was receiving affirmation outside the family circle.

She seemed to recover in the days that followed. I got to wave to my classmates and the crowd from the float, riding with the king, Jimmy Johnson, dressed as a witch, of all things, putting votes in the cauldron. The class that could sell the most votes got to see their candidates receive the crown at the coronation. The school was divided into categories, grades 1-4, 5-8 and high school. Jimmy and

I were crowned in our category and I got a big bouquet of marigolds. I still remember taking the crown off and giving it back to the superintendent after the ceremony, because that is what Mother told me to do.

Outside of our family, other people saw Mom as a quiet person, almost as quiet as Dad. She taught Sunday school and Bible School in the summer, was counselor at camp, sang in the choir, and was active in the Baptist women's missionary union. Her life revolved around us and the church. There wasn't much other opportunity for any other outlet in Willow Springs in the '50's even if she had been inclined to seek it out. She often felt pent-up, wanted to see her sisters more often and felt unappreciated. Daddy was just an average guy when it came to being romantic or being emotionally present for anyone. That was his weakness; he was emotionally distant. Every once in awhile Mom would get very stirred up and say that she was going to leave and go to her sister's in Kansas City. This was her identical twin sister, Aunt Martha. Dad would say, "Let her go". He even bought her a big suitcase for her birthday once. I guess he knew that wouldn't last long, and didn't mind if she wanted to go visit. Aunt Martha's husband, Uncle Irving, was the polar opposite of our Dad. He was loud and scary; very macho and authoritarian. I guess the two of them wouldn't last long under the same roof but to us children her leaving was a very serious and frightening possibility. We would discuss among ourselves whether we would go with Mom or stay with Daddy. Janie would go with her, Judy and I would elect to stay with Daddy.

But Momma was always there. We didn't ever know which version of her we would get from day to day, if she would be calm and understanding, funny and entertaining, or angry and frightening. But there was always some kind of meal at breakfast, dinner and supper. We always got baths on Saturday night and clean sheets and clothes. After we got the TV in 1954 sometimes she would come in after watching some show I didn't stay up for, and wake me up to put my hair up in bobby pin curls for church while I struggled to wake up enough to sit up straight. That was the other thing we could always count on. She gave us permanents about once a year and rolled our hair up in pin curls every Saturday night. Our preacher, Brother Gentry, always remarked on her 'beautiful girls'.

We loved to hear Daddy read to us, as he did sometimes, especially the funnies on Sunday morning. But Mom's stories were off the cuff, from memory or made up, with voices of the three bears or the Billy goats gruff; and then there was that scary one about the 'telepole', which ended in a shout.

Momma was angry a lot. She passed that anger on to each of us. We tried, over the years to understand the source of it or the cure for it. We came to many tentative conclusions. However, I believe now, that a religion that teaches you that you are a guilty sinner and need to be punished, surely gives rise to much of the depression in our society.

Some believe that when we are still non-physical souls, in eternity with Our Source, we choose the parents we will be born to; the ones who will teach us the lessons we are sent to learn. I am glad I chose the parents and the sisters I have had. They helped construct this intriguing life I have lived.

GRANDMA WRIGHT

M Y GRANDPARENTS FARM WAS one of my favorite places. We went there almost every Saturday or Sunday. My Grandpa Wright died when I was about five but I recall the small, wizened man, who reminded me of a dwarf in some of my fairy tale books. He had a long white beard down to his waist. He never said much, at least not to us kids, but he always seemed amused by us, with what seemed to be the small beginning of a smile. He usually just sat in a large padded chair with a straight back, and a footstool in front. No one else ever sat in Grandpa's chair. He became ill briefly and he and Grandma came to stay at our house for a few days. I wasn't allowed to go upstairs to see them and had to stay very quiet. It rained the day of the funeral and they lowered him with some kind of cranks into the grave. It was the only time I ever saw my Grandma cry.

My Grandpa's name was Charles Daniel Wright. Grandma mentioned to Mother that he was related to the Wright brothers, Orville and Wilbur. No one has ever done a genealogy so that is still hearsay; however, everything I have ever read or heard about that family fits. If so, he was of English descent. He did not stay in touch with any of his relatives at all.

My father, Charles Willard Wright was the middle of five children. He had a brother and a sister older and a brother and sister younger. Grandma always called him by his middle name, Willard, to distinguish him from her husband, Charles.

My Grandma, Mary Angeline Wright seemed like a kindred spirit to me. She and Daddy and I were all Pisces, my birthday on February 22, being the day before hers, on February 23 and Daddy's' two weeks later on March 8. She grew up in Arkansas with a tight knit family who always kept in touch with a family letter that they circulated around from one to the other, each adding on until it came back to the eldest. Her father was of French descent, that is, the French who settled in Missouri and Arkansas in the 1800's, and her mother of Cherokee.

Grandma was the soft, plump counterpart to Grandpa. She was rounded, with a soft lap like Grandmas should have, and a soft, friendly chuckle. She would spread out her arms in a welcoming hug to greet us with a smile whenever we came to visit. She grew flowers all around their little frame house including daffodils, snapdragons, peonies, tiger lilies, honeysuckle, hollyhocks and Sweet Williams. She had round rocks which she had brought from her home in Arkansas that she used for making a border around the snapdragons. They were geodes, but were never split open to reveal the beautiful formations that were surely inside. They were interesting enough, just being such nicely shaped, perfect round rocks.

Grandma was a master crafts woman. One of her most outstanding accomplishments was her painting. She reproduced pictures from jigsaw puzzle boxes or calendars or postcards by drawing a grid of squares all over the picture and a larger grid of squares on the cardboard canvass she would reproduce it on. She used oil paints and did a really first rate job of copying. We each still have some of her paintings in our homes. But Grandma was also handy with many other skills. She could wire the bottoms of chairs that were getting loose, together so that they were very strong. When I was grown I took her rocking chair to be refinished. The refinisher took out the wires that she had fastened across the bottom rungs. The chair was never as strong again because his wood gluing was just not as solid as her wiring job. She made the best butter, from the milk of their cows, and big thick shortbread cookies, which she often even put icing on. There were hooked rugs she had made from scraps, and a curtain between the front room and bedroom that was made from milk filters. It is said that she also laid the wood groove flooring in the front room of their little farmhouse because, in Mother's words, "she couldn't get any of the men folk to do it, so she did it herself". I can really relate to this Grandmother.

Once or twice I went to stay a few days with Grandma and Uncle Deb after we moved to Cabool. I loved the country and wandering all over the forty acres. I helped her with mopping the floor and getting things from the garden. Grandma died when I was in my first year of high school. She was in the Texas County Hospital in Houston for a few days. I always remember the nurse saying I had her eyes. I hope I have more than that.

UNCLE DEB

D ADDY'S BACHELOR BROTHER, DELBERT, lived with Grandma and Grandpa and then just Grandma after Grandpa died. Everyone called him Deb, and he was Uncle Deb to us. He was a tall, slender, quiet man with a gentle smile. I felt comfortable around him. Sometimes he would try to engage us in a bit of conversation. He had a way of speaking, very rapidly and like he had cotton in his mouth. He was often hard to understand. I remember his twinkling eyes when he would throw his head back slightly with a short, soft laugh. Everyone in the area around knew him because he was the electronic fix-it man. He repaired radios and later, TVs. He was also good with cb radios when they were popular. He built a special shed to hold all the TVs people brought him. Sometimes they would bring him one that wasn't working and just leave it for parts, because he certainly did get a huge collection of them. After Grandma died the television sets just took over the house. There were TVs on the kitchen table and cabinets and on all the chairs. He brought in extra tables and chairs to set them on. You could hardly walk from one room to the next for all the TVs crammed into a small space.

Uncle Deb carried around a small pocket-sized can of Prince Albert cigarette tobacco. To this day, whenever I see one of those small, red Prince Albert cans with the flip up lid in an antique store I think of him, with a smile. He could roll a cigarette by sprinkling some tobacco onto a cigarette rolling paper and deftly rolling it one-handed. In the sixties when my husband, David, met him, I didn't think to alert him of this characteristic of my Uncle's. Of all the qualities one could choose to admire about this man, watching him roll a cigarette was all it took to elevate him to god-like proportions in David's eyes, which almost popped out the first time he saw it.

Like Grandma, Uncle Deb could fix almost anything. I guess between them, they never had to buy anything new. This family was extremely frugal, which may have been the reason Deb rolled his own cigarettes. He carried a screwdriver in his back pocket and impressed David again when he whipped it out in a timely fashion to fix whatever presented itself. He had an old John Deere tractor, which may have been one of the first ever made. You could hear it chugging for miles, but I don't think anyone was ever able to keep it running after Deb died.

When we were small, Judy and I liked to ride in the wooden milk cart with the milk cans, to the barn where Deb milked the cows. It was worn smooth from so many years of bumping along with the cans. He had a generator to provide power for a small milking machine. We watched him attach the cylindrical suction cups to the cows' teats and listen to the milk come squirting out into the can with a pinging sound. The generator was so loud you could hear it all over the farm, so there wasn't much conversation. Usually there were barn cats, which wouldn't let us come near them, but would come out for warm milk that Deb would give them. They lived on warm cows milk and mice. However, there were two other very special pets at Grandma and Uncle Debs. The large, curly-haired dog named Brownie, and Grandma's big yellow cat, Whiskers.

Delbert Wright was possibly the most honest person I ever met. He and my father were men of integrity, who are rare these days. Working was about all they knew how to do, except for fishing occasionally. I believe his brother was probably my Dad's best friend. Deb was the only person I saw Daddy talk to for long stretches at a time. Their talk was about how things work, what it took to fix something, the cows - one got out, one got sick, how much milk, all those everyday things.

Uncle Deb wouldn't go to church with Grandma, to the little one room white Pleasant View Methodist Church down the road by the cemetery, where Grandma played the organ on Sundays. But I believe he was as near to the heart of God as anyone I ever knew.

JANICE FAYE

WHEN I WAS BORN in Kansas City my oldest sister, Janice was already five years old. She always retained some memories of living there. We called her Janie (that is Jan-ee), until she was thirty something and put her foot down about that. After that we called her Jan. Janie was probably the best big sister anyone could ask for although I didn't give it much though until I was quite grown. The character and quality of your family members is not something you think much about. They are a given, like the air and the state you live in. What is is. She always looked out for us and cared for us. Charlene even observed that she thought she had two mothers when she was small; a remark Mom bristled at. Jan made many of my clothes when I was in high school and I can remember her telling me to let her know if I ever needed her help when she was getting ready to leave for college. Years later she may have been sorry for that when I needed her financial assistance a few times.

Janie was the classic super child that the first born is expected to be. She excelled in school, played the piano so well that she learned to play the organ and played for church sometimes. Obviously, she was very well-behaved, we all were, but she was exemplary in that, too. It was her big sisterly duty to enforce rules of good behavior and decorum when Mom wasn't around. Jan learned to cook and sew just because she wanted to. When we were all about ten, eight, and five Mom got us each a doll for Christmas. Janie's was a beautiful ten inch one with real auburn hair. She named her Anne, for Anne of Green Gables. Janie spent the rest of her youth sewing a wardrobe for that doll. Anne had everything you could think of: dresses, slacks, nightgowns, blouses, coats, hats, formals and more. I don't know if Jan made the patterns for most of the doll clothes of all of them, but she did that, too. She also had a particularly good eye for matching colors and fabrics that went together well.

Janie seemed to stick closer to Mother than Judy and I did when we were kids. She would stay in the house and sew doll clothes or whatever and I'm sure she and Mom shared a lot of conversation that we just didn't know anything about. Judy and I preferred playing on the back porch or outside.

In our house in Willow Springs we all crowded into the double bed in one of the two bedrooms until Daddy built twin beds for Judy and me. Then we slept on the back porch in the spring and summer. During our growing up years Janie always had a room of her own except for the winter when Judy and I crowded into the bedroom with her. If I had a list of the things I wanted more than anything a room of my own would have been at the top of it. However, in reflecting on the self image that all of us came away with, it seems clear that Jan developed a much higher self regard. I do not believe that any of us was any smarter or had any more or less innate capabilities than the others, but we all tend to live up to the expectations our parents have for us.

Once while I was in grade school I had to go over to Janie's class in the junior high building after school was out in the elementary building. I don't remember why, maybe we had to do something after school. What I do remember is how terrifying the older kids were to me. I was downright scared. The boys seemed very big and threatening, the teacher seemed mean, and even Janie's girlfriends were acting weird. I wasn't sure Janie was going to be enough protection if things got out of hand, which to my child's mind, it seemed like they just might. That was one of my first experiences of being overwhelmed by adolescents. It is perfectly natural for a little kid to feel that way, but even when I was an adolescent also, I felt about as strange among them.

Jan finished high school at Cabool in three years by taking extra classes during lunch hour or before or after school. She went on to college at Southwest Missouri Baptist College in Bolivar the next fall. At the end of the year Cabool invited her back to be valedictorian of her class, but Mother didn't want her to. There were many things to resent Mom for; taking that honor from her became one of them. Jan always said that our parents never expressed any pride in her accomplishments. She would bring home straight A's, and not get a single, "well-done" for it. I believe our parents were tremendously proud of her, but they didn't want her to become arrogant - which really wasn't likely. It just wasn't comfortable to them to make a big deal out of anything. After many years of never seeming to be able to win their approval, she gave it up and decided to do whatever she did for herself, and not because she hoped to make them proud of her.

Jan met her future husband when we moved to Cabool. Jerry Dean lived across the street with his parents. Mom was critical of his upbringing because he freely roamed all over town and his parents never knew where he was. She thought he was lazy and unmotivated. He and Jan were together a great deal of the time, frequently at our house. I was the kid sister and Jerry enjoyed teasing to get a rise out of me, which wasn't really hard. Jerry Dean was quarterback on the football team and Jan was in the drum and bugle corps. When Jan went to college in Bolivar Jerry was nearby at Southwest Missouri State College in Springfield.

When Jan became pregnant with her firstborn, Jody, they had to elope because Mom did not want her to marry Jerry Dean. The preacher they went to was Rev. Gentry from our old church in Willow Springs. He made them promise that they would tell her parents as soon as they could before he would marry them. Mom put us all through the trauma of her 'dis-owning' Jan because she was pregnant and married Jerry. I cannot remember any time when a pregnancy was greeted with joy or anything like it in our family. No matter what the circumstances, it was always a source of shame for Mom and she passed it along to us all. Even if a couple was married there was always something wrong with it. They couldn't support a family, or had enough children, or just something.

After her children were mostly grown Jan went back to school at Avilla College in Kansas City and became a teacher; first of second grade and then special education.

She has always been like a back-up parent to all of her sisters, always ready to take us in when homeless, or lend us money, never knowing if she would get it back.

JUDITH KAY

IN YEARS TO COME psychologists would begin writing about family systems. Someone would determine that the second child, particularly if the same gender as the first, was typically the 'scapegoat'. All the negative energy created in the family was placed squarely upon this one, guilty of nothing more or less than being the second born. Whoever came to that insight had surely observed my family.

Judy was given a beautiful name, the name of a queen, but she never recognized it as such, choosing instead, I believe, to recognize the apparent similarity to Judas, the betrayer of Jesus. Our mother bestowed on this second daughter, her own middle name. It was a name Mom had chosen for herself at eighteen, to replace the despised name, Gertrude, which she had been given at birth. As far as I know, Judy was never able to allow herself to receive these birth blessings. Born in the sign of Taurus, the bull, like our oldest sister, she inherited many of the most obvious bullish traits, both positive and negative.

Judy is the most sensitive, gentle and intuitive of any person I have ever met. Her extreme sensitivity has been a burden for her. It is as if she hears whispers that do not exist, and they are all plotting against her. I am using that as a figure of speech, I do not mean that she has lost her sanity, as we define sanity, but how she has not, is a wonder. From the day she was born she seemed to not be quite good enough. There is no apparent reason for this. She was born healthy and beautiful, with no disease or malformation of any kind. There is no reason to believe that her intelligence is any less than anyone else's. But when a person is continually told they are stupid they become something that looks and feels like stupid, because she believes that is what she must be. I remember hearing Daddy call her 'goof', and not in a kidding way. That was his word for fool and he seemed to believe it. Mother was much more scathing and critical of her even than she was the rest of us. She usually got leftovers or second best, and did not have the tenacity to stick up for what she wanted.

She carried this victim identity with her wherever she went. Her teachers at school picked up on it. Her fourth grade teacher in Willow Springs pulled her hair and threw erasers at her and told Mother that Judy was 'crazy'. Our parents actually took her to a doctor, to see if this was verifiable. After examining her he said there was nothing wrong with her, and suggested the teacher come to be examined.

Judy never liked anything about herself. She was taller than the rest of us, and just didn't resemble us as closely. It did no good to point out to her that tall is beautiful, and an all round advantage. She seemed unable to receive these positive attributes to bolster her self image. It only seemed to point out that she was different than the rest of us and therefore if we thought we were okay, we couldn't think that she, being different, was okay also.

The most chilling example of Mother's mean streak toward Judy is a legendary account of Mom trying to teach her to read. Judy was always perceived as a slow learner, which I believe was a result of an inability to concentrate, born largely of a vague fear of what might happen next as well as her own belief that she was stupid. She was constantly vigilant, so could not lose herself in reading or learning like the rest of us can. One evening Mother had Judy sit at the kitchen table and read. She kept stumbling over words. Mother's patience grew thin. Maybe she had told her the same word more than once, maybe Judy was getting restless, I don't know. But suddenly Mom grabbed a kitchen knife and screaming, threw it toward Judy. The knife stuck in the edge of the table very near Judy's elbow. The slit left by the knife remained forever, as a mute testimony to Mother's temper and Judy's struggle. The image of that knife, blade quivering in the table, and the horror of that moment, is seared into my memory. At times I try to imagine that I went to my sister and wrapped my arms around her. But of course I didn't. I was too afraid of Mother. There wasn't any more affection between us than there was from our parents.

Judy always hated school and struggled in it, while her older sister was raking in all A's. She failed classes sometimes, but was never held back, and did graduate from Central High after we moved to Springfield. We were all on the shy side, but Judy most of all. However, her shy smile was one of the sweetest I have ever seen. She was something like a tiny violet growing on the floor of a dense forest; beautiful, but unnoticed except to the most careful observer.

This second sister, closest to my age, was my playmate and roommate. It was easy to embark in imaginary play fantasies with her and keep them going all day. We always shared a bedroom, which sometimes led to territorial disputes, which is probably not that unusual.

After graduation she went to Kansas City and lived with our Aunt Martha while taking training at IBM as a key punch operator, the precursor to computers. This proved to be just too boring for her, and anyway she had a secret ambition to serve in the military. She once told me that she thought that would be a way to earn respect. Persons in our country's uniform were always granted respect. However, she was released during the time the Viet Nam conflict was getting heated up and persons she encountered were not respectful, and she thought even harsh toward her, as a woman in an army uniform.

When she was discharged from the army she was a few months pregnant with her first son, Darrin. Mother was her usual critical, judgmental self about it. When she came home Mom wanted her to hide so the neighbors wouldn't know she was pregnant. As it had been with Jan, after the child was born, all that opposition melted into the background. Darrin's father had promised to marry her, but went back on his word even after several phone calls, talking with the boy when he was old enough to talk, and Judy even made a wedding dress. He finally admitted that he was just leading her on, that he had a family and couldn't marry her. She seemed to draw failure and the role of victim she could never shake.

Judy took the same practical nursing course that Mom had and became an LPN. She was a nurse her entire adult life, working mostly in nursing homes. I have no doubt that she was the most attentive, gentle nurse anyone could hope for. If I ever needed a nurse I would want her.

She and Darrin lived with our parents until she was able to buy her own house. I was very happy for her. It seemed like the best thing she had ever done. But it seemed like she just couldn't sustain such success. After about a year someone she worked with introduced her to the man she married and her next two children were born.

She moved to a trailer with her husband, and never had a house of her own again. He proved to be slovenly and abusive, so they were divorced after a few years. She went to Kansas City and continued working as a nurse.

Always the 'lost child', Judy did not always try to maintain ties with the rest of us. There have been a few times when we did not even know where she was for weeks at a time. She would usually remain in touch with Jan, but didn't call or make any effort to reach out in any way. Sometime after we became adults I began to believe that she had developed a dislike for me. I could think of no reason for this other than differences in philosophy. I was, and always shall be, a war protestor, which, as a veteran, she took personally, and we differ on many political, social and religious views, although I usually had to get this information second hand because she didn't discuss these kinds of issues with me. On the negative side, Judy can be the most critical, judgmental and pessimistic person I have ever been around, often even seeming to outdo Mother in this. I understand where it all comes from. I was there when it was being done to her. Now whenever I can, I put my arms around her and comfort her.

Even after a lifetime of nurturing the victim identity, that her family allotted to her, I wish for Judy that she could find a way to let it go and fully embrace the beautiful spirit that God placed within her. I can only accept that she is learning whatever lessons she came here to learn, as we all are.

CHARLOTTE MAE

O N THE COLD, SNOWY day I was born in Kansas City, on February 22, 1947, my father was also in the hospital. I have been told that he was recovering from jaundice and ate something which set him back. When I was born the nurse carried me into the room and announced cheerfully, "Mr. Wright, you have a beautiful daughter". At which, my Dad, already the father of two daughters, and really hoping for a son to name Charles, groaned and turned his face to the wall. It's one of those birth stories that would have been better left untold, but my Mother delighted in telling it many times over. Actually, I wish the nurse hadn't even told Mother. Years later, I asked Daddy if that happened and he said he didn't remember. I don't blame him.

I am the third of four girls, named for my Father, Charles, and my Mother's twin sister, Martha Mae. I loved being named after my father. It was a great honor to start life with. I liked my Aunt Martha, but I always wished she and I had some other middle name. I did not like Mae. In grade school I always spelled it May, so that it could at least be like that most beautiful spring month. My entire name is a complete sentence: Charlotte Mae Wright, (or, Charlotte may write). For so many years I have asked, "But will she, ever?" It is time.

As if the hospital story weren't enough, when we got home, I was crying, and wouldn't stop. When asked, "What shall we do with her?" My sisters, aged three and five, declared, "Throw her out in the snow". They decided to keep me, however Janie and Judy couldn't say Charlotte. They would begin, "Cha.." then give up and point, "she". So my family's name for me became 'Chashe', from that day on. Someone has said that one of the hallmarks of being unconditionally loved and accepted is that your name just fits in the mouth of the one who loves you. Maybe that is why I never liked to hear anyone but my family call me Chashe. It just doesn't fit right in other people's mouths. My husband, David, called me that, and my lifelong friend, from college, Dixie, but no one else outside of my birth family was ever able to pull it off. When I was in grade school and a friend distorted it into 'sausage' I knew I would always be careful who I trusted with my name.

CHARLENE RAHE

IN DECEMBER OF 1955 my youngest sister, Charlene was born, ending my first nine years as the youngest. One day after we all knew that Mother was going to have a baby she asked me how I would feel about naming the baby Charlene. It was a blow to me because that name is so much like my own and Daddy's, who I was named after. It was almost like being replaced. I didn't want them to name her that but I only said, "Just so you don't call her Chashe, that's my name".

Mother was about the happiest I ever remember her being, during those nine months before Charlene's birth. She ate huge amounts of watermelon, and we watched her laboriously walk up the hill on trips to the doctor. As the day drew near, my Grandma Stewart, Mother's mother, came to stay with us. There were a lot of things Grandma couldn't do, because she had advanced glaucoma, and could see very little at that time. But it was good to have her there as a steadying influence. There was a small community hospital in Willow Springs in those days, so Charlene was born there. When they called to tell Daddy that he had another girl, once again he groaned.

The first time I saw my baby sister was in the car when we went to pick her and Mother up. I looked at her small pink face and the way Momma held her so gently, and knew that life would never be the same. For the most part it was okay having a baby sister. Judy and Janie learned to change diapers and take care of her, so I didn't do much of that. Once when I tried changing her, I stuck her with the pin and she wailed. I didn't want to try it again. It got harder when she started toddling around and getting into my stuff. I would complain to Mother, and she would laugh and say, "Well, she's just a baby". It was also hard being replaced as 'the cutest'.

Charlene was great addition to our family; a sweet, bright, cheerful little girl. None of us would ever know just how grateful we could be to have her until Mother's declining years, when it was Charlene who was the most attentive and took care of her.

Our youngest sister became the most talented musician of us all. She played oboe, accordion and piano but her greatest talent is singing. She would often sing and play for church and other occasions including our Mother's memorial service in which her songs were pre-recorded. I love singing with her on the rare occasions when we have joined our voices together. She still gives a few piano lessons in her home.

In our adult years I have found a great friend in my little sister. We have often had fun together and commiserated about our struggles. She has had plenty of those, which the rest of my story only hints at. She has three lively children, a son and two daughters.

During an already difficult time Charlene went back to school and earned a teaching degree at SMSU, now Missouri State, in Springfield. But like me, she found that adapting to the demands of public school teaching was not what she had bargained for and instead she has found a niche teaching preschoolers in her church's preschool.

Charlene is the one who has stayed the closest to home. Being near our parents and helping them more than the rest of us have.

CHURCH

On Sunday mornings in warm weather I would sit out on the front porch in the big swing and listen to the bells of our church playing hymns while I waited for my parents and two older sisters to get ready for Sunday school. They would play 'Sweet Hour of Prayer', 'What A Friend', 'O'er the Tumult', 'Rescue the Perishing'. Many of the hymns we sang at church were played on the carillon bells that rang out for many miles from the roof of the First Baptist Church. I would sing along softly. I loved those bells, and the hymns they played. . Looking off down the red road, I envisioned our town like a village in the Swiss Alps that I'd read about. Those bells, on a warm spring morning leant an air of enchantment to Willow Springs. The church was about two miles away, but every note dropped like a pearl from the air, clear and sweet. After they stopped I would listen to the birds, look at the beauty of the Missouri countryside, inhale the sweet air, and savor my aloneness. My worship had already begun.

I knew well the place that music was coming from. It filled me with anticipation to be there with my friends in Sunday school at the First Baptist Church. My mother in her Sunday best, hair curled, wearing earrings and lipstick. If it weren't for Sundays we would never see her that way. My Dad and Judy and Janie and I, all fresh from our Saturday night baths, piling into the '56 Chevy Bel-Air accompanied by the eternal discussion of 'who sits by the window', and 'I sat in the middle last time'.

I loved Sunday school and church, being with all the kids I'd known since we were in nursery together, listening to the Bible stories, and singing. We sat in a circle on little wooden chairs and sang' The Wise Man and the Foolish Man', 'Zacchaeus', 'This Little Light of Mine', and "Friends, Friends, Friends, I have some friends I love, I love my friends and they love me, and we're as happy as can be. Friends, friends, friends, I have some friends I love'. I shut my eyes and I can still see their faces, I can hear our childish voices singing in that sunlit room.

The church was the only place where my parents were drawn into community life. There I saw my parents doing things with the parents of my friends, and enjoying it. My mother especially, sang in the church choir, taught in Sunday school, Bible school in the summer, went to camp with us as a counselor, was a leader of the Girls Auxiliary, as well as being active in the Women's Missionary Union, all at one time or another. My father served as usher, faithfully, and cheerfully in his quiet way. There they were Brother and Sister Wright. My friends parents were all Brother and Sister, too, and also the minister. We didn't call people we knew outside the church Brother and Sister because it meant that we were brothers and sisters in Christ. Whenever the doors of the First Baptist Church of Willow Springs were opened, every Sunday morning, every Sunday evening, every Wednesday evening and any time in between, my family was there.

Church fellowship gatherings were usually pot-luck dinners, often after church on Sunday. I watched as my mother, who was often angry, frustrated, and complaining, was transformed into a laughing, joking, enthusiastic woman. I too, felt transformed there. My friends and I would heap up huge plates of fried chicken, mashed potatoes, chocolate cake and every other good thing imaginable and sit down in a corner to stuff ourselves. We had fun running in and out around the adults, the happy babbling noise, and the smells of good food in the church basement, shuffleboard, the women cleaning up in the kitchen, laughing and chattering.

Revival meetings make me think of jelly doughnuts and hot chocolate early in the morning before school. Once or twice a year an 'Evangelist' would come, mysteriously, from 'Somewhere'. He would hold services, early in the morning before school and work began and again in the evening. The Early Bird Services were when we had the doughnuts and hot chocolate. He was loved and adored immediately by our church community, and placed in a high position of esteem. He would pound the pulpit even more loudly than our regular preacher, and shout at us about hell's fire and brimstone, and how we should be bringing in sinners from the highways and byways to be there at church, with us, and how we should do this and not do that, we were all sinners, and would never be worthy to deserve God's grace. We would weep, and go forward, sometimes in mass, to rededicate ourselves to winning souls for God. It was misery, and it was an awful burden of guilt, but we went back again and again because for this we were assured a place in heaven. It must have been then that I began to imagine that my place in heaven would be a little like my place there.

During those times of being alone outdoors, walking around the apple trees, holding my soft purring cat close, sitting down in the tall grass, I would ponder the incongruities of life. I really didn't want to believe the things I was taught at church. It didn't really explain much, and much of it made me feel really bad, although

I avoided thinking about that at the time. Many of the stories stretched my credibility to the breaking point, such as seas parting, and people rising from the dead. How could the world be so much different now than it was then? On the other hand, if I didn't believe it I would go to Hell when I died. I decided I would rather believe it and be wrong than not believe it and be wrong. So I told my mother I wanted to be baptized and join the church. Thus began my lifelong struggle to 'believe', and make the Christianity that was being handed down to me, from centuries of teaching handed down, fit my reasoning and experience.

One Sunday morning when I was nine Mother went with me as the congregation sang the invitation hymn. I took our pastor, Brother Gentry's, hand and answered ' "Yes", that I believed in Jesus as my Savior. Shortly after, I was baptized by immersion in the church baptistery with two of my friends. The preacher held up his hand and intoned, "I baptize you, Charlotte Wright, in the name of the Father, Son, and Holy Ghost". As I went under the water he said, "Buried to sin", as I came up, he continued, "Rise to walk in newness of life". I did not understand the meaning of it, except that now I was expected to be a better person because I was 'saved'. Any grace there was, was lost under the weight of what I must do. For much of my life baptism by immersion remained for me a powerful symbol of Christ's death and resurrection, and the most meaningful of Christian ordinances, which I later named sacrament.

The other ritual that Baptists call an ordinance is the Lord's Supper. About four times a year, as part of worship, the deacons would pass around plates with bits of bread that was more like small squares of hard pie crust. After everyone in the congregation was holding a piece of bread the preacher would say, "This is my body broken for you. Do this in remembrance of me". Everyone would put the bit of bread in their mouth and eat it all in unison. The church was filled with a rumbling, grinding, chewing sound that started out loud and gradually tapered off. Before I was baptized I didn't get any, but only observed. After the bread was eaten the deacons would pass around the heavy trays filled with tiny glass cups of grape juice. Everyone would take a cup and hold it until everyone in the congregation had a cup. The preacher would say, "This is my blood, shed for you. Do this in remembrance of me". Then everyone would drink the juice all together. What followed was another thundering, rumbling sort of sound as everyone put the tiny cups, now empty, into the holes in the backs of the pews. Baptists perform this ritual perfunctorily, as a duty, because Christ commanded that it be done.

Sometime after my baptism I began to imagine myself preaching to others, and explaining the 'plan of salvation' to them. I was really excited about it and felt perhaps God was calling me to ministry. When I told a friend about it, she put it to rest with the simple statement, "You can't do that, you're a girl". I didn't think about it again for about thirty years.

WILLOW SPRINGS

We moved to Willow Springs from Kansas City in 1947, when I was less than a year old. The first house we lived in was a simple two story frame house with a garden space for Daddy to plant vegetables. The old black and white photos Daddy took with his box camera help to preserve the memories I still have of playing there with my sisters and the boy across the street.

My Mother's cooking was as varied as the rest of her moods. Sometimes it was very good but often she would get distracted and burn something. One evening after he was home from work, my Dad was out in the garden pulling weeds. I went out to see what he was doing. He said, "Is supper ready yet?" I answered, "I don't know, but I'll go smell". Dad chuckled over that for the rest of his life.

My cousin, Jerry, from Kansas City was the son of Mother's twin sister, Martha. He and Janie had been playmates when they were just toddlers, before we moved and have remained close all their lives. After we moved Jerry came and visited us almost every summer. Those visits became part of his cherished memories, also. He added extra vibrant energy to the household and sometimes things could seem more chaotic. For instance, the time everyone got ready for the Sunday evening service and classes at church, piled into the car without noticing that five year old Chashe was not with them. I was still in the back yard playing on the swing. I heard their voices and

36

the car pulling out of the drive, but by the time I got there they were already gone. About the time they got there someone had asked, "Where's Chashe?" So of course Daddy came right back and got me. It couldn't have been more than ten minutes, but to my childish mind it was hours. I was very mad at them for that and actually stayed mad well into adulthood. I thought it was a message that I was unimportant and unnoticed. I suppose a modern parent would smooth it all over by taking the child into her arms and saying how sorry they were, and talking about how I felt to be left behind. But parents didn't have those skills in those days. I'm sure mine would have done those things if they had ever been told that was important to building a child's sense of security. It just didn't occur to them. Mine just laughed it off.

Our family was not physically or verbally affectionate. We were polite and respectful, never used coarse language or called anyone a name, but if we ever got hugs it was before I was too young to remember. Decades later some self-help gurus and psychologists made the amazing discovery that hugs were healthy and the nation, it seemed, learned to hug one another in churches, family gatherings, anytime people were together; except for teachers, who could be arrested for that sort of thing. So my family learned this new wonder along with the rest of the world, but by then we were grown. I'm not very sure our children even benefited much from the new found freedom to hug.

There was always enough. We had everything we needed. In spite of that there was always an air of not having enough hanging over us. I always felt poor even though I had as much as anyone and more than some. It was born of the Great Depression which our parents lived through in their childhood. They transferred that mentality, of saving and not wasting, to us. No scrap of food or fabric or water or anything was ever thrown out. The worst was the extreme conservation of water. I never checked this with any of my friends because it's just too humiliating, but I don't think anyone else had to take a bath in the same water the rest of the family had already used. One can of Campbell's soup was rationed to the entire family for a meal, along with a can of vegetables and fruit. Sometimes Mom would make salmon patties from canned salmon. Most days there wasn't very much of anything, and certainly nothing that was much trouble to fix. But on Sundays or when someone was visiting Mom could come up with really good fried chicken or chicken and dumplings, or pot roast when she really tried. She could make good pies and cakes, too. It just wasn't a daily occurrence. Maybe one problem was that Daddy wouldn't eat meat. He said it gave him indigestion. Even on the rare occasions when we were at a restaurant, he would order the 'blue plate', which was just vegetables and fruit. There was hardly ever anything to snack on when we got hungry between meals. We were told that if we would eat our meals, meaning clean our plate, then we wouldn't get hungry. It is true that sometimes I just wasn't hungry enough to eat whatever there was at mealtime. We would snack on saltine crackers or raw oats or potatoes if we were hungry enough. It seemed like we could always get scolded for eating anything between meals.

All of us girls were very skinny when young. I tried to gain weight so hard when I was in college that I developed the belief that it was not possible for me to gain weight. I truly believed that I could never have too much weight. I could eat anything I wanted day and night and never get past being skinny. I weighed 98 pounds when I was married at 22 until I became pregnant at 36. Since then we all have always had just a bit too much weight, but not any more than other middle aged American women.

A game we must have learned from our boy cousins was one we would play when there was a thunderstorm, which there are lots of in the spring and fall in Missouri. When we heard a roll of thunder beginning, we would yell, "Hit the dirt!" and fall down before the thunder got loud.

My family thinks that I had the worst temper because occasionally I would throw temper tantrums. I could go into a screaming, stomping, throwing rage if properly provoked. Jerry was good at bringing these on. Actually, I don't think I had anymore anger in me than any other member of the family it just seemed that I was the designated "steam valve". After awhile it was expected that I would react this way to some things. I learned this behavior, and permission to carry it out from Mother, who I was unconsciously imitating. Mother often told me that I was going to have a heart attack if I didn't stop. She worried about the health of my heart because I was born with a heart mummer. However, that went away sometime in childhood. Others were angry often, maybe more often than I, but after raising their voice for awhile, they would become silent, pouting, passive aggressive. Not me, I might take a nap after a temper tantrum and wake up refreshed. Everyone had been properly punished.

Nightmares were a common occurrence in my childhood. When I was very young, it would often seem like a large furry animal was rubbing up against me where I lay with my sister on a bed on the floor next to our parents' room. I would begin screaming, certain I was

39

going to be mauled or eaten alive. Daddy would come in and carry me into bed with him and Momma, where I was safe from the monster.

Later the dream became very abstract. There was a swirling vortex that was trying to pull me in. I had no strength to resist it. I would wake up screaming, "Momma, Momma". She would come, and assure me that everything was alright and give me some ice cream. She would ask me what it was about, but I had no communication skills, no language to be able to begin to express that experience. I would just say, "I don't know". And all these years later, all I can remember is something like a swirling whirlpool, like a black hole trying to pull me in. There were probably other nightmares of being chased or some other terror, but that one occurred more than once and has stayed with me.

My kindergarten teacher, Mrs. Rickard, was a sweet woman, about the age of my grandmothers. We colored, cut, pasted, and played with really neat toys that I didn't have at home, like pegs and puzzles, and she read to us. We had midmorning snacks from lunch boxes that we brought from home, and ate there in the room. One day Mrs. Rickard said she was going to peel her apple all in one long piece of peel. If it didn't break she could make a wish and it would come true. We watched intently to see if she could do it. I think I was as much interested in what her wish would be as if she could peel the apple without it breaking. She peeled it in one long piece and we all cheered. Her wish was that her son could come home from the war soon. That was the Korean conflict. Her wish was so different from anything I would have wished, it made quite an impression on me.

One day in the spring two high school students came to our class to pick two girls to be flower girls for the spring celebration. They were the king and queen candidates, and that was the way it was done. They looked at all of us and we all looked back at them for a few minutes. They conferred briefly together and then pointed to me and my best friend, Donna. So that was how we got to be the flower girls for the high school ceremony and drop flower petals just like at a wedding.

Donna had a round cherubic face that was always smiling, and long dark brown sausage curls. The same color as mine that framed my face. I was very sorry when her parents moved away to a nearby town. I got to go and visit her once after they moved.

Before I started to kindergarten we moved to another house down the road and up a hill from the school. You could see the new school clearly from there. Every day I would walk home for lunch, though everyone else stayed and ate lunch in the cafeteria at school. I'm sure the exercise was good for me except in really bad weather. Mom always made me wear slacks under my dress to keep my legs warm. This was in a day when it was unheard of for girls to go anywhere wearing anything but a dress. I really didn't like to because no one else's mother made them wear anything on their legs and I had to take them off in the restroom after I got to school. What a bother!

At the new house there was even more room for Daddy to plant vegetables. Mom had a lot of work to do to can all of it in the summer, and of course we all had to work at it. Jerry still remembers shelling peas and snapping beans for hours on end when visiting us in the summer. Daddy dug out a basement under the house one wheelbarrow full of dirt at a time. He took a pick and a shovel and dug for months on end until there was a room about ten by twelve feet. Then he mixed cement and plastered it up for walls

41

and a floor. It was probably rather rough looking, but it was so much cooler to snap beans there in the heat of summer in the days before air conditioning, and Mother had a place to do the laundry.

There were large beautiful maple trees in the front yard that were the most glorious gold and red-orange in the fall. One of them had branches just low enough that a small person about four feet tall could jump and grab hold of, then pull herself up. After that the climbing was easy, like climbing a ladder. I would go up into the leaves to hide and watch Judy come looking for me. I wouldn't make a sound. It was like a hideaway.

In the winter an ice storm covered all the trees with thick layers of ice, which is not that unusual in Missouri winters. Two small cedars in the front yard were bent over so far their tops almost touched the ground. My parents and sisters thought it was an amazing sight, so much ice. But when I saw it I began to cry inconsolably because I thought the trees were killed and would never recover. They tried to reassure me that it wasn't so bad, that the trees would be all right. However, I was not convinced until the last of the ice was melted and the trees stood upright, probably before the day was over, Missouri weather being what it is. I was a tree hugger from the beginning.

Kindergarten and first grade were in the old original school building that was probably the first one built after the one-room schoolhouse stage. I don't know what year it was built, but it was certainly 18-- something because it was very old even in 1952. We were almost the last students to attend there before the new school was built. It was made of red brick, two story, with wood floors, very high ceilings, and long floor to ceiling windows. On the cutting edge of the boomer generation, Willow Springs was the first of two new schools that I got to attend.

We were really excited to start second grade in the new building. One day a new student came from one of the one-room country schools. Her name was Frances. The other kids twittered a little about her 'country' look, with her overalls, red hair and freckles. But I thought she was brave and the most interesting person I had ever seen. She kept smiling as though she was totally unaware of what a stir she was creating. We were doing a spelling exercise in which the teacher would say a word and if you knew how to spell it, you could raise your hand to be called on. Frances just stood up and blurted out the spelling without being called on. The word was 'kitten'. After all these years I still remember vividly Frances standing up very straight, with a great snaggle-tooth smile, proudly proclaiming, "k-i-t-t-en, kitten". Some of the kids snickered, I still don't know why. Our young pretty teacher, Mrs. Skidmore, very gently explained to her that here we wait to be called on before spelling the word. She never made another mistake again, that I was aware of. It was clear that she was very bright.

The day that Frances arrived was the beginning of the first great friendship of my life. It seemed to me that I had already met her somewhere before. We walked home together after school and played together almost every day. I met her sister, Velma, who was always there with us, also. Frances and Velma, became a staple in my life from then on.

I don't think I really remember that day I first met her. That day that my new best friend stopped beside the taller girl with mousey brown hair and smiling her toothy grin said proudly, "This is my sister, Velma". After that we were a threesome like the three musketeers, me and Frances and Velma.

We played together. We stayed together. They came to visit when I had to move away. I went to visit them in the country. The log house their funny, cheerful Daddy made. The bigger one with the tin roof that sang us to sleep on rainy nights. The little rickety frame houses in town, with their Mother's simple clean furnishings.

We could have known it was almost over when Velma married Eddie Hood, even before she was out of high school. Why not? There would never be another cheerful, adoring Eddie, so much like their father.

Then it was just Frances and I for awhile. Then I went off to college. I wrote a kind of prose poem about us because I knew our lives were going on different paths, and I wept for how far apart it would take us.

Then there were all those lost years of being married, having babies, being hurt, learning life's lessons.

When I was through traveling and conquering mountains I came home. And there they were right where I left them. The country, the spring flowers, the fall leaves. Everything the same. Children grown, bringing in grandchildren.

We sat in the shade by the lake and knew that beneath all the things that had changed were the very same souls who had recognized one another in the beginning and said, "This is my sister".

One character I will never forget was Ralph Brown. In the third grade, Ralph was still not toilet trained. He had to sit in his desk up next to our teacher's desk at the front of the room. At least once a day he would have an accident in spite of Mrs. Robinson's efforts to keep an eye on him.

He had a very hang-dog, ashamed look about him. He sort of shuffled instead of picking up his feet at all. There were whispers about the shack his family lived in with dirt floors. He also had a brother, Donnie, in another grade, who was a little better off than Ralph, though not much. They had beautiful long lashes gracing their soft, downcast brown eyes. At the time I just thought they were very impoverished and ignorant, but in retrospect I expect there was a lot of physical abuse going on in their house. Later, when educators started clamoring for special schools and special education, it was not difficult for those of us who had experienced class with Ralph to understand the need for it.

It was because of Ralph that I came to regard Frances as the most compassionate person I ever knew. One day at recess she told me that she thought we should offer to play with Ralph because she felt sorry for him. No one else wanted to go near him, and I had to admit I was one of those. However, we were taught in Sunday School to be kind to everyone and treat others as we would want to be treated so her attitude made me a bit ashamed of myself. I don't remember having much success engaging Ralph in any kind of activity, I think I just tagged along while Frances made some efforts. It occurs to me that someone should have noticed Frances' great aptitude for being a teacher or social worker, maybe even a nurse. Hers was a gift of caring and I'm sure it was greatly cherished by her children and her co workers.

My parents both came from families in which birthdays were not remembered at all, or maybe a cursory, "well, you're ten years old today". A present or a birthday cake would have been rare for them. So they just weren't experienced in the traditions that gained momentum in the fifties. I think that having birthday parties with all the guests bringing presents, complete with cake and ice-cream and games, might be one of the things that consumerism and the Boomer Generation gave rise to. But Mom was reluctant to commit herself to something that was dependent on the cooperation of other people, such as actually planning a birthday party. I never had to go to school on my birthday because it was also George Washington's birthday, and that was a national holiday.

One year I got to have several of my classmates over for my birthday. I had a great big teddy bear, I named Poochie, who was my constant companion and most prized possession. Some of the boys in my class discovered him and I feared for his 'life' at their hands. We managed to rescue him and hide him in the bathtub.

The year I was nine Frances invited me to her house to spend the afternoon. Daddy took me to her house, and her brother, Roger, came to the door. He said, "Oh, they're almost ready." This seemed a cryptic thing to say because I was just there to play. I asked them where they were going, they said nowhere, but I was on alert. By the time Daddy came back to get us, I was very suspicious. When we went in the house there were about a dozen girls from school and church who shouted 'Happy Birthday'. The edge was off the surprise, but it was a great birthday. Lots of presents, of course, and cake and ice cream. One of the first color photographs in all my old pictures is of all the girls gathered for that party. I remember every one of them.

One of the presents I got on that birthday was a small blue five-year diary. So many blank pages. I wrote in it faithfully every single night before going to bed, after reading my daily Bible reading. After I was grown and left home I was rummaging through some old things and found the diary. I was distressed to find that many many times I had written simply, "nothing happened today." How sad. If only I had written one thing I did, one thing I thought, what we had for supper, If the sun was shining, what I wore. Anything. It's distressing to think that I was so unimaginative. But it wasn't that, it was that I thought there wasn't anything that I could write that would be worth the trouble. I thought my life was boring. I believe it is a sign of low self esteem, to think that ones life is not interesting enough to tell anything about it.

In the basement, just under the back porch where Judy and I slept, there was a small door in the stairwell that we could open and throw cans and bottles into a container to be taken to the city dump when it was full. There was a space there where I could put my dolls furniture . It made a fine playhouse. One summer day just around dinner time I went there to get something. A glass jar fell off a shelf and broke. I attempted to step over it, but slipped and cut both my feet. I dragged up the stairs to the kitchen where I stood bleeding on the floor and casually announced, "I cut my feet". Mother was thrown into a panic. She swept me into the bathroom and ran water over them. The blood continued to flow. She grabbed some of my infant sister's diapers and wrapped my feet in them. It was a Saturday and Daddy was home so we made a flying dash to the doctor's office in town. Dr. Perkins put three stitches in the bottom of my left foot and four in the ankle of the right foot. I could not walk on them for several weeks, which meant I had to crawl around on my knees or get carried, and I missed the first two weeks of school.

When Mother was runing water over my feet that day she asked what happened. I said I broke a jar and tried to step over it, but missed. She did not choose to hear what I said. She always told everyone that I had stood on a jar. I have really resented that. I told her the truth, I tried to step over it, I did not stand on it. That would be stupid. I knew better than that. I don't know why she wanted to believe that I was that dumb, and tell everyone forever that I had stood on a jar. I was there, and she was not, I knew what happened. Up until the very day she died she could make me angry by telling someone that I had stood on a jar when I was a kid. But that is not the way it happened.

Buying other people's birthday presents was at least as much fun as getting your own. Our Dad was very frugal, even somewhat miserly, to hear Mother tell it. We did not ever get an allowance, but if we needed something extra for school or a present for a friend's birthday, he would usually give us what he thought was reasonable, which was never as much as we thought we needed. The dime store in Willow had a special fragrance. It was part well-worn wood floors, the hot air in the summer being stirred by the large ceiling fans, but mostly it was the smell of new toys, nick knacks and household items. The counters were divided into sections filled with all kinds of fascinating objects. I loved exploring everything in the store and trying to decide on the best present. The man behind the counter was a friendly gentleman who referred to me as, "one of Charlie's girls" . That gave me a sense of pride and belonging. This was the town where I was known.

Ferguson's Drug Store had a soda fountain where once, with Janie and one of her friends, we stopped and got peppermint ice cream. Movies at the Star Theatre were 25 cents.

When 'The Wizard of Oz' came out we all went to the drive-in movie to see it. I thought it was terrifying, but really, really wonderful. It was also possibly the first movie we'd seen in color. Daddy pulled the car into the space between the speaker poles and attached a speaker to the car window, then turned the knob to adjust the volume.

The summer after the fourth grade, when I had been honored to be the queen candidate from my class, my family moved away from Willow Springs. This was a traumatic event for me, and almost broke my heart. This was the only place I had ever called home. All the people who I knew and who knew me, were here. I felt a part of that place as I have never felt anywhere since. I think that in many ways I have longed for that security and sense of community and searched for it the rest of my life.

The event had been building and looking for something to set it off- catapult it into action. Mother was not happy in Willow Springs, in spite of the fact that she had many friends in the church. There just wasn't anything there for her. Probably her family, who all lived in Springfield or Kansas City, felt sorry for her. At the end of her eighth grade year, my sister, Janice, who was always the star student, wherever she went, was in line to receive a scholarship that was given to the most deserving student going into high school. It was supposedly based on need as well as scholarship. Janice was called in to the principal's office and told that although her grades were the most outstanding, another girl was going to be given the scholarship because her father was deceased. As if that was automatically a given that there was a terrible hardship on the family. That wasn't the case though. This particular family was very well off, certainly more than ours, as the father had left quite a trust fund and other provisions for them. My mother and Janice were furious. My father had already put in for a transfer to Springfield a few years before this but he was always looked over for it. So Mother decided that it was time, and that we could find a way to leave. She wasn't about to let Janice go to school with that kind of atmosphere swirling about. They convinced Daddy that we could at least move to the nearest town, Cabool, while waiting for his transfer to Springfield to go through. So that is what we did. Daddy drove the twelve miles to work and back for the next two years. It may have helped him a little that Cabool was much closer to his parents in Elk Creek.

I did not understand why this move was necessary. I could have much easier understood a move to Springfield because it was a bigger town, with more opportunities for everyone. But Cabool!! What was the point? I may have held it against my Mother and sister for many years, though now I think I'm better equipped to have more understanding about it. When we left our house for the last time it was Janie who asked Daddy to stop so we could look back one last time and say good-bye.

CABOOL

THERE WAS NO PLACE to rent or buy available in Cabool. We finally moved into a very small two bedroom house, probably half the size of the one in Willow. It was very cramped. Janie's 'room' was the front room with the sofa bed. Judy and I were packed into a room the size of a closet. Charlene slept in Mom and Dad's room. We lived that way for about a year and then a larger house came available and we were able to stretch out some.

I began writing letters regularly to Frances and Velma and occasionally other friends. I would put a three cent stamp on the envelope and walk to the post office to mail it. It was a joyous thing to look forward to the letters from Frances.

Life was better for Janie there and probably no worse for Judy. I made some good some friends, though I always had a feeling there was an elite, snob element that did not except me as their equal. I had never been aware of that kind of feeling in Willow Springs. There I had a place and everyone knew me. Here I was forever a stranger. Even if we had stayed there all through high school it probably would have always persisted. I have felt like a stranger everywhere since. It was because Daddy worked in another town, and even though we attended the First Baptist Church, just as we had in Willow Springs, people just didn't know us. I would spend my life learning that small towns are always closed to strangers. Cabool was no worse about this than any town, including Willow Springs, would have been.

There are many pleasant memories of Cabool. I had two wonderful friends, Carol Roberts, and Susie Schnur. We all went to the Baptist Church and were pals for many occasions. Carol and I were in one fifth grade class and Susie was in the other. Carol was the first friend I had who was the child of a single parent. While most mothers were still stay at home moms, her mother worked at a restaurant. She had two younger brothers, Danny and Charlie, who were present for some of our exploits.

Halloween was one holiday that I never appreciated until I moved to Cabool. Carol and her brothers really knew how to do it up right. We dressed up like hobos or something like that and hit the streets with grocery sacks. Images remain of the crackling leaves under our feet and blowing down the street, bare branches against the sky, shouts of other trick-or-treaters, the excitement of filling the bags up to the brim and overflowing. One Halloween we had a big party at church. There was a contest to see who would be the hardest to guess. I dressed up like a hobo and learned the trick of disguising my walk. There were two of us left who had not been guessed and Carol told her brother which one was me. He blurted it out and I lost the contest. I would have won except for that. I was so mad at Carol that I didn't speak to her for several days after that.

Another time Carol and Susie and I produced a party for the girls group at church. Carol and I made cupcakes at her house. She put in too much milk and then kept adding powdered sugar many times to get it to come out right. There was a lot of icing. We sprinkled dry leaves in the basement hallway where everyone would come in, to make it scary like a haunted house and played a record of some classical music which we almost ruined by turning the speed up and down to make it haunted sounding. That was before I learned to appreciate good music. I guess the leaders and some of the moms were concerned that we had taken too many liberties, messing up the church with leaves and all that, but oh well, we had fun. This was in the days before churches decided that there was something evil about Halloween. I'm glad we didn't know that.

Carol and I had a 'sewing club' that was just her and me. Susie lived outside of town and wasn't able to be there every time we devised some spontaneous happening. We got together and sewed clothes for our dolls, sitting out on her front porch steps, comparing techniques for gathering a skirt, trading scraps of cloth. Susie's big contribution was going swimming in the summer. She seemed to be the enthusiasm behind that. Her brother, John, would give her or us all a ride to the swimming pool. I think she went swimming almost every day in the summer and unlike Carol and I, became very tanned. She actually knew how to swim, which we didn't. I took lessons at the swimming pool and learned how to float and I thought I learned to swim, but I never got the certificate that said I had mastered it.

Marching bands were one of the wonders of the world to me. Daddy and I shared a love of parades. He had played snare drum when he was younger. Standing on the side of the street, watching the band pass, I was filled with awe that these were just kids I knew, only a few years older; so majestic, so resplendent in their impressive uniforms. The spirited music filled me with a feeling closest to a spiritual experience than anything I knew. It became my life's ambition to march in a marching band.

So in the fifth grade in Cabool, I began learning to play the clarinet, which was the same one Janie had played for awhile. Our teacher, Mr. Hoover, later became the most well known music teacher in Missouri, going on years later to be band director of the Marching Pride at Missouri State University in Springfield. He taught me what I knew about playing clarinet and band music in general. I became good friends with Crystal Matherly, who shared the clarinet playing in beginning band experience with me. Crystal was always smiling except when she was laughing. We got in trouble a few times for whispering and giggling in our regular classroom.

Our fifth grade teacher, Mrs. Neff, the wife of the principal, was a very 'progressive' teacher. We wrote a play, based on the history of Cabool, and performed it for all our parents, and whoever wanted to come. Frances and Velma came to visit that weekend, and got to see the play. I played the harmonica in it. In fifth grade we elected new class officers about once a month, so that a lot of us got to have a turn. I was pleasantly surprised to be elected as president sometime before the year was over. That was a really good boost for me.

Among the things that Mother considered 'sinful' was dancing. She spoke darkly about the horrible things that it could lead to. It seemed that dancing could just cause people to loose their minds and do all sorts of things. She just drew the line, 'no dancing'. Interestingly, many of the towns in the area didn't hold school dances in those days. Probably because there were enough people who had an opinion of it like Mom's. I don't know which I feared more, Mother's wrath, or the flames of hell. In either case,

I was taking no chances. When a period of square dancing began in music class I refused to participate, stating that my Mother didn't want me to dance. Mrs. Neff tolerated that, but when I would not do 'hokey pokey' in a circle she tried to pull me bodily out of the chair and force me. Actually no one would have enjoyed it more than I, if I just hadn't had that joy taken from me. My mother's response was anger. "The whole world can go to hell if they want to, it doesn't mean you have to". If I had that kind of situation now, I would just enjoy the dancing, and never tell my mother. Life would be fine. But then it was not so simple. I had been taught that God not only sees everything I do, every minute ('Oh be careful little eyes...'), but even knows every thought I think. I knew my mother was not God, but in my heart, she really was. There were discussions in class about it with one of the 'elite', who's grandfather, a well-known public figure, who had died recently, saying tearfully, "My grandfather danced, and he was a good man." Others, who were also Baptist, were asked if their parents objected to dancing, and of course, they didn't. But those persons didn't seem to want to get into the discussion, either. Those days finally passed, but I always felt rather blighted by the experience.

That was one of the earliest examples of a belief that I was compelled to take in because it was given to me by someone else. Someone powerful. There are probably many children who would have gone against their parents' rules in such a case. But for me, the need to do what I believed was 'right' was stronger than being accepted or doing what I really wanted to do.

Many years later, when I was a preacher, one of the best sermons I ever wrote used the illustration of Christmas in Cabool to tell the wonder of Christmas. Even so, as I have learned still later, from the Course in Miracles, "I have given everything I see all the meaning that it has for me". In large part, it says this:

Even though our celebration of Christmas has gotten ridiculously exaggerated, like so many things, we still love it, for the most part. Our frenzy centers around gift-giving, which causes us often to believe that we ought to eliminate that part entirely from our celebration of Christmas, in the hope that this would enable us to focus our attention on the manger, the real meaning of Christmas. But, wait a minute, what is this in the manger, if not a gift. God gave us the first Christmas gift, out of love, and to bring us closer to himself. Maybe if our gift-giving could be an imitation of God, a way of showing our love and drawing us closer to one another, then it can be a true expression of what really happened at Christmas. We don't need to stop giving gifts, but only to start doing it for the right reasons. The very idea of slowing down, of thinking about reasons for and ways of giving brings to mind that other side of Christmas. We don't want to think about the painful side. Yes, that part. I'm sorry to bring it up, but we all know it's there. After all, nothing that happens on this earth is ever pure joy. There are those elements of pain, anxiety, loneliness, fear of rejection, and all the other nameless worries. I think God shares that pain with us when he comes to us as Christ at Christmas.

After centuries of revealing Himself to humankind in ways He thought we could understand, God finally said, "I'm just going to have to go there myself and show them what I'm really like". So He did. It was unlikely enough to come as a helpless baby, but He also came to unlikely persons; Mary, Joseph, shepherds, and in an unlikely place, a stable outside of a small town. The angels' message was the name tag on the gift. "I bring you good news of great joy which will come to all people..." from God, to all people.

I wonder if it was hard for Him to leave His gift there, almost hidden where no one would think of looking, in a stable. He might have had some doubts, if God ever has doubts, along with anticipation of the great things that would happen now that salvation had come. He must have known that some would reject His gift. But God left Him there, at the mercy of the world; wrapped in swaddling clothes, in a manger, in a stable, in the little town of Bethlehem, on earth. And then it was Christmas.

We all know what that's like. Anyone who has ever given a gift out of the deepest depths of love in her heart knows. When I was a child I had a sense of this uneasiness. Something of the wonder of this story and the great love God had for us, came through to me early in life and I wanted to make it the meaning of Christmas, too.

I began by trying to save up some money. The things I made myself just never seemed good enough. I didn't get an allowance, and was only given money for something I needed, so it wasn't easy to save. It seemed as though I saved all year for this special purpose, trying to scrape up a nickel here and a dime there for many weeks. I would count it over and over, trying to figure out if I had enough yet. I would add and divide and subtract trying to figure how much I could spend on the five other members of my family. I'd just about wear that money out counting it, over and over. No matter how many times I counted, it never seemed like enough. Then one day before Christmas, when I had three or four dollars, and there wasn't much chance I would get any more, I would gather up my precious collection of coins, put on my coat, and announce to my mother that I was going downtown. Downtown. It was three blocks straight over to

Main Street, Cabool, Missouri. Downtown was one street, a four block stretch of stores. They had the lights up and some silver garlands draped across the street from one light pole to another. There were lighted candy canes and Santas hung on the telephone poles all along that stretch of Main Street. They played Christmas songs over the loudspeaker. Oh, it was wonderful! It was every bit as wonderful to me then, with those few coins in my pocket, as Crown Center seems today. The dime store, Murr's Drug store, and the hardware store, maybe Ellis' grocery, were about all I would venture into. I knew I didn't have enough money for a real clothing store or whatever else there might have been.

Spending money is always fun, I guess, but it's scary. What if I should buy something in one store, then go to another and see something better? I would always go alone, because I didn't trust anyone enough to help. It was really important. There I was, out to buy the five most important people in the world gifts, with all the money I had. did you ever try to buy five people presents with $3.67? It was a challenge even in 1957. But you can buy some neat stuff with 50 cents. I remember buying my Daddy a fishing lure once in the hardware store. It was probably the most successful present I ever got him. It was made of pretty colored feathers. He actually used it, and he even said it really worked. My baby sister was the easiest one to buy for. She liked everything. The hard part was deciding which toy to get. Mother and older sisters were hard. The pretty things cost too much, and the inexpensive things weren't useful, or they wouldn't like them, or something. I would go back and forth from one store to the next, from one aisle to another, weighing and balancing in my mind until finally, in sheer exhaustion, I would have to make a decision. It was with great excitement and pride, and with some doubt, that I handed over my hard-saved *money for that strange assortment of items - a Santa candle, a potato peeler, a small tablet of paper. Then as I walked home, I would worry. Would this one like that present; would he or she think it was silly? Would it be better not to give it at all? Would it be rejected: Did you ever give someone you really love a present, and as you sat there, completely tense, waiting to see what that person thought, suddenly he or she laughed? No one ever knew what a ritual of caring and love that was. In a home that did not find it easy to give or receive signs of affection, it was a tough thing I did. But it could not have been Christmas without it. I just wanted them to take those gifts, no matter what they were, no matter how useless or absurd, and to say, "How wonderful. You did this for me? I love it, and I love you for giving it to me." That's all I ever wanted. that's the only reason I did it.*

After I got back home, I scrounged up left-over pieces of wrapping paper and ribbon and began wrapping. This was a fun part, too. I didn't have boxes, and I had to wrap funny shaped packages the best way I could. They looked pretty strange. You could tell which ones were from me. I carefully wrote out a tag for each one: To Momma, from Chashe. To Daddy, from Chashe. To Janie, Judy, Charlene, from Chashe. Then I sneaked in by the Christmas tree when no one was looking and left them; hidden under and behind the bigger, prettier packages. With fear and anticipation I stood back and looked at the beautiful glittering tree and the packages. Then it was Christmas.

The sixth grade was more settled, with no major incidents. At about Thanksgiving time in the seventh grade was when we moved to Springfield. We were in the midst of a pottery making project at school. I had just made a small pitcher which still needed to be fired in the klin and glazed. Carol finished it up for me and brought it to me later. I just love that little purple clay pitcher, which I still have. It is an icon of my time in Cabool, my friend, Carol, and the transition to Springfield.

The day we moved my Aunt Faye, who was a teacher at Pipkin Junior High in Springfield, came and helped us. I rode in the moving truck next to her and whoever was driving. My Aunt Faye was the most cheerful, fun-loving optimistic person in Mother's family. She told me about Junior High, which was a strange new world that I wasn't at all sure I wanted to experience. Springfield seemed like a big city which was frightening. Now I was moving even farther from my friends and all that was familiar. I had been to Springfield a lot, visited my cousin Beckie who I loved, and our aunts and uncles who lived there, but I was always glad to get back to the country. It just felt normal and safe. I did not share my Mother's ambitions to live there and appreciate all the advantages of city life.

SPRINGFIELD

THE REAL ESTATE AGENT took us to many houses all over Springfield. Most were the 50's ranch style, but my own personal favorite was a large three story old Victorian with hidden staircases and turret rooms. I have had dreams about that house or one like it since. The real estate agent knew that if the junior high daughter was the buyer, that house was sold, it wouldn't matter much what the terms were. I was so depressed after that they didn't take me with them to see very many more. I was getting tired, anyway. As it turned out, Mother had spotted an ad in the paper for one that was just being completed in a development. The house on Elm Street was possibly the first one we looked at, and the one Mother had her heart set on. Before they were married, my dear Daddy had promised her that one day she would have a 'new' house. This was it. It wasn't entirely finished when Daddy had to come on to Springfield and start working at the State Highway Dept. here. So he was in the empty house, going to work during the day, while we were packing up and preparing to leave Cabool.

It was a three bedroom house with one of those double sliding glass doors going out to a concrete slab referred to as the 'patio', and a fireplace. The garage had a trap door in the ceiling with a cord attached so that you could pull it down to go up into the attic. There was talk about fixing it up for an extra room. Charlene says that when we were all gone, it was fixed up enough that she used to go there and play. However, I don't remember ever going there for anything. It was too cold in winter and too hot in summer.

Dad made a garden in the back yard, but Mom didn't can nearly as much as she used to. Mother had always had an ambition to be a nurse so as soon as she could after we arrived in Springfield she started nursing classes to become a licensed practical nurse. Moving to Springfied was the first chance she had to fulfill this dream. My Aunt Opal kept Charlene often during those days. Judy was a sophomore at Central High School, which was formidable for her. Central was a large, hundred year old rambling gothic structure that was noisy and seemed dangerous. We had never been around people of color before and their exuberance and noisy carefree manner was intimidating to a quiet girl from a small town.

The first day of school the plan was that Daddy would take me to get enrolled at Pipkin on his way to work. However, on the way there we passed a smaller brick building that said 'Eastwood Junior High'. Daddy figured this one was closer, so we should go check to see if maybe this was the district we were in. Up the concrete stairs and through the large door we met a tall gentle man who looked a little like Abraham Lincoln. The principal, Mr. Rollins, talked to Daddy and determined that we were in the Eastwood District. When he started writing out a schedule for me I told him that I played clarinet, so the first thing on my schedule was band. Dad left me there in that strange place with the tall man and I felt very alone.

The jovial music teacher, Mr. Crosby, was in the gymnasium with the band and members of the Christmas play cast. Rehearsing had begun for the Christmas program, so my introduction was to jump in to rehearsing Christmas songs. One of the girls who also played clarinet was friendly and I ate lunch with her and some of her friends after I got more acquainted with things. However, that first day was difficult, finding all the different rooms classes were in. The second hour teacher enlisted a tall girl with a long ponytail all down her back, to show me where the rooms were. She didn't really wait for me, though and I had to try to keep the long ponytail in sight as I struggled to make it down the hall through the crowd of rowdy kids.

Junoir High is a difficult age under the best of circumstances, but it was traumatic for me. I had never had physical education before, and I hated having to get 'dressed out' in the little blue rompers. Even going to buy them at the Busy Bee had been a strain. The class would line up in alphabetical order for roll call and for the teacher to see that everyone was properly 'dressed out'. I believe that was how I got acquainted with Karen W, standing together for roll call. She lived a few blocks from me so we rode the same bus home. Over the next six years, Eastwood, Central and Glendale, Karen would be a really good friend. She even was the passenger in my first car wreck.

In P.E. all the girls grabbed a set of strange wooden objects that looked like bowling pins, and began a routine of swinging them around their heads to the teacher's commands. They were Indian Clubs, which I don't think I have ever seen since, and that is fine with me. The most distressing thing in all of junior high came after P.E. We all were expected to take a shower, and the teacher would stand there to see that we did. I refused to completely strip down for this because I was so small I wasn't even wearing a bra yet, while some of them were larger even than my Mother. It was just an awful experience for me. Every time I hear about the gas chambers at Auschwitz, an image of the showers in junior high springs to mind.

One thing I was really looking forward to was the fulfilling of my longtime dream to be in a marching band. Mr. Crosby had no way to know how important that was to me, and I don't know if it would have made any difference. It was his job to weed out the weaker players going into high school, and assign them to the cadet band at Central. That was like another beginning band, which didn't get to march. I had never taken lessons, but only learned all I knew in class in Cabool and then at Eastwood. He wasn't at all impressed with my playing and thought I should improve before being in the marching band. So my dream was going to be deferred yet another year. That was another low blow.

Eastwood had a great school spirit. For the smallest junior high, we were very proud. But the year my class went into high school was the last year for Eastwood. After that it was converted into the vocational-technical school and a new, larger junior high was constructed. That's how it was for us Boomers, new schools followed in our wake.

As it turned out, being put into cadet band was the beginning of my musical career. I determined that if I had to be there, the least I could do was to be the 'best of the worst' so to speak. So I worked hard on the music for try-outs so that at least I could be the first chair player, something I certainly never was before. The music teacher at Central was Mr. Jay Decker, a man who would be remembered in years to come as the founder of the Springfield Youth Symphony. Mr. Decker was actually a cello player himself, and therefore mostly interested in orchestras. Having to motivate a marching band, with all the rigorous formations and military-like discipline on the field, was probably not the reason he went into music teaching, but he carried it off successfully. He was a more thoughtful, gracious and refined person than the other music teachers I had had, or anybody I had known up till then. I felt an immediate connection to him, which may have been why I wanted to impress him at the try-outs, which I did. After class he spoke to me and asked me if I would be interested in learning to play bassoon. He needed a bassoon in the orchestra and he believed that I would work hard and apply myself to it. I could use a school instrument, but I would need to agree to take private lessons and work hard at it. I guess if Mr. Decker had said he needed someone to jump into an erupting volcano and he knew I was the right person for it, I would have been just as honored as I was when he asked me to play bassoon. I didn't even know what a bassoon was at the time, but that instrument was to become my second voice and my main identity for many years to come. However, it would seem that my goal of marching in a band was being permanently detoured.

I doubt if my parents were as pleased, as I was, that I had been singled out for the special assignment of learning the bassoon. Maybe it was relief that finally I had something to be truly excited about for the first time since arriving in Springfield. They didn't know what a bassoon was, either, and weren't especially enthused at the prospect of having one in the house, but they agreed to let me take lessons. I began taking lessons from Mr. Bill Spence, at his music store, Springfield Music, which was on the Plaza Shopping Center. For the first two years, until I learned to drive, Dad would take me to my lessons, and wait around for what was supposed to be a half hour lesson. We would often be there for an hour an a half or more because the gregarious Mr. Spence would get caught up in a conversation with everyone who came into his store, instead of saying, "I can't talk just now, I'm giving a lesson". He was the only bassoon teacher in town, but not the only music store, so I guess he had to put his priorities there. He seemed rather arrogant and pushy to Dad, who got very frustrated with him. Mr. Spence was never on his list of favorite people. However, he became one of the most important people in my life, probably because of the individual attention. He must have thought he would never teach me to play, but after about two years he began to say that I was starting to sound like a real bassoonist. I prepared a solo for music festival contest in the spring of my sophomore, junior, and senior years, finally achieving a one at state my senior year.

I was exhilarated to be accepted into the Youth Symphony in my junior year, in addition to getting to play in every band and orchestra concert at school, even though I was only in the orchestra. I got to miss a few classes for rehearsals. Youth Symphony is made up of the best musicians from every high school in the area. There I met Carolyn, my bassoon-playing friend from Parkview. They broke the mold when they made Carolyn. She was unlike anyone I had ever met. It would be several years, well into college before I would begin to understand part of the reason for that. For awhile I was just in awe of her. She was a better bassoonist than I thought I would ever be, and she had what seemed to me to be an easy, confident way of bantering with just about anyone. I felt safe to be with her because unlike me, she was not easily intimidated by anyone. We developed a strong friendship and after Saturday morning rehearsals we would go out for hamburgers. We had the shared experience of Mr. Spence's tutelage, and both worked at A&W in the summer. Carolyn had no doubts about her plans to major in music at Kansas Univ. after high school, but I was having a hard time deciding to do it because I lacked the confidence to believe that I could. After I failed at the music festival my junior year by getting a four on a very difficult Mozart Concerto, and having the disadvantage of a less than adequate accompanist, I was very discouraged. Even though I wanted to, I vowed that I would not major in music unless I could get a one the next year. Carolyn was very encouraging, and I will always remember that before I went in to play she said, "Just remember, no matter what you do, we will all still love you". I still think of that when I really need to put things in perspective.

By that time Mr. Decker had gone on to be director of orchestras at Univ. of Missouri in Kansas City. He came back on a recruitment mission, and once again asked me to come there to play bassoon in his orchestra. That was all the push I needed, after landing a one at the music festival my senior year. My parents went with me and I played an audition at the UMKC Conservatory of Music for a scholarship. I was able to get a small one, and every little bit helps, especially in the confidence arena.

The church my family attended in Springfield was Glenstone Baptist. It was the closest to our house, just three blocks west on Glenstone Ave. The first Sunday I entered the girls Sunday school class I'm pretty sure all of us thought I must be in the wrong class. Maybe they interpreted me as they would someone who was of diminished mental capacity. Because I was certainly of diminished fashion sense, which was of utmost importance to junior high age girls. I had been transplanted at that crucial transition time when young girls are beginning to metamorphosis into teenagers, but no one had told me that yet. I would have been perfectly happy to remain a child always, just as I would have been perfectly happy to remain in Willow Springs or Cabool, where I was like everyone else. It had not occurred to me that I was going to have to start dressing differently or wearing makeup. The girls in that room looked a few years older than I, and not just because I was a small skinny girl. I had innocently worn the white anklets and black patent leather shoes I always wore, and here was a room of young ladies in hose and shoes with varying heights of heels. They had not come there to learn Bible lessons or how to behave as Christians toward strangers. They had come there to compare shades of lipstick and twitter about the boys, who possibly could not have cared less. I do not recall any interaction between them then or any time soon. We didn't have much in common. I really wasn't interested in the things they were, and they had no idea what I was interested in.

Eventually when I learned to actually enjoy speaking before a group, along with my progress as a musician, they became convinced that I was a snob. Speaking from any kind of script is often so much easier for a shy person than carrying on a conversation. You have before you the words to say. If your mind freezes over, it doesn't matter. You just carry out the act. When you have to think of what to say off the cuff, well, that's hard.

Even after my Mother realized that I required accessories to create a different fashion statement, those girls were never accepting of me. In addition to being very shy, I had already made a disastrous first impression. There was no going back. In the weeks, months and even years that followed, I changed my dress and appearance to conform to societal standards in order to gain some modicum of acceptance, and not because I liked those standards. In my short years I had gone from being known and accepted, even loved and admired by my peers, to being a complete social outcast. I hated that church as much as I had loved the one from my earlier childhood. My family attended just as regularly as we ever had, so I was in every group for my age that there was. I must have chiseled out some kind of comfort zone and stayed in it, enduring and not speaking. However, sometime during the six years I had to be there, at least one of our teachers tried to draw us into discussion by asking questions about the lesson. Since I was the only one who read it or cared, I was the one who answered the questions. That did not endear me to them, but I was way beyond caring. I believe I just wanted them to know I wasn't stupid. Mother sang in the choir and before Judy and I were out of high school, she wanted us to sing in it also. I don't remember too much about that, except I liked the choir more than Sunday school.

That group of girls from church was probably the first experience I had of feeling real hate. For the years that I was there, and for most of my adult life, I carried hatred toward them. For the way they excluded me, misunderstood me, and looked down on me, I often wished great harm to them. Forty years later, I returned to Springfield, after living other places all those years. I encountered one of them at A Course in Miracles class. She remembered me, and I think concealed her astonishment quite well. She did not seem to recall that I had been an outcast, just very quiet. She acted as if we were old friends and tried to engage me in recalling those days. My bitterness had dissipated quite a lot because I hadn't even thought about all of that for a long time. Seeing her, I completely forgave all of them for just being the kids they were then. They hadn't meant any unkindness, they were so wrapped up in themselves they weren't even aware I was there. This of course, is the greatest indignity - to be ignored. But it no longer mattered, and it is such freedom to leave all those bad feelings behind.

A new friend did finally arrive on the scene during the first year of high school. Connie and her family moved to Springfield from another small town and started coming to our church. She was quiet like me and didn't dress up to the other's standards either. It was good to have someone to sit with in church and the other youth gatherings. She didn't have the extent of resentment toward the others that I did and even tried to be friendly to them. Connie's Dad was a laborer and didn't make much money and was even out of work occasionally. It was curious, the similarities between our families. Her parents had the same first names that mine did, Charles and Evelyn, and her younger sister was also Charlene. We didn't see one another at school very much but were church friends. They only stayed in Springfield for two years and then returned to the other town.

There is probably not anyone who has ever reflected on their life at all, who has not come to that place where they have said, "Oh, if only I had known then what I know now". Well, yeah, that's just the point isn't it? This is about what we've come here to learn. When I was a child in high school, and yes, I was a child in high school.

That was one of the things that made it hard. When I was a child in high school I didn't accept myself as God had created me. I didn't even realize that God had made me this way, and that there was nothing wrong with me that I needed to change. But I was very determined and ambitious. I believed that I could become whatever I wanted to. That is a lofty ideal which may have served others very well, but it was not the one I should have adopted as my own. I tried for many years to be someone My Creator did not mean for me to be. All of the things I tried to be were very good things. They just were not the things that were meant for me.

First of all, I learned about extroverts and introverts. What I learned was that extroverts are the successful, popular, well- liked people and introverts are sick and need to learn to be extroverts if they want to make anything of themselves.

I wanted to be a music teacher because I loved and admired my music teachers more than I did anyone else. Playing in band and orchestra was the most excellent experience I ever had. It was what I loved. I found myself there. I wanted to do for others what my music teachers had done for me. I was not a student leader in music or any other groups, but that did not deter me from believing that I would emerge from college as a full-blown, extroverted music teacher, who everyone would love as I had loved mine.

The first two years of high school were at Central, just down the street from my junior high school. Judy was a senior my first year, but I don't recall ever seeing her during the day. All the Springfield high schools are enormous, by my standards, then and now. I was simply lost there. I didn't even know the people in my classes except to attach a name to a face and some aspect of their personality. I got drawn into rooting for the team, the bulldogs, and enjoying their wins and being disappointed in losses. I was not part of anything except band and orchestra and going to classes. During my sophomore year Glendale was being built. They took us over by busloads on a field trip to see the construction, to try to ease us into the idea of going to a new school. It doesn't seem like that should be a hard thing, but we were going to be integrated with students from our rival, Parkview, and that made it seem like going to a foreign country. They talked to us about having a good attitude and how we were going to be coming together and needed to cooperate and all that sort of thing. I'm sure it helped, at least to know what was expected, but Glendale never became a cohesive community until the third year, or so I hear. One of the first things we thought was important to know about a person was if they came from Central or Parkview.

The last two years at Glendale were not much different socially for me than the years at Central had been. Riding the bus to school, I got there about a half an hour before school started. We just roamed the halls, waiting for classes to start. I was so shy I didn't even look at people or speak to people I already knew. That period before school was the worst part of the day for me. Lunch was okay because I would eat with my friend, Pat who I had known since junior high at Eastwood. I never missed more than one or two days of school in a year, but occasionally Pat wasn't there. On those days lunch time was just awful. I have never felt as alone as I did then in that crowded cafeteria, with happy, noisy students all around me.

I made fairly respectable grades, but I rarely made the honor roll, always missing it by a hair. Maybe I didn't want to be as good a student as Janie had been, because that was her position. I didn't want to appear to be trying to be that good and then fall short, so I didn't appear to be trying. But I wanted to be a lot better than Judy had been because it really did seem to bother Mom that she didn't do well. So I just sort of settled in between. I should have majored in English or literature, but that just seemed too ordinary to me. I wanted to do something to get noticed.

Mother wanted me to go to Southwest Baptist College in Bolivar, but I really didn't want to. I guess she wanted me to meet some nice Baptist preacher and become a preacher's wife. Mr. Spence wanted me to go to Evangel, where he was on the staff, at that time. The main thing wrong with both those choices was that I would have remained at home. There was nothing that I wanted more in the world than to leave home. I used to dream of running away when I was a child, and the thought was never far from my mind. Janie and Judy had both returned after a few years with babies. I made a solemn vow to myself that I would never return once I was gone. That is one vow I really kept.

When I was set on going to the UMKC Conservatory of Music, Mom asked me why it was so important to go there instead of one of the other two. I answered that I wanted to be successful and to do that I needed to go to the best school I could. Then she wanted to know what I meant by successful and I said, to be the very best I could be.

KANSAS CITY

WE HAD VISITED IN Kansas City many times because Mother had two sisters and a brother there. It had always filled me with awe, and a little fear. As a child I remember asking Daddy, as we were driving through the city, "Why don't we have statues and fountains in Willow Springs?" It seemed perfectly reasonable to me that we should have. I thought it was wonderful, and I was proud that it was the city of my birth. However, I had never thought of living there until it was time to go away to college. Even then I thought I would only live there for as long as it took to finish school. I took my cues from my Dad; neither of us liked the traffic and noise of a city. I always thought of myself as a small town or country girl.

At night, looking out at the lights of the city from the window of the residence hall at UMKC, I felt a bit like Dorothy in the Emerald City. Actually I tried hard to be a country bumpkin; I felt it defined me in the midst of all the other girls, whose sophistication I could never approach, so why pretend. Just make it clear that I wasn't in that game. I had a roommate from Fort Scott, Kansas who was majoring in accordion at the Conservatory. The idea of anyone majoring in accordion at a conservatory of music was astonishing to me, and I soon found out, to a lot of other people. They were some of the best students, and the accordion orchestra played excellently executed concerts of the same symphonic literature that we did.

However, a hundred accordions playing at once sounded like cacophony to us, who cherished the tonal rainbow of traditional instruments. I had good friends who were accordion players, but we learned that there is no good to come of discussing your musical preferences with those of the accordion persuasion. We just let them be who they were.

In the fall of 1965 the orchestra met in a building that was then the Playhouse. It has been replaced years ago by gleaming modern structures but it held a certain charm for me then. It was an old creaking building with narrow hallways and low ceilings. The ghosts were almost palpable in that place. The other bassoonist was John T. He was an excellent player, having taken lessons from the beginning from Mr. Speilman, principal bassoonist in the Kansas City Philharmonic, and our professor at UMKC. John was an affable, rather shy, fellow, shaped a little like a bassoon himself, tall and thin. I was so amazed to be there at all I kept saying to myself, UMKC Conservatory Orchestra, wow. Here I am. I thought it might be possible that I was the least talented musician there, but that is only because there were so many really talented ones. Those first days, sitting there surrounded by all these great musicians, it was reassuring to see Dr. Decker up in front directing us just like back at Central High School.

There was so much to take in I didn't take note of the ones sitting closest to me such as the oboe and flute players directly in front of me. So a few days later when a smiling young man came up to me and inquired if I was "the bassoon player", I didn't recognize him from orchestra. I replied that "I am a bassoon player". Not to be mistaken for the only one, mind you. I remember that moment of introduction. It is crystallized in my memory.

Those were the first words David Crabaugh and I ever spoke to one another. He had noticed me, even if I hadn't him. For many years I marveled at that. But there came a time when I almost wished he hadn't.

DAVID

WHEN I WENT AWAY to college I had a great ambition to become a music teacher, but my most pressing goal was to get away from home. David and I became inseparable very quickly. After a few dates, we would meet for almost every meal together at the University Center. However, the first time was a real revelation about the difference in urban and rural Missouri culture. We agreed to meet for dinner. I was there at 12:00 noon, but no David and he didn't call that evening. I was still of the mindset that a respectable girl would never call a boy, so that didn't happen, either. I went to supper with my roommate and some of her friends. The next time I encountered David was at the bus stop the next day. At first no one spoke. Then he inquired testily why I had not been there for dinner yesterday. I replied that I had been, but he wasn't. It didn't take long to realize that my 'dinner' was at noon and his 'dinner' was the evening meal. After that I almost dropped 'dinner' from my vocabulary for a long time. I referred to breakfast, lunch and supper.

One day the intercom in the dorm announced that I had a visitor on the landing. When I got there David was there dressed in old stained worn jeans and shirt. He was dressed as he liked to be most. For some reason he got concerned that I wouldn't like him as much if I saw him so grubby so he thought it was important that I see that side of him, too. It's no wonder he would be uneasy about that because that's exactly what he had done to me.

When the weather began to get cold I brought out my long thigh-high, colorful, warm stockings. I really liked them, and hadn't had a chance to wear them because they were rather new fashion that fall. It turned out, he didn't like them. He thought they were immodest because they attracted too much attention; in spite of the fact that they kept me warm and were really fun to wear. Of all the conversations I would like to go back and rewrite, that one is at the top of the list. Now I would say, "You don't like my socks, you probably don't like me". But I regretfully put them away and never wore them again.

At the time we met, David, who had been raised in the Christian (Disciples of Christ) Church, was exploring Christian Science. I was an ardent, hard-shell Baptist. It had never occurred to me to question any of the beliefs I had been handed by my parents and the church. I considered David's questioning a test of my faith, which I clung to tenaciously. I had been warned that there would be those who would try to shake my faith and I was determined to be ready for any onslaught from the 'devil'. I considered it a sign of weakness to seriously question any part of the religion I was brought up in. Their indoctrination was thorough. David respected and understood my beliefs even though they were more fundamentalist than he had been raised in. He didn't seem to require that I embrace his views, but only talked about what he believed. When he did it did seem like it was important to him that I agree. When I couldn't, I was sure that he thought I was dumb or narrow-minded. It might be that he did, but it also may have been that I felt dumb so believed that he thought the same. In time I began to evolve a broader perspective and what I have learned to call 'chemicalization' began to occur. I began to realize the narrowness of those beliefs and a lifetime of trying to grow beyond them began. However, I realize that wanting him to accept me and the fear that he might not, had a lot to do with all the changes I went through in college.

Playing jokes on people was as natural to David as breathing. If he forgot to tell you that it was a joke, well, that just made it a better joke. Loose Park was a peaceful and beautiful place that we liked to walk in. We especially liked the ducks on the little lake there. Once when we were walking around it and I was admiring the ducks and geese, David remarked quite solemnly, "Yes, they really look real, don't they?" I was astonished at the idea that they might not be. "Well, of course they're real!" In his best scientific, authoritarian voice, David carefully explained how they had tracks under the water which moved them around gracefully. I was totally bewildered. "Most people don't realize this". Some weeks later my parents were visiting Kansas City. We took them to see the ducks in Loose Park. I said to them quite earnestly, "They really look real, don't they?" David began to laugh, "Oh, you didn't really believe that, did you?"

My parents may have been a little amused, but probably more surprised that I would believe such a tale than that David would tell it.

David's best friend was Bill S but I didn't like Bill. Bill seemed overly self-assured, even egotistical. He claimed to be an atheist, which I found alarming. I thought he was coarse because he peppered his conversation with words and images that I found offensive. He smoked and drank some and generally tried to impress with his suave witty manner. I was not impressed.

I was alarmed that David would pick such a person for his friend. He would always be there when we went for dinner at the University Center. Often there was a large group of us; Mike, Fred, Bill, David, Howard, Bill's roommate, Mark H., John, and others. Bill's girlfriend, Dixie and I were the only girls. We had rowdy meals. We were loud and obnoxious, but we really had a lot of fun. Bill's saving grace was that he was genuinely witty, but actually maybe we all were. Bill and David tried to outdo each other, of course. I laughed so much; I don't know how I ever got anything eaten. Sometimes though, especially if it was just Bill and David and me, what seemed to me like Bill's foul mouth, just got to be too much. At one point I thought of telling David he would have to choose between us because I couldn't stand to be around him. Instead I just said, "I don't like him and I don't want to eat supper with him any more." So we started eating by ourselves. The second year it was no problem because Bill moved in with Gaylon, and didn't eat at the center anymore.

David sometimes would try to smooth things between us because Bill wasn't impressed with me either. The best thing about Bill was Dixie, who was usually around when he was. Dixie was a talented flute player from a small Missouri town who had the broadest warm smile I have ever known. Dixie and I became fast friends and I guess that's what helped me get past the things about Bill that were hard for me at first. We became a foursome and our lives became intertwined for the rest of this lifetime.

Over the years Bill became like a brother to me. He was fearless when it came to producing ideas that might shock a person; ideas I would never have been aware of, and certainly not examined, except for his influence. Others would think of this as a 'bad' influence because it was drawing me away from the safety of old familiar beliefs. However, I will always be grateful to Bill for helping me to understand myself better. He brought to light many neurotic patterns in my thinking and helped me see myself as others see me. He was as powerful an influence as David in starting me on this journey.

I remember clearly that it was at Christmas, 1967, my third year, that we began smoking marijuana. I can still see the Christmas tree lights at David's parent's house when we lay under it and looked up through the branches after smoking a joint. The lights were alive and seemed to move about, tossing glittering colors off of every shiny object.

The subject had come up some weeks earlier. At first I was appalled at the idea. But gradually, I was made to believe that I just had the wrong idea about the weed. It was only for mind enhancement, according to David and Bill. They believed that as artists, it would contribute to their ability to be creative. It was only in the quest to be great artists that they needed the uninhibiting influence of marijuana. Furthermore they were convinced that any studies that had been, and there weren't that many in those days, were just not done scientifically, or were biased for some reason. I think the most classic was that the government just didn't want regular folks to have their consciousness raised. We would get to thinking about the injustices and plain old stupidities they were pulling off. The government was outlawing it because it would make us too smart. That kind of statement sounds just like David in those days. He could make me believe anything.

It is true that some things were being said about the

immediate effects of marijuana smoking that proved to be just plain false. That is unfortunate, but the real reason my resistance was worn down was what could be termed 'peer pressure' from David and Bill and Dixie. If Dixie could have refrained from pot smoking I'm sure I could have also. But she didn't seem to have any doubts about it at all. And Bill was always more slick and reassuring than even David. In my mind it was assumed that if I didn't participate in everything the rest of them were that my relationship with them wouldn't last. I could not imagine being with the rest of them, having a good time, going to a movie, or concert, or playing board games, or any of the things we ever did, while the rest of them were getting high, but not me. If I was in a group where everyone else was smoking cigarettes and not be smoking it would not make any difference at all. But this was different because it was consciousness altering. They were going somewhere else and I wanted to go too or else I would feel I had been left behind.

I don't know when the first time was that we all got together and passed around a joint. Maybe it was at Gaylon's place. Gaylon U was one of our friends from the conservatory, a percussionist. He and some buddies had an apartment on Brush Creek above a Laundromat. I believe it was one of his roommates, who wasn't a student at all, who first turned him on to marijuana. It snowballed from there. We would have gatherings of a dozen or more conservatory students there sometimes. My memory is a blur. I guess we played records, jammed on various percussion instruments, had lengthy metaphysical discussions or whatever. There was a lot of noise and smiles. Best of all, I was with David and our friends and I was one of the group.

At that time, hemp grew wild along the rural roads and highways all around Kansas City. That is the marijuana we smoked. Eventually we went scavenging for it ourselves; usually at night. The police began to be aware of it about the same time that we were. They started a campaign to eradicate it, mostly by burning and fining any farmer who had it growing on his land. In the last century when the area was being settled the hemp was used to make rope. I don't know if many of the settlers knew of its smoking potential. But in a few years after the 60's generation started smoking it there was hardly any left at all.

My Dad had bought me a little Renault Dauphine, a small French made car the size of a VW bug. It was not a very good car, and it is no wonder there weren't many around even then. But we had a lot fun running around in it when it was running. One rainy evening after we were no longer living in the residence hall, David decided to go out scouting for marijuana growing along country roads around Independence. We were not familiar with the territory, but he was sure we could find some. We had the cover of darkness so we wouldn't be caught. We would pick some, put it in the trunk and dry it out in the oven when we got back.

He maneuvered a curve a bit fast and lost control on the rain slick pavement. The car rolled down an embankment and came to rest upside down. Very disoriented, we managed to scramble out, and immediately were met with bright headlights blasting in our faces and the silhouette of a man holding a rifle pointing at us. A gruff voice demanded that we put our hands up and come forward. David tried to explain that we had an accident and meant no harm. I was too confused and frightened to think of anything. As soon as we reached the top of the slope where our accusers were, and they saw that we were just a couple of frightened kids, they were willing to help us. They had a salvage yard there and lately someone had been coming at night and stealing things. When they heard the noise of our car crashing, they thought it was the thieves. They took us into their humble house and we called David's parents. They were actually very kind and helpful. The younger man had a wife who was very sympathetic and comforting to me. We had some coffee and visited with them while waiting for his parents to come. I don't think his parents ever questioned why we would be out for a ride on a night like that. They were very trusting and knew that David was a little eccentric.

David introduced me to his family, who lived in North Kansas City. I have replayed many times, the moment he brought in his junior high age sister, Diann, and said, with a twinkle and a bit of sarcasm, "and here is my 'darling' sister, Diann". I thought he was completely sincere and overlooked the teasing and rivalry that went on between college brother and junior high sister. His Mother probably enjoyed running interference between them. I don't know if it is fair to say his Mom spoiled him. She just really loved being a Mom. It's hard to put any criticism on her for anything because, in stark contrast to my own mother, she was possibly the sweetest, most optimistic person I have ever known. She made wonderful box dinners for us every Sunday, when the University center was closed, and they brought them over to us. There were really good sandwiches such as meat loaf or ham, and pie or cake in the boxes. We also ate at their house for Sunday meals frequently. After dinner we played card games such as pit, spades, hearts, or water works. I don't know when I ever had so much fun, or laughed so much; at least as much as with our college friends, maybe more. David's Dad was a good natured, practical man, proud of his German roots. He had a good position with the KCS railroad, and had been in the Navy Sea-Bees in the war, and sometimes referred fondly to that experience. In addition to the fun times at home, we also took camping and float trips to rivers in south Missouri.

Scouting had been an important part of David's experience. His Dad had been a Scout master and he and his brother and Dad all were members of the Tribe of Mic-O-Say, which isn't going to mean a lot to anyone who isn't into scouting, but it was important to them. He was an Eagle Scout, and was always eager to show off his knowledge of nature, camping, and the outdoors. Luckily, I enjoyed these things also and became an avid canoeist. Some of our best memories are of canoe and camping trips. David and his Dad, and later, just David, would plan everything down to the last detail, such as where the drop off and pick up spots were, the food to take, and how far we would go each day. We would paddle downstream until evening and camp on a sandbar, out under the stars. There were a few times when we just went to a State Park and put up a tent. That was just as fun, also. These were things I had never experienced with my family, or anyone. One memorable trip was one my Dad and younger sister, Charlene, went with us on, with Dad in his kayak he had made.

COLLEGE LIFE

CAROLYN TRANSFERRED TO UMKC our second year. She had begun to annoy me during the summer as we were planning our room, which we would share. There were so many things that contributed to our becoming distant and pulling apart. Many of her habits continued to annoy me; my other friends didn't like her, and even poked fun at her. The things that finally pushed me over the limit was that she would come in drunk and create a scene getting back to the room. Usually I continued to pretend to be asleep when she would come in like that while she tried to be quiet. Possibly the main thing that caused me to practically hate her was that she took my place in the orchestra. I can still remember that audition with Dr. Decker. I felt it was so futile to try to play even as well as Carolyn. It was possibly the worst playing I ever did. After that I just could not help being angry at her for what seemed like ruining my life there.

I asked the 'dorm mother' at the residence hall if I could change rooms and have another roommate. It was not possible. In desperation, I simply ran away from school. One day I packed my suitcase and left David a note, without discussing it with anyone, I caught a Greyhound bus home to Springfield. This is a pattern of flight that I have repeated a few times in my life. When I didn't show up at curfew time that evening they questioned Carolyn and David. Carolyn didn't have a clue, but David told them I was at my parent's in Springfield. They called and

Mother talked to them, and I also told them I just couldn't stand to be in the room with Carolyn another day. They thought I might be leaving school, but I assured them I had bought a two way ticket, so I had every intention of returning.

The residence hall authorities must have done some juggling, because that was when I moved in with my Japanese roommate, Yosko. She was a very sweet girl, who struggled mightily with English. She gave me a Japanese name, it was something like 'Uri', meaning, 'Lily'. But I don't think I ever asked her how to spell it. Another girl asked her why that name, and I will always remember Yosko saying incredulously, "Well, just **look** at her!" I enjoyed this quiet, well-mannered roommate after the turmoil of living with Carolyn.

My resentment toward Carolyn just built after that. One evening there was a banquet at the University Center for the residents of the Residence Hall. It was a very nice atmosphere, with round tables seating six or eight. The colored ball in the ceiling was throwing rainbows of light all around. I was with David, looking for a table with two seats left open when we approached the table Carolyn was seated at. I couldn't believe David was actually walking toward it. I simply turned and walked away. I would have gone hungry before sitting at a table with her. David was very angry at me for walking away because I had embarrassed him.

It was probably about a year after that when David and I left school and got married. I never saw or heard from Carolyn again, though I have wondered about her often.

The next year the University opened up an apartment building for student housing. Almost everyone who had lived in the Residence Hall for a year or two was grateful to have it to move to. However, I was fed up with the control of University housing and just wanted to be on my own. I planned to rent an apartment with a graduate student from Springfield, who I knew briefly through our church. But she changed her mind and decided to go with the University apartments. So I was left with the apartment and no roommate. It was a little scary to be there alone and I don't know how long I might have lasted, but an urban city type incident propelled me back to the residence hall.

One evening there was a knock at the door. I asked who it was, a male voice said there was a telegram for me, I had to sign for. Instead of asking, "Who is it for?" I said, "Is it for Charlotte Wright?" Of course, it was. I still shake my head at that. It's hard to admit that I was ever so dumb. When I opened the door a young black man pushed his way in. He held a knife on me and tried to sexually assault me but I screamed and the lady across the hall came, but not before he fled. The police were called and came and questioned me. David came and took me to the residence hall. I stayed with Dixie, who just happened to not have a roommate. I was so shaken up, I couldn't believe how dirty and sick I felt. It just seemed like my very soul wanted to throw up, even though he hadn't actually done much at all.

After that I was Dixie's roommate for that year. That was the best arrangement I ever had. We really enjoyed being roommates and reminisce about it to this day. But I still had issues with the rules at the Residence Hall and had run-ins with the 'judicial board' and other archaic stuff girls don't have to put up with these days.

During that year Dixie became pregnant and had an

abortion. Abortions were not legal in those days, and she and Bill had to hustle around to find someone to do it. They also had to borrow money from almost everyone they knew. That really shook me up, too. I really hadn't given much thought to abortion before. But I must have assumed, like those in the church I was raised in, that it was just not done. Period. It wasn't being talked or written about so much then and I really hadn't heard many discussions of it. I was shocked to the core that it was her automatic decision, without hardly having to consider it even for a minute, and it saddened me terribly. I was not judgmental at all, just sad. I am sure I was not much support to her during that time. The Pharmacy student who was helping them make connections with a doctor who would do it, made that clear to me in a phone call one day. He gave me a sound scolding for not being more supportive of her. I was actually in too much shock, maybe needing some support myself, to deal with it. I was still a virgin at the time. I really did have resistance to all the social changes that were happening in the world in the sixties.

Any time I think of Dixie's abortion I feel sadness. Life would have been very different for all of us if they had a child. Maybe we wouldn't have done all the things we did and I can certainly understand why they just weren't ready for that at the time. It was probably the best decision for them and I am certain they didn't have to think about it for a minute. I could never make the decision to have an abortion. I still think sadness and regret is the appropriate feeling response when it is necessary. However, I also believe that our nation is a democracy. What that means is, to quote my political science professor at SMSU a few years later, "We are free to go to hell in a handbasket if we choose". That is why I am pro-choice. God gave us the freedom to choose, we have to grant one another the same freedom. We cannot legislate morality.

The next year I decided to try apartment living again, this time with a roommate. My roommate was Carol, an oboe player from Carthage. We got along well; she taught me how to make white sauce with chipped beef in it, which I still make occasionally. The apartment, on the third floor, had a balcony looking out on Warwick, just blocks from the Conservatory.

Dixie was down the street, sharing an attic apartment in a stately old house, with a viola player. Bill had graduated and went back home to Indiana for the summer. However, he realized he couldn't live without Dixie and they were married at the Unitarian Church in October. Dixie wore a dark red floor length gown that she had found at a thrift store. They found rings that were made of jade. We stood with them as best man and maid of honor, which they also did for us at our wedding. David and I spent several days and hours making large candles for the ceremony. It was our gift to them. We got large cardboard tubes somewhere. My memory is that they were larger than the tubes aluminum foil comes in. We melted wax that comes in a box at the hardware store and poured it into the tubes. After it hardened we peeled the cardboard off. We made about twenty of them, and they had them for a long time.

David and I had been working at Linda Hall Library of Science and Technology, which is on the University campus, though not a part of the University system. As pages at the library our job was mainly to shelve magazines, journals and books and to search for things the librarians requested from the stacks where the patrons could not go. We liked working there, it was peaceful, quiet and there was always plenty to do. The library is an awesome, spacious structure. It was practically a spiritual experience to be there. The main floor is all glass looking out on the immaculate landscaped grounds. The atmosphere of the downstairs kitchen where we had breaks always reminded me of a country cottage. I would have liked to live there.

David was living in a basement apartment two buildings down from my building. Bill and Dixie lived in a basement apartment also. Neither of us returned to school in January of 1969 and we were married in David's parent's church, Hillside Christian, on February 7, 1969. The church had done some adding on and remodeling and our wedding was the first one in the new sanctuary. I made a short dress out of white velvet and put lace on the neckline and cuffs. David said he didn't like to wear a ring so it was only a single ring ceremony. I would certainly change that if I could go back and redo things. David wanted to have rock music played; I didn't, so we didn't have any except the organ playing Bach when we came in. We had a cake made and I carried a modest bouquet. The entire thing cost us $21.00. There were probably about 30 friends and family there. Then I moved into the basement apartment with David.

I had huge misgivings about getting married. It scared me more than anything ever has. If I was counseling someone now who was that worried about it, I would tell her to wait and see if her concerns could be reconciled before committing to marriage. However, the only persons I had to talk to were David and his parents. One day just a few days before the wedding I told David about my misgivings. He told his parents I was about to back out and they came to visit me. They thought it was just a simple case of jitters that a new bride often gets and that it didn't mean anything. They tried to reassure me, and actually if it weren't for the Crabaugh family, I might not have had the courage to marry him. A person should always realize that they are getting into a family and if you don't feel good about them, you really shouldn't get into it. To this day, I can say his family was one of the best things about being married to him. But the day of our wedding in the room we waited in before the ceremony, if Mom and Dixie had not been there, or if either of them had said, "You can still leave". I believe I would have.

That does not mean I didn't love him. That is what made it hard. You want to believe that if you love each other, everything will just work out. We had no plans for the future except very vague ones. You could say we had great ideals, but no concrete plans. We knew only that we didn't want to live lives like our parents. They seemed to us to be trapped. My Dad had to go to a job every day of his life that he didn't really like much in a place and around people that gave him headaches. Mother was frustrated by the closed in feeling the four walls of our house gave her. We didn't know how to say what we wanted; only what we did not want. We spoke of 'freedom', thinking that meant 'never having to do what you don't want to do'. Perhaps to spite my Mother's best advice: "You should do something every day that you don't want to". I never thought to ask her if she thought a person ought to do something they wanted to do every day.

The thought of just moving in and living together did not even occur to us, except to flicker past and be immediately dismissed, like a fly brushing past your face. It was not an option. That would have been like choosing between our parents and one another. It was probably more inconceivable than abortion or bombing a bank (the latter, of which David wrote a song about a few years later). That would have been even more frightening than marriage because it would have meant severing the tie with our parents. Our generation had a revolution, and many changes happened.

Committing to a life with David was frightening because he was unpredictable. I didn't have the feeling about him that he was solid. He wasn't. We had had a conversation in which he expressed the wish to just work at some uncomplicated day job so that he could be free (there's that word again) to be a creative artist in the hours he wasn't working. He was thinking of Charles Ives, who sold insurance during the day and wrote great music in the evening in a shed in his back yard. That appealed to him more than being a college professor or any other white collar position, which everyone thought he ought to go for. Because he thought that in those positions you never really get time off that the worries and concerns of it never leave your mind so that you can create art. Little did I know all that really meant was that he would not commit to responsibilities. Yet, my inner self, who I didn't know how to listen to, was screaming at me, "Don't do it!!!" I didn't know of anyone I could go to and discuss my doubts and fears.

Long hair became the distinguishing mark of young men who were against 'the establishment', which David certainly was. This meant they were against the war, middle class values, and probably smoked marijuana. David started growing his hair long shortly after we were married. He continued to grow it and wear it long for the rest of his life. I let mine get even longer, also, in an attempt to keep it longer than his. I don't think his ever got longer than mine, which was some sort of comfort to me. I really disliked his long hair, and continued to hate it more each year. He might have been surprised at this, because I never expressed that to anyone, in fact, I felt guilty for not liking it. However, his beard was acceptable because I thought he actually looked better with it.

David disappointed his parents terribly by not graduating from the University. He was one hour short and just decided there was not anything he could actually do with a degree in music composition that he really wanted to do. I think the real story, that he tried to conceal from his mother and me, was that he was annoyed at an art professor for giving him a bad grade in a subject that I suppose David felt he knew as much about as the professor and that he was going to have to repeat that class in order to graduate. I really don't know, but I wish there had been someone to help me interpret all the red flags that his behavior was sending up. There was also the fact that the four years the draft board allowed young men to go to school, before being drafted into military service, was up.

Yes, the Viet Nam War was in full swing. At that time the economy was stable so a draft had to be instituted. In years to come those of us paying attention notice that if jobs are scarce they don't need a draft because many young men will go to war just to have a job. David and Bill were full blown war protesters. They were among those who disagreed with the government's policies in getting us there and in continuing it. They were especially irate at the prospect of going there to die for a cause they didn't believe in. Because they didn't believe it was for democracy and justice, but rather for Big Oil. Listening to them, I came to believe they were right, and I still am rather pleased that they were intelligent enough to see through the lies.

Right after we were married, the draft was the first crisis we faced. David had the address of someone in Canada, where he was prepared to flee if necessary. The Marines called him up and in spite of having flat feet and smoking cigarettes laced with iodine, to make his lungs spotted, he was classified A1 and given a date on which to report. As a last resort he went to a psychiatrist and convinced him that he was emotionally unstable for service. The doctor wrote a letter to the draft board explaining that in his professional opinion this man should not be drafted. It was necessary for David to be in a mental hospital on the day he was to report for it to be valid. So he was there for a few days. I went to visit him there and it was an intense experience. The people who worked there seemed to be in a different place psychologically, as much as the patients, some of whom were quite conversant. I am so grateful David didn't have to stay there very long. I'm also grateful that he didn't have to go into the military, because he would probably have gotten himself killed or a dishonorable discharge. He always thought he had 'put one over' on the doctor and the draft board because he had studied up on psychosis from books at Linda Hall and thought he knew all the right things to do and say. However, I think their decision was correct, and in the best interest of all concerned.

David's brother went into the army and came back after three or four years with shrapnel wounds, a Purple Heart, and cancer.

During the time that he was struggling to figure a way out of going to war, it hurt me that David didn't think it had anything to do with me. I once said how disruptive and difficult the war was for everyone, even those who didn't go and he said, "Well, it isn't your problem, it's mine. You're not the one being drafted." I don't think he ever grasped that being married means you share everything. And he certainly didn't understand that it was causing me distress too. The first days and months of our marriage were some of the most difficult of my life. I felt as close to wanting to end my life as I ever have. At one point I had reason to call the doctor he got the letter of deferral from. The doctor didn't even know David had got married. A person likes to think that getting married is a joyous occasion which you want to share with the world. However, it seemed like he didn't want to talk about it to anyone. It made me feel stupid, ashamed, and helpless.

Before the social revolution that finally occurred in the sixties, a wife was a little like 'the mother you're allowed to have sex with'. So even though I worked at the same job and same hours that David did, it was always my job to do all the grocery shopping, meal preparing, cleaning, and laundry. Meanwhile he was getting stoned, playing the guitar, writing songs, and any other creative endeavor that caught his fancy. He saw that as his real calling and work. I wish I had been able to have the same philosophy. I would not have been able to quit school and take back the only bassoon I had to play on, and to give up on myself and my dreams.

One day I came back from grocery shopping to discover that he had taken the entire bottle of pills the doctor had prescribed for him. It was Meladril and I had no idea what effect it would have on him. I took the bottle to the corner pharmacy and the pharmacist told me it wouldn't really harm him; he would just have to sleep it off and his mouth would be very dry. Another time I got so distraught I left and drove to my sister, Jan's, in Belton. After a few hours I came back and we continued blundering on.

Every once in awhile there was a 'drought' on marijuana when none was available for a few days. Maybe it was during one of those times David was desperate to get high. He had heard that morning glory seeds would do it. They were coated with a poison to prevent this, but it would only make you feel sick for awhile and then you would have a splendid high. He soaked them for a bit, which may or may not have removed some of the poison. We took them together. I don't remember the sickness; it may have been pretty bad. I just don't remember. I do remember parts of the high. There were brilliant colors and moving shapes, more spectacular than any fireworks, or anything I had ever imagined. We were lying on the bed together, clinging to one another very hard, because it was as if there was nothing else solid in the universe. Everything was gone and there was nothing but just us. I knew then that no matter what happened we had to hold on to one another that all that was real was one another and if we kept holding on one day we would be at peace. That may have been the closest we ever were. It was as if our souls were joined in that experience. When I remember that, like being lost in space and time together, I realize that we were in fact, soul mates.

Bill and Dixie moved to Los Angeles just a couple of months after we were married. They had been working at the post office and saved up enough to rent a U-Haul and move out there. We would go down to the Osco on Main Street to use the pay phone to call them about once a week. It was the high point of the week to talk to them.

They had found an apartment in Hollywood and had jobs with Los Angeles County at the Dept. of Public and Social Services as case workers interviewing clients for assistance. Bill assured David that they could get a rock band together and become rich and famous. This is why Bill picked Los Angeles over San Francisco. He thought they would have better luck in the music business there.

Shortly after Bill and Dixie left we moved to a third floor apartment in a building just down the street. We had a little cream colored tomcat we named Walter, (after Walter Cronkite), who was one from a litter that Bill and Dixie's cat had. David's Dad, Papa Crabaugh, laughed about how Wally jumped up on the couch as they were bringing it up all those stairs, and just rode along like he was King Tut. The apartment, which was what you would call a flat, had a balcony and a little back porch. We were much more comfortable there, and life became a little easier.

We also had a beautiful black Burmese cat, Myron. He was the most unusual cat I ever knew. We got him from some friends of some friends who also worked at Linda Hall. Our friends told us that Myron's first owners blew marijuana smoke in his face when he was just a kitten. We always attributed his strange behavior to this. He was very frightened of strangers, and even though he was affectionate to us, sometimes for no reason he would get a strange startled look and begin bolting through the apartment, from one room to another, as if looking for a place to hide, and not finding one good enough. It was as if something was after him that only he could see.

During the next year we continued to work at Linda Hall. David kept perfecting his guitar playing and writing songs, which he would send to Bill. David's grandparents died and we inherited several items of furniture, many of which I still have. His brother, Donald, came back from Viet Nam and married his high school sweetheart, Mary. We stayed around for the wedding and then followed Bill and Dixie to Los Angeles.

Before deciding to go there we took a trip to L.A. in our newly purchased blue VW bug. We had nothing but car trouble, and spent many hours and days waiting for tow trucks, money being wired to us, and David trying to fix it himself, which he did several times. At one point it was a wheel bearing. It was such a problem getting from where we were camped in a state park to a place where we could get parts, finding someone who had time to fix it, and all of that sort of thing. We finally got to L.A. and had a wonderful memorable visit with Bill and Dixie, although Dixie was working some of the days we were there. David and Bill and I went to Griffith Park, the observatory and a lot of other places. We all went to the beach together when Dixie could go with us. I kept a journal of the trip in a little book I bought in Manitou Springs, Colorado in the first day or two of the trip. I might not remember much of the trip except for that journal. I wish I had done that with all of my life.

We were like a family by now. It was brother Bill's idea to move to Los Angeles; not David's, not Dixie's and certainly not mine. I didn't want to go, didn't like it much, and were glad when we came home. I never knew I was from the Midwest until I went there. We would tell someone we were from Missouri and they would get a puzzled look and say, "Oh, that's somewhere in the Midwest, isn't it?" Is it? Until then, if someone had asked, I would have said the region I am from is the Ozarks. I just didn't identify with being 'Midwest'. I would like to say to them, "In Missouri we learn about all the fifty states, (you do know there are fifty?); where they are, and something about each one. What do you learn in school here in California?" But the ones who really sealed my resolve to return home were the ones who said, with a smug smile, "If you stay in southern California for a year you'll never go back." Watch me. I could never trade the constant haze and smog alerts for spring, fall, and winter.

LOS ANGELES

WE PILED EVERYTHING WE owned into a little U-Haul trailer about as big as the VW, and tied the table and chairs on top of the Bug with strong Boy Scout knots. Donald and Mary were going to use Grandma's dining room furniture for awhile so we didn't have to take it with us, but Mary certainly didn't want it permanently. Seriously overloaded in this manner, we said our goodbyes to David's parents in North Kansas City and started out for Los Angeles on a sunny spring morning in 1970. As we chugged and crept across the Chouteau Bridge about a mile from their house, the realization dawned that we would never make it to California in this manner. So we returned to rethink how this was going to happen.

The problem was that we didn't have much money saved for the trip and didn't think we could afford a larger truck. Papa proposed the idea of taking out a loan against the life insurance policy they had for David. It seemed like a plan so arrangements were made and the truck was rented. We didn't much like the idea of driving both vehicles so we tried to figure out a solution. As I write this, there is no one left to refresh my memory. It seems like the logical thing to do would be to hitch the VW to the truck. But I have very clear memory of trying to get it to fit into the small trailer. The middle of the Bug was the widest part so when they got it that far it wouldn't go any farther. It was a hilarious sight. David and his Dad finally gave that up and it was decided that I would drive the Bug and David would drive the truck. I really wish I could remember why they thought that was better than hitching it to the truck. After reloading everything it was probably the next day when we finally started out again.

I still have the photo I took of David in the truck through the rear view mirror. The cats, Wally and Myron, were in the truck. They stayed under the seat the whole way to California except for creeping out with their little pink tongues panting while going across the dessert.

It was probably somewhere in Colorado that we picked up a couple of hitchhikers; two young boys, also going to Los Angeles. I suppose David was intuitive about people, still it was unnerving how he trusted them so swiftly sometimes. It was soon decided that if they all took turns driving we could get there a lot faster. The guys were all having a blast exchanging stories of the adventures of getting stoned, and the various means of doing this. We would stop occasionally to eat or for a rest, but not very often. After three days and nights of nonstop riding and driving, I was so tired of riding I was practically whimpering to stop by the time we got there. As we rolled into L.A. the guy who was in the VW with me was driving. Between us we had a very sketchy idea of how to get to Bill and Dixie's. Plan A was to follow the truck. Upon arriving in Los Angeles freeway traffic, we soon lost the truck. It was too late to work on plan B. I guess we must have taken the right exit but after that it was guess work and luck. These were days long before cell phones, which would have come in handy. I may not have even had their phone number on me. We drove around Hollywood for a bit trying to remember where they told us to turn, and finally joyously reached their apartment where the truck and David, with the other hitchhiker were wondering where we were.

Hitching rides was very common in those days. There were other trips when we picked up hitchhikers. We might have been going to Big Sur or San Francisco. Once there was a boy and girl who were students at Berkeley. Another time it was two young guys who were real Star Trek fans, who thought David greatly resembled Spock. It was mostly Freaks, as we liked to call ourselves, helping Freaks. But on this day, when we arrived with all our worldly possessions to begin the greatest adventure yet, these two young wanderers, who had so harmoniously shared it with us, drifted off into the L.A. haze and became a memory.

It seemed most urgent to find a place to unload the truck as soon as possible so we could return it. Bill and Dixie said they had to live in a tent in someone's backyard for a few days while their stuff sat on the truck. They had a cat, too. We didn't want to have to shell out that much for the truck so we felt fortunate to locate a place rather quickly. The problem was it wouldn't be ready for us to move in for about a week. So we negotiated with the landlord to let us move everything into the garage, which went with the place. After that was accomplished we stayed with Bill and Dixie until we could move into our place. Myron and Wally were tomcats and their Stanley was a female, Wally's mother, so we had some riotous times with them. It might have cost the cats more than one of their lives.

The apartment we moved to was on Montana Street in the Silver Lake area, which dead ended at one edge of Elysian Park. It was a lovely, quiet spot. The apartments were strung together like a motel. Sometimes when we would take a walk in the park Wally would tag along with us.

The third anniversary of our wedding was February 8, 1971. At 6:00 a.m. on that day I was awakened from dreams by the feeling that David was thrashing about on the waterbed, making me think of a storm at sea. At the same time the wind chime in the hall was ringing as if there was a storm blowing through. As I reached for consciousness I realized the entire building was swaying as if it were made of rubber on a windy day. David had staggered to his feet and mumbled, "It's an earthquake". While rapidly throwing clothes on and trying to think what we were supposed to do in an earthquake, the rolling stopped. We raced outside to see what the world looked like. Our neighbors were doing the same but other than people outside reassuring one another, there was nothing else out of the ordinary in our neighborhood. Wally and Myron bolted out the open door and we didn't see them again for two days.

It was the Sylmar earthquake, which did some serious damage in the San Fernando Valley. Where we were, in Echo Park, there was only minor damage, such as cracks in walls and pavement. We went on to work, but kept feeling aftershocks all day, and for several days. So there was another experience we had never had back home. I couldn't help thinking; at least with tornadoes you get a little warning.

Wally liked to go out 'cating' around and one night he got in a terrible row with another cat. He had open sores on his front legs. We put antiseptic on them and waited for them to get better. I will never stop regretting that we didn't take him to a vet. They got worse and he became ill. One Sunday night he lay and groaned all night, in pain. I couldn't get a vet because it was Sunday. By the next morning he was very weak. By the time I got him to a doctor there was nothing he could do but put him to sleep. Grief was compounded by guilt; he was a sweet funny little cat.

Sometime after that Bill and Dixie's cat had kittens and we adopted a sweet black and white tuxedo kitten who we named Ruby. In spite of our heroic efforts to keep our cats inside they always managed to get out and get pregnant. We thought getting them spayed was too much of an expense. After trying unsuccessfully to find homes for Ruby's kittens the next year I had the most wrenching experience of taking her beautiful black kittens to the animal shelter when they were three or four months old. I guess I wasn't working at the time so I got stuck with this most unpleasant task. They escaped from the box I brought them in and were running wildly all over the shelter so I had to chase after them.

The first job I got was with a temp agency which sent me to a stockbrokerage downtown. I walked about four blocks to Sunset Blvd. and caught the bus downtown every morning. I remember standing on the swaying bus wearing a poncho I had made from shiny brown fabric with nap like velvet only stiffer. I helped the stockbrokers by sorting and alphabetizing various kinds of stocks and bonds into piles. I believe I could have stayed on and maybe moved up in the business, but after a few months I was dissatisfied with being inside a building all day and the sameness of the routine.

Eventually all of us, Bill, Dixie, David and I were all employed with the Los Angeles County Dept. of Public and Social Services (DPSS). Bill and Dixie were caseworkers, who interviewed clients. But David and I were only unit clerks. David worked in food stamps and I did secretarial type duties for a unit of eight caseworkers. We were all in the same building on Beverly Blvd. It felt safe and sometimes fun to share the same work experience. It gave us a lot of fuel for jokes and commiserating about people we worked with and also clients.

There were dozens of other free spirited young persons like us working at the county. We made friends from among them and the people they knew. David and Bill got together a rock band consisting of Ron C, themselves and Carl, the drummer. Bill and Dixie moved to the first floor of a house a few streets over, which had a garage where they practiced and got stoned almost every evening after work. I went with David regularly for awhile, but eventually it got boring, especially after Dixie went back to school at UCLA, and was studying almost constantly. I was expected to offer some kind of critique of their performance, which I really wasn't up to. David's true style was a folk style with acoustic guitar. I liked his songs and singing well enough but it took awhile for me to really like rock music. He would not have liked for me to compare him to John Denver because he thought Denver was trite. But it was sometimes obvious that he had been studying him and especially Bob Dylan, who he admired greatly.

I had always wanted to play the guitar, myself, and it is curious that back in school when David decided to begin playing, I had already been thinking of it, too. I didn't want to bring it up after he began because I didn't want it to become a competition. It's really tragic that that was the only way I could see it. I had a lot to learn.

Several years later I was to have the opportunity to write a monthly column which will become clear as the events of my life unfold. On one occasion I used a memory of Thanksgiving in LA as the topic. I wrote it like this:

Autumn is a season of golden golds, of reds, oranges, and yellows. The pumpkins, mums, leaves overhead and underfoot, all singing praise to their Maker. Autumn speaks to me of home more than any season. It has been that way ever since that long ago Thanksgiving in a far away place called Los Angeles, where autumn is not quite so golden, before I became a responsible adult and got serious about life. We had a motley group of friends around us there; all of us refugees from the home and parents where we were loved and missed.

What to do for Thanksgiving became a mission for me that year. We knew the basic thing about Thanksgiving is that you have to have a big feast with turkey and all the fixin's and have a lot of people over to help you eat it. The first real concern was who is going to prepare this feast? Mom wasn't there. That was one of the early occasions on which I learned that if you want something badly enough you can make it happen – "with a little help from your friends". I still remember the conversation in which our friend, Bill pointed out, "Well, all those recipes are written down somewhere aren't they?"

We wanted to invite all the new friends we had encountered since coming there and we didn't have a table big enough to seat everyone so we found three long, wide boards. We made a long narrow table out of them in the front room of our little apartment by placing them on stacks of books and bricks and things. We invited our friends and they all came. They came with their long hair, patched and embroidered bell-bottoms, and beads. Not only did they come, but as each one arrived they had someone with them who they had invited to come along. We needed more chairs than we had and became very inventive creating places to sit. Boxes and pillows and things you don't normally sit on appeared, just so we could all be around the table together.

We were just a bunch of kids, trying out a new thing, trying to discover who we really were and what we could do with the gifts God had given us, even though at the time we wouldn't have put it in those words. I had been a little hesitant to suggest such a 'normal, middle-class America' thing as a Thanksgiving dinner. But here they all were, more than I had imagined. There really wasn't enough of anything except turkey, but it didn't seem to make any difference.

There was that awkward silence in which we all realized that probably someone ought to say a prayer of thanksgiving. My husband, David, offered up in a conversational tone, as if God were standing around the table with us, "Hey Man, good show. Thanks a lot." We ate quietly almost as if in awe at the significance of this event. That group looked more peaceful and pleased than they had seemed at any other time. They looked grateful, as if to say, 'this was a good thing from home. Thank you for reminding me'.

None of us liked working at the office. It wasn't what we wanted to be doing and was stifling because of that. Every morning we had to drag ourselves reluctantly out of bed and to the office. We took turns quitting for awhile. David quit at least once when the band got a practice studio and began practicing full-time. They had a few gigs in coffee houses and places like that, but never made any money at it, just were playing to get exposure. Much to my dismay, they called the band, "Mumble, Toad, and Gravy'. I thought it was the stupidest name I ever heard.

One evening a man came over to talk to them about

producing a demo record with them. He had a song, which he or somebody else had written, which he was sure would be a hit if he could find someone to play it. They talked about it for hours. Personally, I couldn't see what the harm would be in doing it. It didn't seem like they had anything to lose. But I guess they didn't like the terms, and besides, they wanted to play their own songs. I don't know what the problem was, but they let that opportunity go. As far as I know, there never was another one. There were hundreds of bands like theirs in L.A.

A couple of times I quit working at the office, too. Once it was to try to start sewing things to sell. I like to make dolls and stuffed toys, and when we went to head shops and boutiques I would see bright creative clothes that would be really easy to make. So I thought I would try it. I spent days sewing, but just like the band, I didn't sell much either.

There were a lot of head shops around, on Hollywood Blvd and all around which sold paraphernalia for smoking grass and other drugs. There were black light posters and strobe lights, lava lamps, roach clips, pipes, incense, records, and hip clothes that only a hippie type person would wear.

"Guinn and Macguire just a getting' higher, in L.A. you know where that's at….."
The Mamas and the Papas

Getting high was a full-time occupation with Bill and David. They both became very adept at rolling joints with Zig Zag papers. David enjoyed sifting through the grass and taking out the seeds to plant and also because they made a little pop when they burn. There was an abundant supply of weed most of the time. I don't know where they got it or from whom. They just knew someone who knew someone. Every once in awhile we went to a strange house, a different one each time, where we would meet a dealer who let us try his wares. It was usually for hashish or some particularly potent grass, maybe laced with something. After we were all properly stoned they would buy some and we would leave.

We had interesting conversations while there on such topics as the latest music out by our favorite rock bands, or the current curiosities at head shops. Occasionally there were urban legends floating around that we could pick up on. I didn't really enjoy tagging along on these expeditions much mainly because I was usually vaguely frightened because we didn't know them. I did enjoy seeing the interior decorating of other pot heads. We never referred to ourselves or anyone we knew as 'hippies'. We used terms like freaks or heads for ourselves and our friends.

The 'drug culture' was just exactly that; a whole world of its own. The blacklight posters hanging on our walls would hardly be appreciated fully without the benefit of weed. Then there was the paraphernalia, the roach clips, hash pipes, rolled up match book covers. There were certain books which were favorites, for whatever reason; books that pointed to strange new worlds, or new ways of seeing and being in this one. But most of all, it was the music. Any Friday or Saturday evening would find us seated in a circle on the floor of someone's abode, passing around a joint to whoever was there. There was usually wine or beer as well and lots of 'munchies'. Pot seems to make one hungry. Incense was partly intended to mask the fragrance of the marijuana, and the smoke rising was lovely to watch. The music that would be playing would be something like Beatles, Grateful Dead, Dylan,

Jefferson Airplane, Jimi Hendrix, and so many more. This was our community, our new church. The grass was like a sacrament, communion with one another and all others who wanted to change the world and didn't quite know how.

By some miracle Bill and David knew better than to ever try any of the hard drugs that we knew to be addictive and destructive. We stayed far away from heroin, opium, and cocaine. However, we dropped acid and other hallucinogenic substances frequently. Taking any hallucinogenic trip is a very powerful experience. We always felt the need to leave spaces of about 3-6 months between them. During the time we were in L.A. I may have taken a trip like that about 6 times, though the others took a few more than I did. We would talk about them between times, trying to put that experience into the context of what we knew as 'reality'. One of Bill's favorite questions was, "What is Reality?" Many years later that was to influence my theology and my concept of God greatly.

Most often it was just Bill and Dixie and David and me, almost always at their house. We had Owsley's acid at least once. It was the finest. The trip starts off so gently, colors become sounds, the smallest sound becomes magnified into an entire symphony. You are hearing overtones and timbres you never noticed before. Conversation becomes impossible, but we didn't know that. We thought we were discovering the meaning of the universe, and would excitedly try to express things to one another. Later we couldn't remember any of that, so one time we decided to tape record the trip. It was complete gibberish to our non-stoned minds. The wisdom of the universe has to remain out there somewhere. All of this sounds like foolishness to anyone who has not been there. Like all experiences, it has to be experienced to be known and appreciated. I value those forays into other-consciousness as one of life's experiences.

There are only a few specific incidents from hallucinogenic trips that I can recall. Once we took something we called 'elephant tranquilizer'. I do not recommend it. I became very ill after it began to take effect and thought I was going to die. After that it was a pretty good trip. We were all sitting in a circle on the floor and I saw colored lines coming from each one of us to each of the others, connecting us. It was powerful enough that I remember it all these years. It was a picture of the connection that we all had to one another. Probably the most important reason we never had any really bad experience, such as we often heard about, with people getting traumatized and doing horrible things, is because of the level of trust among us. We were in familiar surroundings, with people we trusted and cared about. It makes all the difference. So instead of having trauma and horror, we had really beautiful trips for the most part.

On one acid trip at their house Bill was having some kind of difficulty; some kind of distress. He went into the bedroom and was holding his head and groaning and Dixie, also stoned, was trying to understand what he was experiencing. I knew that was going on and my reaction was to think that Bill should just 'get over it' so we could all have a more pleasant time. I was just standing in the middle of the floor turning around and around tossing a colorful cup into the air and catching it over and over. Suddenly I took the cup into the bathroom, filled it with water, went in where Bill was and threw the water on him. He was so startled he couldn't breathe for a moment. The suddenness of the water jarred him out of whatever he was imagining. Later he said that was the best thing anyone could have done, that it brought him back and may have saved him.

That may have been the same occasion which, as I was coming down from it, contemplating the insights, and there always were, I 'heard' a voice, not audible, but the way you 'know' things in a dream. After a sound enters your head through the ears, it touches off synapses in the brain that give you the message. This was like the message appeared in my brain without having come first through my ears. The message was emphatic, **"Don't come this way again"**. The meaning was immediately clear to me. I was being instructed not to ever take another hallucinogenic trip. And I haven't. Even though the others did a few more, and I felt left behind, I never regretted it much, but have felt gratitude for that One who was looking out for me.

After about a year we moved to a house on Allesandro Street. It was made in a Spanish style, with a lower floor that was almost a basement, an upper floor, and a little turret room on the top. We lived on the lower level and a Hispanic family lived on the upper floor. They spoke only Spanish, so our communication was very limited. They played a lot of Mexican music, which we didn't care much for, at least, not as a steady habit, so we countered with a lot of Beatles, Dylan, Woody Guthrie, Jefferson Airplane, Jimi Hendrix, and so on.

We suffered two robberies while in L.A. One at each of the places we lived. On Montana St. David had an electric guitar stolen and I lost a sewing machine. When the police came to investigate the robbery, they seemed more concerned about the huge hookah pipe that David had made from a five foot wine bottle, than with the break in. We had no reason to think that they cared about finding our stuff or the intruders, so at the second break in we didn't even call them. We believed it was people who lived in the building next to ours, who took a huge hunk of our record collection. We kept hearing our records coming from that house after that. Without some kind of backup, we were at a loss as how to recover our property.

While we were living in the place on Allesandro I took another hiatus from working at the office. I wanted very much to make clothes and other things to sell. One morning while I was home working on things David came home after being gone only a few hours. He had a very tiny calico kitten that was so young she wasn't even weaned yet. Someone at the office had found her in an alley and David thought I would be a good mother cat. I guess he was right about that. I fed her with an eye dropper and held her in my lap all day. She thrived and became one of the funniest, frisky kittens we ever saw; bringing us much joy. She had the most beautiful calico coloring that people often admired. Instead of naming her the traditional 'Calico' I thought of calling her 'Paisley'. She became Miss Paisley, or sometimes Peesil. Ruby seemed to think of herself as a mother even when she didn't have kittens so she adopted Miss Paisley and washed her and slept with her even though she couldn't nurse her at the time. Peesil wasn't even a year old when all the cats contracted cat fever. We took them to a vet and Ruby and Myron recovered but Miss Paisley died. I went through a period of grieving because I had loved the little kitty so much. Because I had cared for her when she was so young we had a bond almost like mother and child.

There was a lot of backyard space that we tried a couple of experiments in at the Allesandro house. First David made a small fish pond just under the back porch, by lining a hole with black plastic. We discovered that the water had to be running constantly to keep it fresh for them. After about a month of this the elderly woman who owned the property made a trip to the house personally, to see why the water bill was so high. I guess we knew she was coming, so David turned it off and she still didn't know what was happening. I felt awful about it, and expressed the opinion that we should stop trying to have a fish pond.

The other experiment came just as we were trying to decide to leave L.A. Whenever we went to the mountains to escape the city smog we hated to come back so much. We both preferred the country and it got harder and harder to live in the smog, traffic, noise and all the artificial and phony things that were part of living in the city. Sometimes we would encounter someone who would engage us in a conversation about how unhealthy life in the city really is. We dreamed of having a place in the country and how we could get from here to there. David wondered if we would know how to grow vegetables without having any experience at all doing it. So we planted a garden in the back yard area. We put a lot into it, fertilizer, mulch, seeds and all. I reminded David several times that my Father had the 40 acres in south Missouri, which I was sure he would let us live on. In the early spring of 1971, after planting our garden in Los Angeles, we took a trip back to Missouri to look at the north forty and discuss the idea with my parents. They were of course, delighted at anything that would bring us back home. I'm sure that my Mother thought it wouldn't work and that we would wind up in Springfield. She certainly didn't know David's attitude toward my hometown. It was about this time that he declared his opinion that Springfield was 'a black hole in the universe'; just to make sure that I knew he had no intention of ever spending more hours there than he had to.

After the trip back we decided to move back to Missouri. We felt certain that spring was the right time to go so that we would have the summer to grow vegetables and get a place ready to live in by winter. Rather than wait an entire year, we sped up the process and moved within a few weeks. There was the garden we had just planted in Los Angeles, just beginning to take off. David told the neighbor kids in the welfare family down the street that they could help themselves. I wish it was possible to know the ripples that garden may have set in motion. I like to think that those kids might have been inspired by David and his garden to become gardeners themselves.

As we were packing a little tiger striped kitten, probably about two months old, appeared on the back porch. She seemed certain that we belonged to her, even though we made a good effort to find who lost her. I carried her around the neighborhood, asking if she belonged to anyone. No one claimed her, so naturally she came home with us. Maybe it was the Universe returning Miss Paisley to us. We named her for the city of her origin, L.A., which became Ellie. She was our last gift from the city, and she was a great one.

David and Charlotte Crabaugh with Ruby, Los Angeles 1972

ELK CREEK

The Tent

OUR FIRST STOP WAS Kansas City, where we unloaded most of our worldly possessions in the basement of David's parent's house. While there, Ruby gave birth to two kittens. David's Mom kept her long enough to get the kittens weaned and find them homes. She brought Ruby to us later. Myron escaped the madness while in Springfield. Mom didn't want a cat in the house, so we left him in the Volkswagen during the night while we were there. He pushed open the side vent and made his getaway. We called and called and looked far and wide for him the next morning, but he never appeared. It was wrenching to me because I knew how terrified he must be. He was always scared even in normal circumstances. After the trip across the country and now this, he was not waiting to see what would happen next.

So David and I and Ellie, the L.A. kitten, arrived at the north forty in April of 1973 and set up camp. We lived all summer in a tent the Crabaugh's gave us. We should have taken it down and let the bottom dry out a few times. Because we didn't, it rotted out and was never any use after that. Ellie often brought me gifts of field mice which she would lay carefully by my head next to the sleeping bag so that I would see them immediately upon opening my eyes. She was such a sweet kitty.

We carried water from either Deb's house or the little creek close to the highway. Whenever Dad was there with his truck we would go to the bridge over the creek and let down a bucket on a rope into the water. After drawing it up, we would pour it into milk jugs and let the bucket down again. But we got all the drinking water from Deb's. We had to wash up by taking a sponge bath in a big pan. The Coleman camp lantern, a flashlight, and candles were our lights at night. David's Boy Scout technique for a bathroom was a shovel and a roll of toilet paper, which we would carry out into the trees whenever nature called. It wasn't long before my Dad made us an outhouse. David thought it was amusing that he made it with a great big picture window.

We planted lots of vegetables right away. David picked out a nice fertile area right in the center of the property for corn and beans. It worked out well except for the deer. He used to mutter about getting one of those 'corn-fed deer', which was quite a threat from someone who was in no way a hunter. The other problem was watering it during dry periods, of which there were many. We had to carry loads of milk jugs with water out there in the back of the Volkswagen, which had become a real multi-purpose vehicle. Everything we did was a great deal of work.

The Trailer

When the weather started getting cold my parents brought out an old travel trailer for us to live in. Mother had bought it from her brother. At the time no one could understand why she did that because my family was not much for camping or even traveling. Maybe she had an idea that Dad could use it when he retired and started working on his house there. Although, I have to admit, that doesn't seem like Mom's kind of reasoning, since she didn't really want Dad to go there when he retired. However it came to be there, we put it to good use. It was good to be inside and be warm, but the propane for the heat and cooking was an expense.

Carrying the water the way we did was a major problem. It was back breaking work and we had to be so careful not to use too much or we might run out. In rural Missouri drilled wells are the source of almost all water unless you are lucky enough to live near a spring. All you have to do is drill a hole, and eventually you will hit water. There are various ways, new and old, to determine where is the best place to drill. That is, where the water is closest to the surface so you won't have to drill so far. Dad tried his hand at 'water winching' and picked out a place to begin to drill for water. Uncle Deb had an old antique water drilling rig that looked like it might have been used by the earliest settlers. Even though none of us really believed it would work, we thought it was worth a try. They set it up in the spot Dad had picked and began to drill. The soil is mostly rocky hard clay and it was arduous work. Every hundred feet or so they would put in pipe casing and drill some more. After many weeks and several hundred feet, they gave it up.

The rain catcher was one of David's more exotic ideas. First we spent many backbreaking hours carrying large rocks from where my Dad had piled them over the years, along the road, to a spot in the cleared area in about the center of the property. It was only clear of trees; there was a lot of brush and tall grass there. He dug a shallow hole about five feet across. It was shallow largely because the gravely soil was extremely hard to dig out. Then we piled the rocks all in and around the hole. He built it up to make a bowl with the rocks and coated it inside with tar to make it water tight. The finished bowl was about ten feet across and stood maybe five feet from the ground. It might have held about fifty gallons. He got some huge sheets of plastic, possibly thirty feet long, and stretched them out on poles from the rock container and laid them across the field.

The first time it rained after we had it all ready was a tense moment. Rain coming in a forested area is a dramatic moment if you stand still and listen. We could always hear the rain coming across the trees before it reached us. It was a sound like wind only silvery, first very softly and then growing louder. When we heard it coming, David shouted to me to run out and pick up a side of the plastic to hold it high so the rain would be funneled into the rock container. It didn't work. We weren't able to hold the plastic taut enough to get very much water in. It was hard to say if the rock bowl would have held water, since we weren't able to get much more in than the rain itself would have got in it. At such ridiculous moments I really wished David could see the humor in the situation. But he was always so serious and got upset because the plan didn't work the first time. I felt that he probably blamed me for not being a more competent helper. He tried a few other things I think, but eventually gave up on the idea. We just wound up with a nice rock tank that more rational people could come over and shake their heads about.

Not long after we came to the north forty I started to work at the Lee Plant in Houston, about eight miles east. What reason did I have for wanting to put on my life's resume', 'hemmed cuffs at a clothing factory'? I didn't, but our savings had run out and it was the only job available. It was pretty awful. It was a large, noisy building, with scores of sewing machines, all geared to a specific part of the assembly of Lee pants. My part was hemming cuffs. It took me awhile to get the hang of it because you have to hold the fabric in your hand with just the exact amount of cloth curled around your fingers, and just the exact amount of slack, and hold your mouth just right. I really wasn't too bad at it and sitting at the machine and sewing all day wasn't the worst part of it.

There were no windows anywhere, not even in the break room, where most had lunch. I would get there just before daylight and leave at about sundown, so if I didn't go outside to eat my lunch, I would never see the light of day. How the other workers could stand such an existence puzzles me even yet. But some looked at me curiously because of my habit of going outside alone and sitting under a tree to eat. There were no chairs or tables outside, so no one else did this. The atmosphere toward workers was hostile, as if management was doing us a favor by giving us a job, which in that area was exactly right. Maybe it was because of people like me that they eventually moved to Mexico, but I think employers should treat their workers with respect, and there was none there. Some days we would sit almost all day with no work coming down the line and then at four-thirty the supervisor would come along and tell us that we would work overtime. There was no asking; only telling us this. There was no overtime pay, just lose your job if you don't comply. What if a single parent had to pick her kids up somewhere or go get groceries before going home? In my case, there were days when David had the car and came to get me. There was no way to let him know he was going to have to wait for hours. There were other practices that were unjust, which I can no longer remember. Even though there were no minorities at that plant, just the working poor of south central Missouri, I believe many of the social reforms of the civil rights movement caused them to have to change many of their practices. Rather than reform, they just relocated to other countries. Towns like Houston really suffered economically when the plants shut down.

We were required to join the union, which was a sham. The officers were picked by management and no complaining was allowed. My supervisor was the most sour person I may have ever known. She had a little pedestal at the head of the line where she read her Bible at periods throughout the day. She never had a kind word and was critical and suspicious. I far as I could tell, she set back the cause of Christianity at least a few decades.

I probably had complained a few times about the practice of making us work overtime with no warning, but one day I just had all I could stand. When Sourpuss came along and told us we would work overtime, I just said, "I don't think so," and walked out. That was the end of my career as a factory worker. That was not the last time I was to quit a job in that manner. I was so relieved for that episode to end. When I got home I thought it seemed like all the trees on the north forty were clapping their hands for me.

During the first year on the land David started working at a sawmill. He got much of his pay in lumber. He liked interesting pieces that might not have been good for building with. Even before we had left L.A. he had started making pictures and patterns with different grains and colors of wood. He began perfecting this, making tables and boxes with designs on them. One of the first was 'the four seasons', a long trestle table with an image inspired by a season at each corner. He called the process 'intarsia', though many who saw it wanted to call it inlay. Without any instruction, using a router and skill saw, he figured out how he wanted to do it, which was his way with all of life. He kept getting better at it and I helped by making cloth linings for the boxes.

David also made wooden earrings and necklaces. When I lost my wedding ring he made me a wooden one from cherry and hedge apple. It was made in layers so it looked striped, and had an irregular shape. On my thirtieth birthday he made the 'snake box' for me. It is a very nice cherry wood box eight by four and a half inches and less than four inches deep. There is a three dimensional snake with yellow stripes draped across it from one side to the other. I think maybe a snake was something easy to make that way, and he said it was for protection of whatever valuables I put in it. It is really very eye catching once you get past the natural revulsion most of us have for snakes.

The guys who worked at that sawmill were virtual outlaws. David was soon to lose his urban-college boy veneer. In winter they would sit around the wood stove at break times getting warm and throw bullets into the flames just for kicks. When they realized they were going to have a pickup truck repossessed for non-payment they would take it out and drive the hell out of it, literally destroying it by driving over logs and rough terrain and crashing it. I don't know if that worked for them. There were a lot of other outlandish disrespectful habits, some of which unfortunately David picked up. I never could understand why he would want to emulate such people in any way. I was totally revolted by them, never wishing to be around these men who didn't seem to regard women as real human beings. He seemed to actually be awed by their macho disregard for the law. I began to believe that maybe someone should have encouraged David to actually be a bit more mischevieous when he was a kid instead of putting such value on being a 'good' boy. It was almost as if he had never experienced the freedom of misbehaving, and relished it.

While we were living in the trailer Mama and Papa Crabaugh came to visit. I always enjoyed their visits. They were a lot of help and Mama especially, was always so optimistic. Everything David ever did they supported completely and never questioned or made judgments. David could get a lot more enthusiasm for his ideas from them than he did from me. After all, they weren't going to have to live with it. But I could complain to Mama and she seemed sympathetic to all I was going through. They just seemed to think that David was full of great ideas and one day it would all pay off.

It was right after they left that I had the 'dream of transformation' that I have pondered for the rest of my life. I hold every event, before and after that dream up to it, like it was a prism through which to view it all and to try to discern its meaning.

We didn't have very much interaction with other people during the years at Elk Creek. Edgar and Rhonda were our only friends and we had contact with people we worked with. Edgar was not educated but he had a curiosity about things and was very interested in reading things David would suggest to him. He was like a student who David mentored. Rhonda was good natured and hard working and she was good company to share the experience with. I once suggested the book <u>Be Here Now,</u>

by Ram Dass. She thought it was absurd and didn't make any sense at all so I didn't try any more after that.

Many times we thought it would be so enriching to have a community of persons who were trying to work out living on the land together to work things out with. We could all encourage one another and share the load. We did encounter two other couples who were trying to make it there just as we were but no kind of alliance came of it. Often I had the feeling that there were other people not far away who were also trying to make the world a better place, and with whom we could communicate the deepest hopes and aspirations of our hearts, who would not only understand but be able to help us in that endeavor. I knew they were out there, I had a certainty, but I didn't know how to find them. Many years later I was to learn that my intuition was correct. Only two counties over from us, to the northwest a group of people were establishing the Worldwide Headquarters of the School of Metaphysics in Windyville and also the School of Metaphysics in Springfield. If David had not been so convinced that nothing good could come from Springfield I wonder if we might have found them then. But it is really more likely that we just weren't ready yet for the wisdom that I have only recently discovered through them almost forty years later.

The Shack

After he had accumulated a little lumber from the sawmill, the first structure that David built was what we called 'the shack'. He wanted to experiment with making a building whose walls were not at ninety degree angles. David didn't seem to get it that the reason some things are always done the same way, such as walls at right angles, is because it's the best way to do it. On the one hand, it seemed like he just wanted to step out of the box so badly that he would put up with any inconvenience to do it. But also, he wanted to be creative and see where it would lead him. The two room shack was quaint. It was actually more room than we were used to. He put it way off in the woods at the extreme northeast corner of the property. We had to take a hike to get to it from where the car was parked. It had large windows on the north, east and west sides. He put in a drain pipe so that when water was poured out we didn't have to go outside. We found a wonderful old 1920's gas stove in mint condition at an auction barn. It was clean and worked well and leant real charm to 'the shack'.

While Mama and Papa Crabaugh were visiting us a nest of little sparrows, which lived up in the rafters, started learning to fly. We have a photo of Grandpa holding one out on his finger. It was especially exciting with the cats there, but they all escaped. While we lived there was also when David acquired Fang from someone at the sawmill. He was a bouncing, lively puppy of probably German shepherd, coyote mix. He was a good humored jokester, who loved to play, and went everywhere with David.

Ruby and Ellie were good buddies, and seemed to love one another like sisters should. They did everything together, even having kittens. I guess they must have gone out in the woods and entertained the same tom cat because twice they had kittens within the same day, before we got them spayed. One of those occasions was while we were living in 'the shack'. We had a box with towels in it beside the bed, but that didn't seem to mean anything to

Ruby. I was awakened one night by the feel of something wet in the bed. There she was, already giving birth to her kittens right in bed with us. We moved them all to the box. Ellie was fascinated, and had hers sometime the next day. They didn't seem to know or care whose kittens were whose. They had a communal home with both mothers taking care of all ten or twelve kittens. When they were big enough I took them to town and gave them away to people who came to the Dairy Queen, and friends of the other employees.

Uncle Deb made a joke about Ellie, saying that I should keep an eye on her or someone might think she was a coon and shoot her. Not funny.

Edgar

In the midst of the lawless, earthy behavior at the sawmill David discovered an uncut diamond in the rough, who became a friend for life. Edgar Underwood was a quiet, soft-spoken guy, in whom David found a kindred spirit. His one-quarter Cherokee ancestry showed clearly in his black hair and dark eyes. He shared David's love of nature and dreamed of living off the land. He was married to Shirley, a sultry, acerbic strawberry blond. They had a little boy, only a few months old. Their marriage was shaky, and didn't last very long after we met them.

The witty, lively Shirley was a friend who made life interesting at times. It was she who pierced my ears with a large darning needle, using ice cubes to numb them, so that I could wear the earrings David was making.

David and Edgar became involved in an enterprise that was suggested by David's brother, Donald. He was living near Weston, a town in north Missouri, in an area where tobacco was grown. (Curiously, this town was going to become an important part of my life years later.) He thought that if David could find a way to make tobacco stakes from some of the cast off lumber he could sell them and make a profit. They located an old abandoned flat bed truck, that Donald helped them get running, to transport the stakes on.

The two sawmill workers rigged up a sawmill with two table saws for cutting the stakes on, not far from the dome. One saw was for cutting the lumber into small sticks about an inch and a half square and the other one was for sharpening them. The stakes had to be pointed at both ends so they could be stuck into the ground and the tobacco speared onto the top. They recruited me to learn how to sharpen stakes. It took some practice to get it just right, but before long I was making pretty good points.

They would take orders for a certain number of stakes, and then work like crazy to get them all finished in time. There were times when it seemed to me as if they had put themselves right back on the treadmill of commerce they so despised. After a load was ready they would pile them on the flatbed and drive north to Weston to deliver them. They made some extra cash this way, and had dreams of making a much greater enterprise of it.

Edgar once made the remark, "I would be better off if I was an orphan." It was clear why he would feel this way. His father, who looked even more distinctly Native American than Edgar, was a violent, abusive alcoholic. His parents had endured a tempestuous relationship for as long as Edgar could remember. It finally ended in divorce during the few years we were there. His mother was a sweet, tough lady who could make the best hot rolls I ever ate. Of his two or three brothers, one he was particularly close to had been killed in Viet Nam. This had affected Edgar greatly, and he grieved this loss.

Even before he was completely separated from Shirley, Edgar appeared late one evening at our house with Rhonda. She was just a kid, about fifteen. She was very pretty, with fluffy dark brown hair framing her round face. He said Rhonda's mother was looking for them and would have him arrested if she found them. Edgar was frequently employed as a trucker and he was going to have to take off on a run to the west coast for the trucking firm he was employed by and couldn't take Rhonda with him, although she really wanted to go. He wanted to know if she could stay with us while he was gone. I felt immediate sympathy for Rhonda's mother, and didn't really want anything to do with it, even though the shy Rhonda seemed like a sweet girl. David and I went outside to consult about it. I suggested to him that we might be in trouble also, if we were found hiding her from her mother and the sheriff, who were looking for her. David reassured me that everything would be fine and we agreed to let her stay while Edgar was gone. Rhonda and I became great friends and she was a source of comfort to me at a difficult time a few years later.

Edgar built a cabin on the far west side of the forty acres and he and Rhonda became a part of our lives. His cabin was one room on the bottom with a loft for sleeping on. It had a large front porch, the size of the interior, with a very large picture window. They had a small wood stove, and he, at least, was happy as a lark. Rhonda told me about the mice that came at night and played in her hair while she was sleeping. I was appalled. It didn't seem like anyone should be expected to put up with that, but

I guess you could say that about almost everything we were experiencing.

The Dome

David started buying up plastic straws, large pink pencil erasers, and straight pins. He sat for hours each evening making models of geodesic domes, using the straws for struts and cut up bits of erasers for the hubs between. He had been reading Buckminster Fuller's <u>Nine Chains to the Moon,</u> which was largely what got him to thinking about geodesic domes. He decided that was the kind of house he wanted to build. He talked about all the positive characteristics of domes; easy to heat and cool, very strong to withstand storms, and esthetically pleasing. There were other qualities, harder to describe, about the energy that is generated in a dome that makes it a very positive vibration to be in. That it was a weird house, made out of triangles, did not bother me much at that point. I was happy to be talking about a permanent 'real' house of any kind, with running water and electricity.

David had wanted to live on the land for awhile before deciding on the exact spot to put the permanent house. I believe he also wanted to see how 'tough' I was, and if we were really going to make the life on the land experiment work. We decided the most beautiful spot on the forty acres was a rise of land in about the east central part. There was a meadow right in front of it, which wouldn't be too hard to clear, and beyond that you could see for miles. But this time he was going to be cautious. Since he had never built a dome before, he wanted to build a trial one in another spot, just to get some experience building one, and to be sure it would work.

So that is how we came to build the dome on a spot a little to the south of the most perfect spot. He started by sinking eight posts, soaked in creosote to retard rotting and bug damage, into the ground in the spot the dome was to be. This was the foundation. The first floor, which was to be the kitchen, was octagon shaped with the walls slanting out from floor to ceiling so that the floor was slightly smaller than the ceiling. The ceiling of the little octagon room became the floor of the dome.

David carefully cut the struts and hubs for the dome and marked them so he would know how to put it all together. Then one day that summer, just about all of both of our families came to the north forty and we had a dome assembling party. Everyone came to help; David's parents, his brother and wife, Donald and Mary; his sister and her husband, Diann and Roger; my parents, my oldest sister, Jan and Jerry Dean, and their kids, and Uncle Deb.

If our living there and building that dome never served any other purpose, at least it can be said that it provided the most beautiful memory of all of us working and playing together that day. David's Dad had enough understanding of the mathematics and mechanics of the dome to be of valuable help. David was on the ground, still making adjustments with the saw. He sent up the pieces while his Dad would help oversee the assembly from the top. For several hours we sweated and laughed, pondered and wondered how it would come out. At the end of the day, there stood the perfect skeleton of the dome, like giant tinker toys, on top of the octagon kitchen.

Papa Crabaugh devised a 'circular' staircase going from the first floor to the dome in order to save room.

Actually, it was slightly bent, rather than straight, but it took a lot of figuring to do it that way. The post, that was the truck of a tree with the bark peeled off, which David put in as a support between the two floors, became a real curiosity to everyone who ever came to visit the dome.

When we took a break for lunch David had fun riding Jan and Jerry's kids, Jody, Donna and Jon, around the grassy top of the property in the VW. They may never forget weaving through the tall grass, not able to see where they were going, shrieking and laughing the whole time. Meanwhile their Mom and Dad were playing on a swing in front of the dome. It is interesting to think of now, they and Judy's were the only nieces and nephews we had at the time. We could do a project like that now in double time with all the ones that came later now that they are all grown.

My Uncle, My Teacher

Several years after we lived on the north forty and built the dome my nephew, Jody, wrote the following paper about his Uncle David for a college class. When I read his words I see David through his eyes. He makes our back to the land experiment seem almost bigger than life. His words give another perspective to us and our life there that refreshes my memory of our time there.

When I was old enough to realize a little of what life had to offer I couldn't learn fast enough. In those days the children of my family had the opportunity to stay with Grandmothers who lived in Springfield or Cabool, MO. This led to some rather active days of shopping, visiting, or whatever our little

Charlotte Crabaugh

hearts desired. The Grandmother that lived in Springfield also had 40 acres in a rural part of Missouri called Elk Creek. This was a great retreat, even though we drove 1 hour and 30 minutes to get there on weekends. These forty acres soon became home to my Aunt and Uncle who had just returned from California where they were social workers in the Los Angles area during the late 1960's. My Uncle also played in a rock and roll band, but he didn't make much at it.

I can recall my first meeting with my Aunt and Uncle together. They seemed strange to me at first, because they were what people considered "hippies" in those days. They dressed themselves in the loose fitting and colorful way that seemed to pronounce to the world that they wouldn't give in to the fashion statements of the greedy power hungry society. My Uncle always wore a ponytail, which seemed to say he couldn't accept being just like everybody else. This rebellious behavior affected both my father and I. I still wear a ponytail today. They were highly educated so I soon learned that you can't judge a book by the cover, so to speak. This was an invaluable lesson for me, which I still use every day.

My Aunt and Uncle considered many alternatives of living and chose the country as their home. Their lifestyle seemed very open and "back to nature", so I considered this a new interpretation of successful living. This, I believe, is where I got the idea that country living is far better for your mental wellbeing.

My Uncle came from a highly educated, very loving, and enjoyable family. This only encouraged me to get to know him better, because it seemed to me that my family was lacking in this respect. My parents never seemed to slow down long enough to pay much mind to the children. I felt that if I got to know them that maybe, just maybe I could start to be just like my Uncle David. I felt that almost everybody I knew

134

just didn't measure up anymore, because of their materialistic views.

My Uncle David had peculiar habits like rolling his own cigarettes (and material from his special crop). He was also fairly health conscious because he would not consume junk food, or high doses of sugar, or chemicals in the processed foods. I can remember retrieving water from a certain creek three times a week, mind you, not just any creek – this one was spring fed. Getting to the creek was never a problem in his VW Beetle. He told me once that, in dealing with cars, the simpler the better; which was why he owned the VW and I still own one today. He also said he could learn anything even though he wasn't mechanically inclined, in that respect simpler was better.

One summer, upon arriving in Springfield my Grandmother told me if I wanted to, I could go to "the farm" and stay with Uncle David and Aunt Chashe for a week of two. I considered this to be a privilege since I hadn't seen them for several months. I thought this was going to be just another visit, with our agenda being filled with romps through the woods. I couldn't have been more wrong. My Uncle had been working on plans for a Geodesic Dome. He later told me that he had planned to teach me how to design and build my own dome some day. I think he was really surprised at how well I took to the idea, because he recommended several books for me to read, which I did.

After a few days of enjoying the serenity of the back woods – nights laying on the deer blind looking at the stars which looked as though you could reach out and touch them, we then started what seemed to me to be the impossible project. He told me that the best way to get the materials was either to tear down an old structure, or visit the local sawmill, of which he did both.

My Uncle's love for learning was so great that even though clumsy at times, he still pursued this current adventure. He would often tell me not to get discouraged with anything in life, anything you set your mind to can be accomplished. He proved this to me in building this dome because there was a hub he was designing to hold the structure together that took several failed attempts. We finally mastered the design of the hub which was indeed an accomplishment in itself. This just made me feel like there was nothing in life that was impossible if you just set your mind to it.

The dome envisioned by my Uncle was to be only 26 feet in diameter and 2 stories with a loft. This dome would also have decking around the structure on the second floor with plenty of windows following mainly the suns path of winter.

He also taught me along the way that when building a dome you need to consider a treed lot so as to avoid extreme heat on your structure. Because of the extremes in temperatures, without trees, your dome would have leaks. The spot he chose for the dome was very dense with beautiful towering trees that seemed to accept the challenge of protecting his masterpiece.

Upon crafting the supports for this dome, my Uncle made sure I knew how to use the "tools of the trade" with professionalism. He would not allow sloppy work on his creation nor would he endure horseplay (that came later). He enjoyed teaching me along the way as much as I enjoyed learning from him. I think he could have been an excellent teacher.

Although I didn't get to help him assemble the pieces we made, I still have a proud feeling about that dome. My family and I went down to Elk Creek for Thanksgiving to see the finished product. My Uncle built his dome around a tree he had shaved down for added support in the middle. He also had consulted with my Father to find the best wood finish, which he used. The wood on the floor was so shiny and the grain so clear that a person would feel guilty about walking on it. My Uncle and I started a fire in the Ben Franklin stove on the second floor, and then left for several hours. When we returned the thermometer was registering about 110 degrees. I couldn't believer how energy efficient this structure was. Today only the squirrels live in his masterpiece. I am sometimes jealous of those squirrels.

When everyone had gone David spent the next weeks covering the frame with plywood and making windows with Plexiglas. There was a huge window from floor to ceiling facing south, the direction of the road. The center of the dome, in the tallest part, was at least twenty feet and the width across was about the same. There was a loft for sleeping on the north side, where we put the mattress and our chest of drawers. There was a row of smaller windows, one triangle apiece, under the loft. The floor sanded and varnished, was glorious, as Jody relayed, but there were one quarter inch gaps between each board. Dust and debris sprinkled down mercilessly into the kitchen below. David pounded small strips between most of the boards to try to stop this, but dust and dirt continued to rain down. He never did seem too interested in a permanent solution, such as ceiling tiles, because the esthetic effect seemed more important to him than comfort or livability. He built a ledge for a sofa, next to the big window, and we covered it with thick foam and some dark heavy velvet fabric that was once a stage curtain from a school. The inside of the dome was painted white and very nice cherry wood strips were placed along all the seams of the triangles. It was shaping up to have some very good possibilities.

The wood in the lower floor kitchen was mostly light colored ash. It was very pretty when the inside walls were up and a sort of pantry was put in one wall. Each wall in the octagon lower floor was a triangle a little larger than the triangles upstairs in the dome. The pantry wall was a triangle with the pointed end at the floor. He built in a table under a window which was made so it could fold down to make more room, but we never folded it down. It was sanded and varnished smooth but the boards didn't fit exactly, so it was uneven. There were spaces for drawers but they never were finished. There was a hole in the floor next to the supporting post for the cats to run in and out.

We had a wood-burning cook stove that we got from the same auction barn as the gas stove in the shack. It had warming ovens over the cooking areas, which had four covers you could lift off to put wood in, a water reservoir off to the side, and an oven. It was in great condition except for the oven door, which would not stay closed without a stick levered under the handle. We tried to think of several ways to fix it, but never were able to. I cooked on that stove and even canned vegetables on it, for the two or three years we lived in the dome.

We got electricity put in with the help of my Dad and Uncle Deb. After that we were able to get a refrigerator, which was a very old one; I believe it had been David's grandparents. It seemed like the most wonderful luxury after using an ice box for so long. In the winter we had been putting milk and other things in the ice chest to keep them from freezing and then set it outside to keep them cold.

Running water never did arrive at the dome. A few months after we moved into the dome Dad hired a well drilling company to come and put in a well. While they were there we had them dig a trench from the pump house, a few hundred feet, to the dome. It surely would not have been incredibly hard to run pipe and hook it up in the dome. However, that never happened and over the years the trench gradually closed up and became a ditch.

Edgar wanted David to experience truck driving so David went with him on a trip to Los Angeles. They were gone for only a few days, but Rhonda and I were left at home. We started having a pity party about the second night, commiserating about how hard things were, and how they were having a great trip to see the world and there we were. Suddenly I remembered a tab of acid that David had stashed away. It was a few years old and I had heard David remark that he didn't know if it would still be effective. We decided to go ahead and try it. We split it between us and had a very good time waiting for them to return, which they did before it had entirely worn off. They were too totally astonished to be angry. We got to hear about one another's trips later.

Not long after that Rhonda started going with Edgar when he was driving. Once they went to the Gulf of Mexico and brought back an enormous catfish. I didn't even know they were back, and certainly not that they had brought anything. Opening the refrigerator I was startled by the huge whiskered fish with its mouth wide open.

There were many things that didn't make sense to me. Of course, the entire experiment of living on the land as we were trying to do didn't make sense to other people, but that wasn't what bothered me. There were things that would have been so simple: the water that never got in, the rotted tent, the perfectly fine Flexible Flyer sled, in mint condition, which was ruined by being left sitting out in the weather for a year or more. These and many more just didn't seem like the person I believed David to be. I began to suspect the years of marijuana smoking, which continued, were taking a toll.

David grew plenty of marijuana now that we were in a place where it was very easy to conceal it. If he ever sold any, I really didn't know about it.

Once David made a trip to Kansas City to make arrangements regarding the tobacco stake business. I was left there to take care of things, which mostly meant watering the corn and beans, which I would have to carry out manually, two jugs at a time. This would take me several hours. I had not understood when he was getting back, and on the evening of the day I thought he would be back I waited and waited until long after dark. Finally Fang and I walked and ran across the fields to Uncle Deb's place. Fang thought this a grand adventure, a walk through the tall grass in the moonlight. At Deb's I called the Crabaughs to see what was going on. They were all sitting around laughing, and eating cake and having a great time. He said he wasn't planning to come back until tomorrow or the next day. I guess I was supposed to know that. You could almost feel Uncle Deb's judgment of David growing by the minute. He didn't say much, of course, but I could tell the entire episode made him angry. At least Fang and I got a ride back in his car. When David returned he was upset with me because I had not watered the plants enough and they suffered for it.

The old flatbed truck, David and his brother had

salvaged from a field near Weston, where it had been abandoned. Donald was a good mechanic, so he was able to get it up and running. However it never was extremely reliable and I am sure the butt of many jokes on the highway. One fine day in early summer I went with David in the truck down some of the winding blacktop county highways to fetch some more lumber. I'm not sure what kind of place it was where we got it, but it seemed like an old back country lumber yard that hardly anyone knew about. After completely loading the truck with as much as he could get on it, we started out. Shortly we came to a very precipitous uphill grade, possibly about a forty five degree incline. The truck wouldn't go any faster than slow, so we didn't have to slow down. Almost eerily the front wheels lifted gracefully off the pavement. The truck rocked back and I thought we were surely going to go pummeling down the hill backwards. Neither of us spoke, except perhaps a soft, "Oh shit". Time stopped. For an eternity we teetered between heaven and earth. It was long enough for several possible courses of action to flit through my mind, like making a run for it. David commanded me to sit perfectly still and not breathe. He didn't have to ask twice. Numerous possible endings for this adventure occurred to me as I sat there not breathing, listening to the truck creak as it swayed gently, trying to make up its befuddled old mind which way was back to earth. Birds sang in the still air. It seemed most likely that we would be ending up in a pile at the bottom of the hill with truck and lumber on top of us. The brakes held and I never knew how, but somehow, by sheer patience, and maybe some trick of physics that only he knew, David was able to bring the wheels back down to the ground. Slowly, slowly, with much prayer, we inched up the incline. Upon reaching the top, I breathed a sigh of relief I shall never forget. I don't know if I was able to speak, but maybe I said, "Good job".

Not long after I quit at the Lee Plant I started working at the Dairy Queen in Cabool. During the year that I worked there I became acquainted with not only the Maupin's, who owned it and their three sons, but also the other employees, who were mostly high school kids. I enjoyed their companionship and got to know them while working with them. They were fascinated with the dome and liked to bring friends there to see it. However, David didn't like them much and grumbled about "babysitting high school kids".

The old blacksmith shop in Cabool was the source of some of the finest lumber David ever acquired for building. He and Edgar helped pull it down when it was decided that it was too rickety to leave standing. The oak timbers were some of the strongest and most beautiful any of us had seen. David used them in building our dome.

I always feel a tinge of nostalgic sadness when the old things have to pass on. My brother-in-law, Jerry, who grew up in Cabool, had some fond memories of the old blacksmith shop, also. But I was glad that at least David was there to salvage the old lumber, probably some of the first ever cut from the hills around Cabool.

Dome House in Elk Creek, 1977

Back To School

"Life is hard" was a belief that I had carried with me from childhood but after so many years of poverty and scarcity I was willing to admit that it really doesn't have to be *this* hard. Soon after the dream of transformation I began to try to think of ways to claw my way out of the poverty trap. More than anything else, that was my motivation for returning to school, finishing my degree and teaching music, as I had originally planned.

After being away from music for seven years I should have been reasonable enough to change my major, but I persisted in trying to make it work. In 1974, at 27 years of age, I entered Southwest Missouri State University as a student. I drove from Elk Creek to Springfield at least three times a week. Often I stayed overnight at my parents or in a house they rented, when it was empty.

David, Edgar and Rhonda worked very hard keeping the tobacco stick business going. Rhonda made the meals for all of them in the dome kitchen. Whenever I came home it must have been like the mother bear returning to the lair for them. I had to go to the store for food they had run out of, do the laundry, and generally get things straightened out. I fussed a lot about the way things were so disheveled.

While I was a student David began to try to find a venue to sell the boxes and tables he was making with intarsia designs. Also, a friend from school was very adept with macramé. So he and David collaborated on some wood and macramé hanging tables. We took them to a craft show in Weston, where they had been selling tobacco sticks until the season was over. We sat out in front of the grocery store on the highway with tables, boxes, panels and some of my dolls. It was a long day, and I don't remember that we sold anything. But it was then that I got a good look at Weston and fell in love with it. It is an old historic town that has many houses which have been preserved like they were at the turn of the 20th century. The quaint old houses, Main Street, and the churches seemed idyllic, and beckoned to me. I decided then that I would absolutely love to live there.

We also discovered a store in Lampe, at Tablerock Lake where he could actually have an art show of his items. The proprietor was an energetic woman who was a potter. Her store was stocked with her original, creative pottery art. She had an apartment above the store and we spent the night there when we had the art show. She was enthusiastic about getting the word out about his show and David sold several pieces. But one of the main rewards of it was the boost it gave to his morale; just to have someone appreciate his art that much.

One of the many persons who came to see his art show was a woman who was a handwriting analyst. I was writing cards to put on each piece, with the name, and a little about it. We got in a conversation about handwriting, which I have always been intrigued with. By looking at my writing, which slanted greatly backward to the left, even though I am right-handed, she could tell that I was extremely introverted. When she learned that I was in school training to be a music teacher, she suggested that I need to do something to become a bit less introverted, as that would help me in teaching music. I was willing to try anything so she suggested that I write my name, filling up an entire page, each night before going to bed, writing it slanted forward as much as possible. I began that very night to do that. The first pages I did were very messy, I found it hard to slant my writing the other way, but I kept at it religiously. I was totally astonished to find, after a month, that I really was becoming more outgoing. That was a huge learning to discover that not only do things like handwriting indicate some character traits, but those traits can actually be changed by changing the behaviors that indicate them. That was perhaps the first step I had been able to take to overcome deeply ingrained shyness. I owe that woman a great deal, but her advice cost me nothing.

It was a journey between two worlds, going from the dome in the woods to a university campus. I had to arrange to study, write papers and practice while I was home but I did fairly well in my classes. I never did get back to the level of skill I had achieved when I was a student at the UMKC Conservatory. The muscles of my face and jaw, the embouchure, never did get back to the strength they once had. As a result, I wasn't able to maintain a solid pure bassoon tone quality for the hour that my senior recital required. The tone began to quaver and waver and it was hard to hold it in tune. I struggled so hard the muscles in my face were shaking almost like someone clinging to a wall with their fingers slipping. Fortunately the last part of the recital David was playing duets with me on his oboe. That helped some, but it is almost embarrassing to listen to it on the tape, even yet.

As a music education major, I was counseled to take the courses necessary to become certified to teach vocal and instrumental music in grades K-12. So I was in the SMSU marching band. We played and marched at all home games and took at least one memorable road trip to Indiana. Since bassoon is not a marching instrument, I played the clarinet, which I had not played since junior high, when marching. I should say, I held on to it for dear life and tried to keep up with the rest of the band with my feet. I certainly learned a great deal about the exacting art and science of choreographing a band show.

In addition to my life-long habit of feeling estranged from the rest of society, I now had the added difficulty of being an older than average student, not only living off campus, but in a really eccentric life style. I did not make friends with any other students except one small French horn player, the macramé expert, who possibly felt outside of things also because of his homosexuality. Maybe our outsider status was something we had in common. It was nice to have a friendly face among the crowd at football games and other times the band gathered.

Of course, I did have interactions with the other students. Angie B. was a small, blond rich kid from Kansas City, who was the star bassoon player. She was friendly to me, and we shared a common distain for the other remaining bassoonist, who was simply a social cripple. I felt fortunate to be on speaking terms with her, because since she was popular with the others, it seemed like a kind of protection. As the bus was loading for the road trip to Indiana, Angie grabbed one of the sack lunches, prepared for the band, as they were being loaded. She tossed it to me, where I sat on the bus. Everyone on the bus at the time saw this. Shortly Mr. Scott, the director, pounced onto the bus and demanded to know who had the other lunch sack. He had some choice words about irresponsibility and such. No one said a word. You never saw such an innocent band. As for me, it was clear that it was a test. It would not have been worth the scorn and vindictiveness it would have cost me to give it up, whether I reported where it came from or not. So Mr. Scott stormed off without finding the lost lunch. I thought I had at least demonstrated that I understood how teen-age gangs work. As a future teacher of teenagers, perhaps that would be important.

The supervising teacher that one is assigned to when doing student teaching is of critical importance. That person is the one to put the finishing touches on the kind of teacher you will become, and sends you out with confidence or uneasiness. I had met the instrumental music teacher in Mountain Grove, the next town over from Cabool, the year before my student teaching, when I had gone there to do some observing for a class. I knew he would be a really good one to have as my supervising teacher and had even spoken to him about it. However, the next year when I asked to be sent there, I discovered they had a new teacher. This teacher was not near the quality of the one I had observed the year before, and I would never have requested to be sent to him. My student teaching experience was not productive, and I felt very uneasy about being in such a position myself. As it turned out, that was his only year there, and I was even interviewed for the position, but I did not have the confidence to step up to it even if it had been offered.

It was traditional for the band to play for graduation ceremonies. At my graduation, on May 13, 1977, as each graduate who had been a member of the band came forward to receive their diploma, the band burst into spontaneous applause. But when my name was called, and I came up to receive mine, the band did not stir. It was a stinging final rejection and I was glad to be out of there.

SPARTA

I APPLIED TO JUST about every school district in the
state that had an opening for a music teacher. I was
interviewed maybe four or five times. I was about to give
up hope of ever finding a teaching job when I was hired
at Sparta . We found a wonderful old house on the banks
of the Finley River in Lindenlure, not far from Sparta.
Living there was definitely the best thing about that year.
Lindenlure was a group of vacation houses built up along
the Finley River. In the winter no one was there but us.
When there was a beautiful snow and school was called
off, we walked back among the houses and marveled at
the beauty of the frozen river and the lacy ice covered
trees.

The original conversation between us when I decided
to go back to school was, "Okay, if you can get a job
somewhere nearby, so we don't have to move." But after
all I went through to graduate; there was nothing available
in Cabool or Houston, or anywhere else within driving
distance. It was heartbreaking to leave the dome and the
north forty. Neither of us wanted to. I had hoped with an
income we could finish doing all the things we had talked
about. We really did hope that we would be able to return
and make all the dreams realities.

Disaster followed disaster after we moved. To
begin with, the first day of school I returned home and
announced to David, "If you think I'm going back there
tomorrow, you're crazy". It went downhill from there. It

was the most grueling, horrible, hateful year of my life. In addition, a few days after we moved and school started David returned to the dome for the rest of his tools, only to discover that lightening had struck the shack and burned it to the ground. He brought back a lump of aluminum about two inches long and sadly observed, "That was my sander". That was as good a guess as any.

The beautiful lumber he had carefully saved by putting it under the shack, was gone, the lovely old gas stove, everything. Thankfully, the dome itself was fine, except for the kitchen clock that had been knocked off the wall and the fuses blown.

A lively little black female dog of uncertain genetic makeup arrived on the scene shortly after we moved to Lindenlure. We named her Wags, and before long she was pregnant with Fang's puppies. One evening, sometime after Fang had been killed, I was at home alone with her. She began pacing and acting strangely. I think she really didn't know she was going to give birth. When the puppies began arriving, she didn't know what to do. I cut them out of the membrane bags they were in, because she was frightened at what was happening to her, and was dragging them around with the bags attached. It was upsetting to me; I had never seen anything like it. After I cut them out, I got her to settle down and laid them beside her. After that she knew what to do and began licking and nursing them. They all looked a lot like Fang, and were very cute puppies. I took them to school and gave away some of them, and we found homes for the others also.

It was nice to live in a house with running water and electricity and be warm without having to make a fire, but the rest of my life seemed like pure hell. In those days I still operated under the illusion that no matter what, I must not be a 'quitter'. If I faced something as unpleasant as that now, I would resign the job and return to the dome, or find other employment. I struggled constantly to try and reason out if it was the school I had landed in, or my inexperience, or if I simply didn't have what it takes to be a music teacher. Actually I think it was a little of all those things. It is probably an understatement to say that I could not maintain any control in the classroom. The students were shamelessly disrespectful and I had no confidence in my ability at all, a disastrous combination.

The only part of music teaching I had ever really been interested in was the instrumental. At Sparta there were six or eight instrumentalists in what we called 'the band'. There were three students who were siblings, who played saxophone, trumpet, and clarinet. There was also the drummer, who refused to learn to read music and another saxophone and flutist. I was able to organize a beginning group of about the same number. I thought I did a pretty good job of getting them started on their instruments and they made good progress. The instrumental groups, small as they were, saved my life, because I felt that I knew what I was doing. But as for being a choir director, or even elementary music, I was a fish out of water. I couldn't play the piano well enough to accompany, and relied totally on a stereo record player for accompaniment until it quit working late in the year.

One pleasant surprise that happened sometime during that year was that Bill S. from Los Angeles came to visit. Dixie had to stay home and work but Bill brought Nathan, their son, who was three at the time. He also reconnected us to Gaylon from Kansas City. It was a wonderful reunion. We trekked back to the north forty to show them the dome and had a great visit. After that

David and I went on some canoe trips with Gaylon and his friends from K.C. Among them was Lynn, who together with Gaylon, was a great uplifting spirit whenever she was around. She and Gaylon remained together for the rest of her life, the next twenty eight years, even though they never married.

David used the big upstairs room in the house for a workshop and continued to develop his skills at intarsia. He accumulated more tools, including a router, and began making boxes, panels and tables with pictures on them.

After a year of a constant stream of students from the music room to the principal's office, and rather bad music programs, in addition to constant complaints from the students and the music teacher, I'm sure I wouldn't have had my contract renewed even if I had asked to. When I was faced with the prospect of looking for another teaching job, I actually considered trying for another year there, which seems incredible. I thought that with the summer to get myself together, maybe I could make it work. Then I began to think that maybe if I only taught elementary music, and didn't have to deal with the high school and junior high, I could do it. So even though it meant giving up the idea of instrumental music, I took a job in Maysville, teaching only elementary music.

MAYSVILLE

W HEN OUR RAGGED LITTLE Volkswagen rolled into the quiet town of Maysville in August of 1978 no one could have guessed that little burg would never be the same. Not because the woman riding inside was to be employed as music teacher for the next nine months, but more because of the man who was with her.

With the help of the superintendent, Mike Lord, we located a wonderful old farmhouse on a blacktop county road five miles outside of town. It sat on a hill overlooking miles of rolling farmland with a wide veranda encircling two thirds of the house. The spacious rooms on the first floor were enough for us to live in comfortably, and the four bedrooms on the second floor, and even the attic, became David's domain. He used the two larger rooms for his woodworking shop. Another became a kind of office and drawing room and the remaining one was so small it was a general catch-all storage space. There was also a damp, moldy basement, a large garage close to the house, and an old barn sitting out in tall grass in a field beyond the house.

The house had previously been rented to some athletic coaches who had moved on, and there were several reasons for the extremely cheap rent of a hundred fifty a month. Nothing about it had been repaired or renewed in the many years since the family who owned it had all grown up and moved out. It needed new everything but the worst was the water, which was so bad it was yellow. We had to carry in drinking water, just like back on the north forty. Even dishes turned yellow from being washed in it. In the winter the winds sliced through every crack and loose board in every room. David remarked, "This house is just wonderful….. in the spring, summer and fall." But the winter was something to be survived. The landowner, Mr. Fore, allowed us to use a wood stove because the furnace was unreliable. We got some ceramic tiles and made a beautiful tray for the stove to sit in so coals wouldn't drop out and burn the carpet. In spite of all that, we thought we were in heaven. Sitting on the front porch, passing a joint between us, watching spring creep across the rolling fields, we felt like we were living in a Renoir painting. In that house, and in that community, for awhile we felt like we had come home.

That David had the soul of an artist could not be denied. He had decided to express himself by using the grains and colors of wood. He loved to work with wood, and he did intend for someone to buy them. It was an affirmation of himself as an artist when someone admired his work enough to buy it, but that was his excuse for making the pictures.

One winter it snowed. It snowed eight or ten inches all down the road. It snowed all down the driveway, all over the fields. We looked out at the vast landscape we could see from the large front window of the old farmhouse. There was snow as far as the eye could see. It drifted. For several days we couldn't get out or go anywhere, and no one could get in. Then it got colder and snowed some more. Then it snowed some more. If it warmed up it wasn't enough to melt and the sun glared off the whiteness; snow on snow. Even after we were able to dig out and go into town, for almost eight weeks we never saw the earth; only whiteness.

It gets to you, so that you feel like you have to do something about it. So David did the only thing he could do about it. He went upstairs to his shop and chose two large white slabs of pale hackberry. They had smooth flowing lines like snow laden clouds and snow drifted hills. Out of some dark wood, he cut the tiny shapes of a farmhouse and a barn and silo. He placed them down in the midst of the lighter pieces.

His pictures were a kind of abstract; people didn't always see the same thing he was thinking of when he made them. But when I saw it I knew immediately what it was about. I said, "Snow". It was more than just recognizing the scene that was represented. He had captured the feeling of that winter. It was the feeling that came over me looking at it; of knowing I had survived a rough winter shut up alone, isolated from the world with the only person I've ever known whom I could have endured for that long. Then I asked, "Can we keep this one?" so that one is ours. 'Winter in Goose Hollow' was never for sale and it hung in a prominent place in every house I ever called home for many years.

Mr. Fore's family had grown up in that house and he treasured it for all the memories it held for them. He was an elder in the Christian Church in town and invited us to come. It was natural for David, having been raised in that denomination, and his parents always revered Mr. Fore for that. We started going, and because we were so starved for human companionship and being part of a community, we jumped into every happening with enthusiasm immediately. It was wonderful to belong somewhere. We became great friends with the minister, Mike Christianson, and his wife, Gail.

We soon became very active in the Christian Church. David helped out with the youth group; I attended the women's group meetings. We played a lot of different roles there. The third or fourth year there David was put in the position of chairman of the church board. It was really difficult and he made a few enemies. Many personalities there were very hard to work with, and David didn't have much in the way of people skills. But maybe it only seemed that way because he thought so differently than other people.

One of the main things that were a bone of contention was the work that David agreed to do for the church in the way of woodworking projects. He was on his own schedule and many thought it was just taking too long. First he made a stunning cabinet for some old historical artifacts they wanted to have a nice place for. That went pretty well, and everyone was pleased. Then they commissioned a very large panel to hang in the sanctuary. It was an intarsia picture of John the Baptist baptizing Jesus and the dove alighting on Him. The panel was approximately nine feet by five feet. He had to make a special table to put it on in the upstairs hallway area of the house where the stairs came up into the open area outside of all the bedrooms. It took up the entire space for many months. It was a masterpiece which he worked on diligently. The few hundred dollars they paid for it was nowhere near what a person should consider an income for most of a year. But then of course, he had to take time out for flying airplanes and getting stoned.

In the spring Mike came out and tilled up a place for a garden with his tiller. He was an avid gardener himself and it gave him great joy to share his enthusiasm with us. The rich north Missouri soil was astonishing to us after the rocky clay to the south. As we planted and weeded, we kept exclaiming, "There are no rocks!" You could plow up an entire garden and not find a single rock. It was unbelievable. David helped with the planting a little, and after that I was on my own, so of course, it became a source of embarrassment for me. I recall a row of zinnias, a lot of huge zucchini, some corn and beans, but mostly weeds, in spite of hours of hard work weeding. There was a cherry tree and a patch of asparagus, which produced plentifully.

The house was made with two front doors on either end of the large porch. But since the driveway came right up to the back door, one would have to walk past it to go to the 'front doors', so naturally, they were hardly ever used. From the back door one entered into the kitchen. This is the way farm houses are made. Whoever said, "Home is where you can plant flowers by the door", was right. I planted a bed of gladiolas and poppies right by the back door. They were beautiful.

Sometimes in warm weather we put the cat's food out on the back step. Possums would come up and help themselves. One morning we heard a loud rough, rasping meowing. We were shocked to discover a large striped tomcat limping on only two feet. We took him to the vet, who said he had probably been caught in a trap. He was able to restore one leg to health, but 'Captain Hook' was always a three legged cat. He was always so good natured and grateful for any attention; I really enjoyed old 'Cappy Cat'. He stayed with us for two or three years and then one day he just wasn't there anymore.

David loved to go walking in the fields around the

house and often I would go with him. He would find many things like bones, mushrooms, wildlife, and other things that fascinated him. There were old decaying outbuildings that he scavenged for weathered wood for picture frames. He collected random bones and put them together in a grotesque creation. It was the skeleton of a creature made up of perhaps the skull of a coyote, the tail of a squirrel, and leg bones of cattle or something like that. He was so proud of it; he hung it in the front room above the couch. I endured it.

We had only been in Maysville a couple of months when we had to make the trip back to south Missouri for Uncle Deb's funeral. It was a sad event and a long trip. We hardly spoke all the way there and back. Our relationship had become very strained and both of us would rather try to pretend everything was fine than to try to talk about it. In his heart, David blamed me for every bad thing that had happened. When we got home after midnight, I lay down exhausted and had some disturbing dreams which I recorded in a journal. In the dream I was trying to escape a sinister man who was supposed to be my husband because David had sold me to him. After the dream I woke and David was still up, I could faintly hear the guitar softly comforting him.

Our friends, Les and Mary Kerns and their children were involved in 4-H. When they were looking for someone to teach woodworking, David was the obvious choice. He began teaching a group of them in his workshop on the second floor of our house once a week. He enjoyed it and it brought a lot of noise, enthusiasm and new energy into the house. He taught them how to use tools properly and safely as well as making simple projects. Many of them will remember those sessions all their lives, I am sure. I still have a newspaper clipping from the Dekalb Herald with a picture of David and one of the students and an article about his woodworking classes.

That first year in Maysville I taught elementary music. There is not much to be said about it. It was a very nice music room in a fairly new building. It was well supplied with good equipment and lots of bright music books. However, children are still children and I was still me. I traveled between two towns with three days in Maysville and two in Clarksdale. The teachers in Clarksdale were hostile about my being a poor excuse for a music teacher. They were as hard to work with as the children and their attitude did not help me either. The best thing I can say about Clarksdale is they had really great cooks in the cafeteria. Having lunch there was the best part of the day.

I had to put together a program for Christmas which the whole town turned out for. Michael, who was a musician, himself, tried to be complementary about it but it was only so so. David didn't even go to it.

I had a lot of difficulty keeping order in the classroom, just as I had in Sparta. The kids didn't really learn much and I yelled a lot. One of our friends from church was on the school board and toward the end of the year when contracts were being discussed he called me to get my version of what happened because some parents were complaining. I no longer remember the situation, but it was very uncomfortable at the time. Once again, I was extremely glad for the school year to be over. I can't believe that I would even consider going back for another year. How much punishment should a person put themselves through, anyway.

Admitting that I was a failure at teaching and leaving

it was emotionally wrenching for me. I questioned myself mercilessly because I had thought that was what I wanted to do ever since junior high. I asked myself why I had thought I wanted to, and all the reasons why I had failed. I came to the conclusion that it was a person I wanted to be, and I thought being a music teacher would make me that person. But the reality was that I did not like being the person I became in the classroom. I did not want to be a disciplinarian and I was too frightened and insecure to be able to learn how to be both gentle and teach. Perhaps that is a rare combination.

There was one very good thing that came of my teaching music. Although I never could play the piano adequately, I could sing. Teaching helped me to find my voice. I began to sing solos for church, and I directed the cantata at Easter and at Christmas for the Amity United Methodist Church, when they didn't have a director. David and I would try singing together, but I never thought it was very good because I couldn't sing harmony just naturally. I had to hear it plunked out for me and practice it and David just never gave me enough time to get it right. I found that I was always struggling for a pitch all the time we were singing, and it felt like it was usually wrong. So naturally, I wasn't singing very confidently, either. Even though I quit teaching, I always sang for every church I was in from then on. Later I sang for funerals and weddings, also.

I didn't want to try teaching any more, but neither of us wanted to move again. We enjoyed being a part of a community, and wanted to try to put down roots somewhere. This was to become a theme that was to color the rest of my life. So we decided to stay there and I would try to find other employment. Since people knew me I had a form of networking to help accomplish that.

HEADSTART

As it turned out, that was exactly how I got my next job. Maxine Long, whose grandchildren had been in my music classes, and who was connected to our church, was director of the HeadStart program in Maysville. The program was administered from a corporate office in St. Joseph. They were starting a home visiting program and I was hired to be the first Home Visitor. I traveled to homes that were too far away from the HeadStart Center for the children to attend and visited with the mother and child together. We played games, made fun things, and had a snack. The goal was to teach the mother things she could do with the child to prepare them for success in kindergarten. As with any HeadStart, the program also included nutrition and health education, as well as any special needs, of which there were many. The social opportunities were provided by monthly trips to St. Joseph to interact with the children in the centers. The most popular of these trips were for holiday activities like Halloween, and Christmas.

I liked being a home visitor with HeadStart. Even though I didn't make nearly as much as I did when I was a music teacher it didn't matter. I liked the work with children and their mothers. I felt as if I became a good friend to the families and became involved with their joys and struggles. I liked the other home visitors I worked with in St. Joseph, who I met with every Monday to plan our lessons and activities. I liked the freedom of making my own schedule and even being out in the countryside driving several hours most days. I felt that the work was significant and it made me feel like I was making a valuable contribution. I think for the first time ever, I felt that I was doing something valuable and doing it well.

There were so many things about life that I was still trying to figure out that sometimes I was only dimly aware of the things that were better than previous years. It would have been good to stop and be thankful. It was a vast improvement from our time on the north forty to be in a community of other people at all. There may have been those who wondered why we put up with the drafty old house and yellow water. They didn't know we had lived where we had to dig a hole for bathroom duty and carry water in jugs from the creek or well. We each had created opportunities to influence the world around us in some way, and that was an improvement to being isolated as we had been.

THE DREAM CRASHES

ALL MY LIFE I had wanted to be a mother. I envisioned having several children. I wanted to be the kind of mother I wished mine had been and wasn't. When we first got married we both talked about and agreed that we would have children 'some day'. After the first three years, when we left Los Angeles I didn't use any birth control. Yet I never got pregnant. I had no pains; my periods never skipped a beat. So as the years went on, after I turned thirty, after my dream of being a music teacher fell flat, I became more and more concerned about having a child. I began to want to find out what was wrong and fix it.

Maybe David and I were never really happy except for moments here and there. Those moments were enough to sustain us and keep hoping for the next time joy would emerge between us. They became fewer and fewer and farther apart. I wrote the following words in my journal the day before my thirty third birthday in 1980. I had started writing how I didn't want to smoke marijuana anymore and hadn't wanted to for a long time, but every time David would light a joint I would go in to the room where he was and share it, even though I really wished he wouldn't smoke it, either. It seemed the height of duplicity for us to go out into the community and be respected solid citizens, a teacher and church members, and then to come home and smoke marijuana. I had a hundred reasons for wishing it would go away. Then I wrote this:

"I have been in such a state of emotion for the past several

weeks that it's beginning to make me ill now. I feel weak, lightheaded, and nauseous. My stomach sometimes feels like a live thing that has teeth; it draws up and spreads out and bites and turns over and over sometimes when I'm taking a nap or when I wake up at night. If I lay down during the day, when I'm first waking up, I don't know if it's morning or night, or where I am or what day it is or why I'm laying down or anything.

I'm not sure I know exactly how it all got started, but I think it was the scene we had the day I was supposed to have the doctor's appointment.

The appointment was for January 25. I thought while I was off work in January would be a good time to go find out once and for all why it is that I've never been pregnant. So the day before the appointment I said to David that it really wasn't going to do much good for just one of us to be examined, and since the test for males is less expensive and more simple, it would make sense for him to go with me and be examined. I guess he didn't make any reply at all, at least I can't remember any. Whatever his response, I knew he wasn't going to go with me.

The next morning he went out to do something to the car, in a little while he wanted to know what time I had to leave. I replied that I was not going. For some reason that made him angry and he huffed out of the room. I was mad at him all day for not going with me.

A few days before this he had had a temper fit while trying to call some business establishment in St. Joseph and could not get through. In a rage he picked up the phone and smashed it down repeatedly so hard that he broke something in it and it went dead. He also threw a cup across the room and broke it on the cabinet. I think it was before the doctor appointment incident because I called the doctor from the phone upstairs. When that happened I knew he was breaking the phone. I wanted to jump up and yell at him to stop, but I didn't. I just sat there and listened to him destroying it. When he is that angry I'm afraid of him.

Back to the story – I can't remember for sure how it got started, the first thing I remember now is lying in bed and hearing David start in on one of his "why-don't- you-ever-try-to-do-anything-to-please-me" speeches. One of those lectures that make me feel worthless like he just thinks I never try to do anything better, I never put out any effort, he does all the 'work' to keep the relationship going and I just pull him down. And ends with "why don't I?", "What do I expect him to do?", and "what do I have to say for myself?"

Just to avoid having to listen to any more of it, I got up and came in the front room on the sofa. He came in to try to smooth it over, and I explained how it seemed like I was the only one who wants to have children, like it's not our *problem, it's* my *problem. I said I thought if I had a baby it would give me a whole new outlook on life, I would be different, I'd be happier, more relaxed. He would like me better because I would like myself better. I will never forget how I felt when he answered that. He said he was afraid if I had a child I would like it more than I do him, and that I would give him 'even less' attention than I do now. That if I would become more involved in his work so that I could communicate with him about it more and so on, that he would feel better about it.*

He couldn't have done it better if he had slapped me clear across the room. I think I have hated him ever since that moment. I ended the 'discussion' by saying that we could never work it out by ourselves and I would try to learn more about art if he would agree to go to a counselor with me. He said alright.

A few days later I got a lot of books about art from the library. He never mentioned anything about a counselor again. No, I never read the books and even if I memorized them all he still would not think I had done anything.

I have spent a lot of time trying to figure out where to go and what to do when I leave."

A month later it was David's birthday. We had Mary and Les K and the new pastor and his wife, Gordon and Rebecca P over for cake and ice cream. We had a good time like we were a happy, normal couple, and I must say, so did they.

Two months later I went to a counselor. David said that if the counselor thought he should go after I had visited with him, he would. So the second visit he went, also; but he didn't like it. Neither of us ever mentioned to the counselor that we smoked marijuana. I felt that it would be the most enormous betrayal I could ever make of David. He would never forgive me for that or trust me again. I don't know how many visits I or we had been to when I wrote the following in my journal:

March 14, 1980 "The thing he said that stays in mind the most is, "You hold all the aces". It really seems funny now that I never thought of it that way before. To have someone support me in the way I have always thought and felt about our situation was such a relief. Just to have someone finally say, "You're right; you're being taken advantage of." When this is over, I don't know if I will have David, I never have had him yet; but at least I will have myself, and I've never had myself before, either.

Dr. H actually suggested that I might have to leave for awhile in order to convince David that I meant business, in order to get his attention. I hold the aces, when he said that phrase and began elaboration on it, saying, "He knows you do, but he doesn't know you know you do. (I didn't) You have more power than you think you have".

I remembered the time back at school when David and Bill first taught me to play hearts. Dixie wasn't there. I won the game by running the hearts. Naturally, I didn't know what I was doing, it being my first game, but I won simply because of the cards I had been dealt. It seems symbolic now. I didn't tell the doctor about it because it didn't seem important."

April 28, 1980 My children are worse than dead.
    They were never conceived.
    Don't tell me I don't want them.
    I do. I miss them.
    Is there no one who will grieve with me?
    Don't tell me they would only bring me
    pain and sorrow. I know.
    I know.
    I would gladly exchange that pain for this.

May 13, 1980 Now I am really certain that I will be leaving. I'm trying to collect my thoughts so that I will be able to explain why, probably to myself as much as to anyone.

From the very beginning I was so afraid to get married so I told myself, and David too, I think, that if it ever got so it felt like a trap I would end it. I didn't want a miserable marriage like every one I had ever known had. I wanted a happy one or none at all. All the things that have happened to me have been my own fault, for not believing enough in good things.

I did not feel comfortable to marry David, I did not like his friends, or believe in the things they believed in, but instead of being strong enough to leave and say, "I love you but we don't belong together, this isn't me, I tried to be 'strong' by changing and telling myself the things I thought weren't as good as the things David thought. And now I am caught up in a life that doesn't seem to be mine.

It just seems that we have such a different set of values that there is no reconciling them. I try to explain that I need for David to be a provider, to take care of me, and to want a family to raise together so we would have some common purpose. But these things mean nothing to him. He says, "I'm a Great man!" As if the ordinary things I want are beneath him. I don't know if he is a great man or not. I don't care. I don't want a great man, I want a loving husband. He takes my words and either exaggerates or twists the meaning. Saying that all that's important to me is money, or that I don't want him to enjoy life, I want him to have some miserable job and be miserable. This is the image of myself that he has been holding up to me for years; a crabby, complaining, melancholy, stupid, cold, frigid woman.

He said to Dr. H that he could get some fantastic job, and do all these things I say I want, and I still would not be satisfied. I can see that he might be right about that, and it makes me more miserable than ever to think of it. Why am I so dissatisfied? Why can't I believe in myself, or love anybody? What's wrong with me? Do I really have to live my life like this, going from on thing to another, one psychologist to another, one husband to another? I would rather die now. I think there is no point to my life anyway.

If it is so selfish and weak for me to leave why is it so hard to do and supposing it is a mistake, is it really irreparable? It is either right or wrong. If it is wrong I will be very lonely until I find a new life again, and the hardest thing will be believing that I will, and that everything will be alright.

169

On August 17, 1980 I left home. It was a Sunday and there was to be a pot luck dinner after church and Sunday school. David was playing the guitar for the pastor's daughter and another girl to sing. It made for some confusion because he had to be there early and the dinner wasn't until after Sunday school, and David didn't want to be there for Sunday school. I took the dessert I made for the dinner to the church.

August 18, 1980 After church he says he's going home, will come back for dinner. I can't believe it, doesn't he know gas is $1.25 a gallon and there's an energy crisis. All the way home no one speaks. I keep my head turned out the window on my side.

At home my stomach is churning, always it's the stomach. David puts on swimming trunks (which he does to stay cool), I say, "Have you decided not to go back for dinner?" He says he hasn't decided. I begin cleaning up, getting things together; clothes, music books, sewing box, HeadStart materials, and my file box. I think, 'I don't want to be wearing this dress when I go and I'm not going to church and pretend everything is hunky dory, not this time". So I change my clothes and continue packing things into boxes and sacks. David might think I'm having a spell of cleaning up.

I followed him upstairs and I said, "When you get like this and you won't say what you're mad about or what's bothering you I can't help thinking you just don't care." He says he doesn't think I care either and I say I care less and less all the time. He says he doesn't think I ever did. I nod and retreat.

He comes in later and asks if I am ready to go, very typical of him to pretend the conversation of a few minutes ago never happened. I'm not going and I tell him there is a banana pudding up there. I meant at the church, but he looks in the refrigerator, doesn't find it and goes on.

I have to force myself in the next few hours over and over again not to think. Just act! For God's sake if you think about it you won't do it. I start to make a hamburger, then I realize he won't be gone long. I have to have everything ready when he gets back so he won't see me packing. Upstairs, everything out of the bathroom; downstairs, all clothes, I have to leave so many things. Don't think, don't think. Reminding myself how I will feel if I don't leave. Dirty laundry, toothbrush, library books. What if it's a mistake. Do it! Hamburger is pretty well done now.

He comes back. Everything I own is in a box or sack so I sit down at the piano and grab a book like I'm looking at it. He comes in, "We're supposed to be at Gordon and Rebecca's at 6:00". Then he turns and softly pads upstairs. He doesn't want to be where I am.

Then is when I actually did what I have never been able to do before. I began to carry my things out to the car. I propped the back door open so it would not make noise. I cleaned out the floor and ash tray of the car, so if he looked out when he heard the doors open, he would only see me cleaning the car. I was terrified that he would come down before I was finished. (I wanted to leave without telling him and without his knowing it, because I couldn't stand the confrontation. It would have delayed my going because he would have insisted that he needed a vehicle and the car was the only one we had. I didn't feel too badly about taking it since my parents had bought it for us and I was the one who needed it for work. Anyway, I was sure his parents would help him get one, which they did.)) *It must have taken me fifteen minutes, but it seemed like an hour.*

Every time I put something in the car I glanced up to see if he was looking. Each time I passed the stairs I thought he was coming down. I couldn't decide what to pick up and carry out next; I kept saying, "hurry, hurry!" What will I say if he comes down and sees it? I was making up replies. I picked up the blue suitcase with my jewelry and other things in it, but I must have left it in the yard. The last thing was the clothes on hangers, just like I planned months ago. As I pushed and shoved them into the back, I thought I could hear him moving upstairs. I put the key in the ignition, it started. I started rolling backwards but it wasn't fast enough, I shifted into reverse. God, what a grinding. If he didn't hear me loading the car he heard me start it, and if he didn't hear me start it, he heard that! Into first, into second , out the drive, up the road. I made it! I made it! I forgot my watch. I did it! Joy. Jubilation. Ecstasy. I laughed, I was exhilarated, Oh, Lord, what a feeling! It was so funny, so terribly beautiful! He was right upstairs!

I stayed at a ratty little motel, The Rose, in Cameron that night. I don't remember if it was the next day, but very shortly I was able to get a small apartment attached to a house. It was only two or three rooms. My family was very worried about why I left. I couldn't understand why that would be such a mystery to anyone, after all the unpleasantness we had gone through, but I guess they didn't know. Charlene and Ron came to visit me, to see if I was alright and what was wrong. It's amazing how difficult it was to put it all into words in such a way that anyone could understand how much pain I had been in. I didn't really mean to be leaving permanently. I was taking the counselor's advice and doing it really to get David's attention, to let him know I was serious about changes. So in probably less than two weeks I was back home.

My leaving was scary for both of us and the climate improved a lot for awhile. We seemed to appreciate one another more and talked again. I felt more confidence and felt less trapped because I knew I could leave again.

During that year David started writing plays for the youth at church and they performed them. He also made a lot of pictures of old farms and farm buildings in the area. They were deteriorating and falling down, but he would draw them and make pictures in wood of what he drew. Mr. Fore and others had him make pictures for them of their buildings. I continued to enjoy my work with HeadStart and I was always learning new things there. His parents helped him buy a used pickup truck while I was gone. His Mom did his laundry and brought him food.

During that year I finally went to a fertility specialist in Kansas City and discovered that I had endometriosis, which was preventing me from getting pregnant. Often women have pain and other symptoms with this condition. I had no symptoms at all except for not becoming pregnant. I took a very expensive prescription for it for a few months. The doctor said we would see what happens now.

It was exactly one year after the first time I left and what happened was that the dam burst again.

July 7, 1981 On June 1, after I got home from seeing Dr. Betts for the last time while on the pills David and I got into an argument about money.

I wish I had started another way, I should have said that on Sunday, the last day in May, we discovered that all the cherries were ripe, or very nearly so. There were enough that we went out and picked enough for a pie, brought them in, washed them, went out on the front porch and took the pits out with hairpins. I then made a pie, which was only half eaten when I left the next day. We had planned to pick and freeze all the cherries during the next week. I am still sorry that the cherries didn't get picked, and probably went to waste. They were so pretty, and there were so many.

David began saying that I owed him or our joint account money. It was clearly down in black and white that I did not.

Thinking back on it, this may be the most incredible outrage of our entire marriage. I was the one who made the income that paid for all our living expenses. David made very little. In a good month he might make slightly over one hundred dollars. It would almost always go for something for himself. And yet, because I asked him to make something for a gift for a friend of mine, he thinks I 'owe' him for it. I think that because no money changed hands, he felt that I thought it was valueless. In a strange convoluted way, one can almost understand the artist's feeling. Apparently I had thought the matter was settled when he brought it up again. It was as if he was trying to con me. I had a feeling of mistrust and resentment.

July 7, 1981 continued. I have been trying to remember how the discussion evolved, and cannot. But it seems that he asked if I would be willing to support him while he went back to school, and my answer was not as affirmative as he would have liked so he said, "Well then, I'm in a kind of double-bind, there's not really much I can do". At which I jumped up and said, "You're right, there is nothing you can do now, you've already blown it".

I wonder what he thought I was already doing. It was

an indication that he totally discounted the fact that I was doing all the providing for us. Without my support he would be living on the street, which he had actually said at other times was an experience he would like to have. I don't think he had any intention of going back to school. He was just saying that to use my reaction as fuel for his defense.

July 19, 1981 When I left on June 1, I called Gretchen (a co-worker in St. Joseph) from the office. She had told me I could stay with her if worst came to worst. When I finally reached her she said, "Is this what I think it is?" I stayed with her until the weekend, and then I went to Janie's. Wouldn't you know it; Janie and Jerry were on the brink of disaster also.

I went back to Gretchen's Sunday evening. Things were a little weird there. She was getting ready to go get her daughter from her Mom's house, to spend the night. As I had been using her daughter's room, I thought it would be better if I stayed somewhere else that night.

I planned to sleep in the office, but on the way I had a bad feeling like I shouldn't. I drove by the house on the off-chance that David wouldn't be there, but he was. So I drove around to the northwest corner of the property, opened a gate, drove the car in, closed the gate, and slept in the car that night. I had a pillow and a spread with me. There was a little lightening and thunder but it didn't rain. That was the most uncomfortable night of all.

I stayed with Gretchen that week, until the house I had located in Plattsburg was ready to move into. It was a sweet, old one bedroom house with a front room, kitchen and back porch. There was a small front porch with a swing. One feature I really liked was a border of stained glass squares around the large window in the front room. Ever since, whenever I see a window with a border like that I think of the house I had in Plattsburg. I didn't have any furniture for it so friends donated some things. I was heartened by a visit from Donald, David's brother and his wife, Mary. They understood perfectly my issues with David and brought me very useful items such as a mattress and springs, and a frame to put it on and some lamps, but the thing I appreciated most was their understanding.

However, his parents always sympathized with him about everything and probably agreed that I was just such a horrible person, how had he put up with it so long.

It was very lonely there by myself and I missed my cats. So when one of my HeadStart families had a litter of kittens I took a little gray and white one the kids had named 'ugly' because her muzzle had a gray spot that looked like she had stuck it in some paint. I did not think that was an appropriate name, because she was a very cute kitten. I brought her to my house and named her Claudy.

During the year before I moved to Plattsburg David had started making and flying model airplanes with a passion. It was a hobby he had started as a child and his Dad was very enthusiastic about it, also. Papa Crabaugh built them each special cases for carrying all the equipment needed to the area where they would fly the planes. He spent a great deal of time making planes and flying them in the fields around our house, which was the most excellent place for flying. I made a small cloth head of a doll for a pilot in one of them. The planes would eventually crash, if they were flown often enough. It seemed like it was a game to see how many flights it could make before a fatal crash or not being able to repair it again.

I tried to be supportive and enthusiastic about his hobby but in the back of my mind I was thinking how nice it must be to be able to play all day while someone else took care of you, like a perpetual child. We were living in poverty. There were so many things we needed and which would have made life more pleasant. But David seemed to act as if none of that mattered, and he had everything he wanted.

I believe the body has wisdom of its own and that my body actually found a way to prevent me from bringing a child into the world under these circumstances. Often I thought how hard it would be, and the changes that would be necessary. David had said he wasn't going to baby-sit because it would interrupt his work.

I liked the little house I was in and if I had a child then, or someone who could have helped me to focus on my intentions for my life, I would have been able to go on from there. But I was constantly drawn back to David because I didn't know what else to do. In spite of so many unresolved problems it was too hard for both of us to voluntarily tear apart the fabric of our lives; the history we already shared, the belief that we could make it work, and the love that was very real.

We reestablished communication and visited one another a few times. There was one memorable time when we had arranged for me to go to the house in Maysville for an afternoon. When I got there he was out in the field flying his planes. The memory of everything I had been dissatisfied with, and all the feelings associated with being there all came crashing back. I wrote a note and left. He got very angry at that and came to my house and delivered a scathing letter, in which he addressed me as Charlotte Wright. It should have been over for sure then, but somehow we pulled out of even that. In a few weeks I moved back home, bringing Claudy with me.

Ellie and Ruby accepted Caludy with a limited amount of growling and sniping. They adjusted after a few weeks. But it was a rough year for cats. One day Ruby just didn't show up. We never saw her again. David said an owl could have got her. I think if he had found any remains he wouldn't have told me, for which I am grateful. Claudy liked to play dare with the swallows who built nests on the large front porch. One day she appeared with a badly mauled eye. The vet said it looked like a sharp object had hit her very hard. We thought a swallow had probably had enough and dived at her eye. That eye was clouded over and she could never see out of it after that.

During that year it seemed like David let up on trying to make me someone I wasn't. It was peaceful but there was an undercurrent of dissatisfaction; as if we were both tired of the same arguments and were willing to just accept things as they were, although it was not what either of us really wanted.

Fairport School was the last of the small country schools in the county. There were about four classrooms with fewer than a dozen students in each. The entire staff was two or three teachers and the principal, Betty G. They even tried to have a basketball team. One of the most pitiful things I saw was the entire male student body of Fairport School, about a dozen boys, pitted in a game against Maysville. The Maysville team kept putting in fresh players while the Fairport boys all had to keep playing with no relief. There had been no try-outs for the Fairport team as there had been for Maysville, just, "Hey, you want to play basketball?" I don't know if they scored any points, and I wonder if they could keep enjoying playing after a few massacres like that. They had a stubborn pride and they didn't want to have to close the doors of their school and go in to Maysville.

During that year, 1981-82, I taught music there for a few hours a week. Somehow I was able to arrange it with my HeadStart schedule. I wasn't any better at teaching music than I had ever been, and some of the boys were very disrespectful. So I didn't last very long and David went over to try his hand at it when I got tired of trying. Not having the constraints of any music education classes to hold him down, he just did what seemed like fun. He put together a program using country music and his guitar. They sort of acted out parts, like a music video. It was highly entertaining, although I can't imagine how any music education was gained from it. The experience introduced us both to Miss Betty, the principal, who was a pretty, youngish woman who was the dreamer that kept the school going.

Sometime in the spring of 1982 I went to the Dept. of Family Services and got forms to apply for adoption of a child. David had agreed to sign them, but I really believe he would have done everything possible to sabotage the process.

During the winter of that year I finally spoke a question that had been growing in me for a long time. Remembering how we thought we were so special, back when we were really young and first met, how we were going to do things better than our parents had, maybe we thought we were going to be more authentic What was it that we were going to do? I said to David, "You know, I can't remember what it was we are trying to do?" His answer came quickly. Typically, not having anything to do with us, how we were together on this journey, he said, "I am searching for truth and beauty".

THE STORM AND
THE TALL GRASS

L ATE IN THE AFTERNOON or evening of June 8, 1982 it all began. It grew dark and windy. The clouds began to boil. It was like being in the bottom of a pan of boiling oatmeal and looking up at it. I have never seen clouds churning that way before or since; turning over and over on one another, bubbling up and rolling over and over. Thunder like tympani; low, rolling like the clouds. Gray, close to the earth, like it could roll down and catch us up in it and carry us off.

He called to me to come out and look. The wind was whipping us about. It was frightening and fascinating all at once. I was more frightened and wanted to go inside. David was more fascinated and couldn't leave. We stood out on the hill beyond the barn and looked straight up into it. Almost as frightening as the wind and clouds, was David's fascination with it. He was mesmerized; the beauty of it, the awesome power.

The rain was coming down in sharp pellets and he was still standing staring up into it. I thought he was losing his mind.

That night we sat inside and listened to it rage. It beat and tore at the house as if trying to get at us. The thunder crashed and rattled the windows. Lightning slashed and cut. Wind. torrents of rain. I can never remember being afraid of a storm before. I have always enjoyed the cozy feeling of being safe inside. But this did not feel safe or cozy. It seemed like it was trying to get us.

David sat and wrote on his Jonah play. He wrote out the rough outline of it while the storm stormed. I went to bed finally. He stayed up most of the night.

When I woke up the sun was shining. It was quiet except for birds twittering outside. David had been there sometime during the night, but now his side of the bed was empty. I got up and got ready for work. There was no electricity. I knew he had gone out to see how much damage had been done, and maybe get the electricity back on.

I had only been at the office a few minutes; was coming back to my desk carrying a cup of coffee, when Stanley B came in the door out of breath, like a wind left over from the storm. "You've got to come home. There's been an accident. David has been electrocuted. He's dead." I tried to hold on to my coffee, or sit it down, or something. I said, "I don't understand." And I didn't. What he said made no sense. David was alive. He had always been alive. The last time I saw him he was alive. There was no life except his. And I was still alive, so he must be. It made no sense. "I don't understand".

My friend, Beverly, was there. She said, "I'll go with you." Stanley was relieved. On the way home in his truck I kept saying, "There's some mistake. He's just hurt. We'll call an ambulance." No one answered me.

When we got there Norwood was there, and maybe someone else. They wouldn't let me see him at first. But I did see him stretched out in the tall grass just a few feet from where I had gotten into the car in the garage earlier. His straw hat was lying beside him. It had surely been the hand of God that covered my eyes that turned my head away that made me not see him there.

Norwood asked, "Didn't you see him?" No, I guess the grass hid him. Thank God. "If you had seen him you might have rushed over to him. Then you both would have been electrocuted. Did you know that?" No. I didn't know if I touched him, I probably would have been killed also. I just didn't see him. Norwood shook his head at the possibility.

David had found the electric power line blown apart, and lying on the ground. He had turned off the power at the source and was preparing to splice it together. However, as the electric engineer later explained to me, there was still power in the line. He said, very kindly, that sometimes even people who work with electricity regularly don't realize that this happens. Everyone who knew David pondered why he would do such a thing. I felt some anger at him for not having more respect for the power of electricity and for thinking he could actually fix it. Why did he think it was so urgent that he couldn't just leave it for the electric company to come and repair? It almost seemed that here was a man who thought the powers of the universe were at his command, or didn't apply to him, or who thought he was invincible, that there was nothing he couldn't do, or maybe he actually had a secret death wish.

When our friend and pastor of the Methodist Church came, he made them let me see David. He was stretched out, holding on to the power line with both hands. His mouth was in a shape like he was saying, "Oh". The ground around him tingled. I was wearing brown sandals.

As we went into the house I said, "If this is one of his

tricks, I'm going to kill him." It wasn't funny. No one laughed.

When the coroner, Pete Bram, and the electric company came. I watched them put him on a stretcher. I went outside without saying anything to anyone. I went over to him, took the blanket off his face and touched him. His hair felt normal but his skin was rigid. His face looked greenish and splotchy. When I touched him I realized finally that he wasn't there. That was the first time I knew he was dead.

A few tears came as we went back into the house but I didn't cry very much until much later. I only sat in shock that day, trying to comprehend this thing. Different people sat with me throughout the day. Jean Ann Bird, Evelyn Bird, Bob Barnett, the Christian Church pastor, are the ones I remember.

Charlie had me call David's folks. But he had me call their minister first so that she would be there when they got the news; and she was. I don't know what we would have done without Charlie there. He said calling them was a very brave thing for me to do.

Beverly said she went back to the office and put her head in her hands and cried. The phone rang. It was a woman who lived out near Weatherby, who had only been in the office once or twice, who really didn't know any of us very well. She asked, "Whatever is the matter there at the office?" as if somehow she had mysteriously received a message that something was wrong. Beverly told her. She said she would pray for us; for me. That was the first of many times I would be aware of someone I don't even know praying for me and also of the telepathic messages that are sent and received between people.

The next day Charlie asked me about the service. It's

amazing how I knew what songs to use without having to think about it very much. It seemed like my hand was just directed to a song I didn't even know, about walking in the fields with God. It was more like David than "In the Garden". The song, "My Way", made famous by Elvis Presley and Frank Sinatra, seemed perfect for him. In later years I have thought back, I guess it's too bad it wasn't 'God's Way', but on that day, the words of that song fit David perfectly. He had always admired the sonorous harmonies and words of Martin Luther hymns, so the congregation sang "A Mighty Fortress Is Our God'. The service was held three days later in the Maysville Christian Church. There were three pastors. Bob Barnett was the current pastor of the church; Charlie was David's friend, and pastor of the United Methodist Church, where he had been going for months. Our old friend, Michael Christianson, who had been pastor of the Christian Church when we first came to Maysville, came back to sing the two songs. The church was filled to overflowing. Edgar and Rhonda stood way in the back, looking so out of place; Edgar with his long hair and truck driver blue jeans, but to me they were about the most important people there.

All of both of our families came. My cousin, Jerry, was there. David's brother, Donald was a skeleton. The cancer he had for ten years was advancing, unstoppable. He was soon to follow David and we all knew it. It was exhilarating to have everyone there. It was a wonderful gathering. I didn't grieve very much that day because it was such a joy to be all together.

Marijuana plants that David was growing in milk cartons were upstairs in the small room where they could get lots of light. I thought of them, and decided if anyone asked about them I would say I thought they were tomato plants. But either no one discovered them, or had no reason to question what they were.

June 12 was a warm, sunny day. The peonies covering the cemetery were in full bloom, making it look like an elegant garden. My sister-in-law, Mary later described an almost other-worldly impression of the gathering around the gravesite. The family had gathered around the grave first. She looked around to see where everyone else was. She saw them begin to appear over the sloping rise of ground beyond his grave. First a head, then the rest of the body, as if rising up out of the ground; at first one or two, then more and more rising up this way; the crowd coming toward us.

As for myself, I was remembering my Grandfather's funeral. On that rainy day a long time ago, the coffin had been lowered down with cranks while we all watched. I had the expectation that was what would happen, so I remained seated after Rev. Barnett was finished speaking and everyone was going. Pete asked me if I wanted to see the coffin lowered, and I said "Yes". So they lowered it, more gracefully than the old cranks, and we all returned to the house where David and I had lived, leaving him there.

The gray granite stone had an etching of the dove, taken directly from the large picture David had made of John the Baptist in the church, with the words, "He searched for truth and beauty". He had spoken his own epitaph.

In the weeks and months that followed grief seemed to swallow me like an ocean. It came in waves, sometimes seeming as if it would tear me apart. Rhonda came and stayed with me the first week or two; the same soft, wide-eyed, runaway girl who Edgar had brought to our dome house so long ago was a great solace to me in those first days. She was the perfect person to be with me. She seemed to realize that it was not necessary to say anything, and never struggled for words. She was just quietly there at my side while I wept. Having been there with us through that strange monumental adventure at the dome house, she seemed to understand the whole depth of my sorrow. When I emerged out into the bright summer air with Rhonda it just seemed impossible that the world was still there. How could it be? It didn't feel like it, but there it all was; the sky, the sun, the birds singing, and the fields; maybe David was out there somewhere. My nephew, Jon, came for part of the summer. We went to St. Joseph and saw ET when it first came out. The little ET being separated from his friends and family and trying so desperately to 'phone home' touched me so deeply in my raw state. My co-workers from St. Joseph came out and visited. Gaylon and Lynn came. I used part of the insurance money to go to Los Angeles to visit Bill and Dixie, who were divorced by then.

All of this helped me to get past the initial disbelief and to try to begin to heal from what Charlie called 'a broken heart'. All of these friends were the strength and healing balm that carried me on from that sad time. The comfort, especially of those who had also known and loved David, was the grace of God beyond all understanding.

Ever since David had first come into my life he had been trying to mold me into the person he wanted me to be. In my deep seated insecurity I had allowed him to do this. He had picked what books to read, what movies to see, what music to listen to, what friends to associate with, and what thoughts to think. I was at a complete loss. I know what a bird, born and raised in a cage, feels like when it is set free. It does not soar joyously into the sky, singing, "Freedom, freedom, I am free!" No, it is terrified. I didn't know what to do. But slowly, gradually, I began to realize that those who live have the last word. My life was just beginning.

End Part One

NOW WE ARE ONE

EVERY DREAM I HAD ever had was destroyed. In spite of all the difficulties David and I had been through, or maybe because of them, I had placed all my hope in the future we would create together. In the weeks and months that followed I tried to construct a way to live without him. I could think of myself as 'widow', but it took several weeks before I could think of myself as 'single'. Single means that you could let someone else into your life. It means you can, or must, decide things for yourself. People had been very kind and supportive through the initial loss and the shock. The people of two congregations, both the Methodist and Christian, were praying and grieving with me.

However, it didn't take long for some to begin to think they knew what was best for me. One older woman was even reported to have said, "Why, she's going to have to sell everything she owns." I never could figure out why anyone would think that. If it had been David who was left alone, that would have been true. But I was the one who knew how to make my way in the world and now there was only myself to provide for. People thought I should move out of the house and into town. They didn't seem to realize that my whole world had been destroyed and I needed to hang on to everything familiar that I could while I sorted it all out. Mr. Fore no longer wanted me to live in the house all alone. He began trying to make things difficult. He did an about face on having a wood stove. He no longer wanted me to burn wood, saying the insurance wouldn't cover it. It hadn't been a problem while David was there. The old furnace burned an incredible amount of oil and didn't work reliably, but he wouldn't do anything to try to fix it. Out of sheer stubbornness, I used a lot of David's life insurance money on heating oil that winter just so I could stay in the house.

An old bachelor farmer lived down the hollow from our house on the hill. I had never met him and was barely aware of his existence. A few weeks after David's death and when no one was staying with me any longer, he started coming over to visit. He made me feel very uncomfortable and I dreaded seeing him coming. He had nothing to say except about the weather, crops, or neighbor's dogs barking. At every visit he would say, "Well, I guess you really miss ole what's his name". I would agree, yes, it was very different now. At about the third visit he brazenly, without any warning came right out and asked, "Would you care to have intercourse with me?" I was so shocked, appalled and frightened I couldn't run to the door fast enough. I demanded that he leave immediately. Shaking, I called Beverly and told her about it. She called the sheriffs deputy, who was a good friend of hers. He came out to talk to me and went over to the old man's house. He told him that if he ever set foot on the property again he would be arrested. Mr. Fore also paid him a visit, with the same message. But it only reinforced his conviction that I shouldn't be there alone. The old man got the message, and I never saw him again.

During this time of trying to find a new direction in life I became close friends with Kay and Charlie Harrison. David and Charlie had been very good friends. David had been going to the Methodist Church since his falling out with people at the Christian Church, and he was preparing to join the Methodist Church, where Charlie was pastor. He had not talked to me about it at all. Just a few days before the fatal accident Charlie had called to talk to David about joining the church the next Sunday. It was the first that I had heard of it, and I made it clear to Charlie I didn't know a thing about it. It rather hurt me that David would do something that important without even mentioning it to me. Charlie was rather taken aback by my reaction. It was one of his first impressions of me, and he never quite forgot it. As it turned out, David never did join because he was dead by that Sunday.

That was the reason both of the congregations were there for me at the time of David's death. I began to attend both churches, going to the service at the Christian Church at 9:30 and then going over to the Methodist at 11:00. Maybe it was one of the things that were part of the grieving process for me.

Charlie was very pastoral and caring in helping me through the stages of grief. We had many long talks and I became a regular at their house to watch movies and eat popcorn with him and Kay and their children.

I continued to work at HeadStart while working through my grief, trying to learn to be single, and deciding if I should begin a new relationship and with whom.

People in town who knew David were also dealing with their sorrow and shock at his death. One woman who was a leader in the Dekalb County Historical Society planned a memorial art show in honor of David's work. I helped her by providing a list of persons who had something he had made. She sent out letters and most of them responded by bringing the items he had made to the Christian Church for an exhibit. Among those who came to see his work was a photographer from the St. Joseph Newspaper. He interviewed me and took pictures of me standing by the large mural of the Baptism of Jesus. There was an article with the picture in a prominent place in the paper.

MIXED BLESSING

I BEGAN TO RELY on our good friend and neighbor, Leslie Kerns, for help with things that came up around the house. He and his wife had been divorced during the previous year. The same storm that blew down the power line also blew the television antenna off the roof. Les came and put it back up for me. When the weather started getting cooler in the fall, he helped put up the old storm windows, that were kept in the garage. This was an autumn ritual in older houses before the advent of air conditioning, which had never been installed there.

One of the most difficult times for me was Sunday afternoons. It was for Les, also, except that he would usually go to his mother's for Sunday dinner after church. Since we both attended the Christian Church he began inviting me there to have diner with them. His mother, Iona, was a sweet, gracious lady, who seemed pleased that we were spending time together. I was there for Thanksgiving and we watched the football game in the afternoon.

In the fall Les invited me to go with him to a singles group that he attended in Cameron. It was a good group to be around and we had some fun times. We had a hayride, and I guess that was the first time Les and I really began to feel close to one another. We kept doing things with the singles group, but more and more things just with the two of us. We went to St. Joseph or to Cameron to eat out. People started getting used to seeing us together.

Leslie was a rather melancholy person. It seemed like a character trait such as the 'Norwegian farmer' type made famous by Garrison Keillor in 'Lake Wobegone Days', even though his father and grandfather had farmed there in the Missouri heartland. That was his home where he had lived his entire life. Everyone knew him from his heyday as a football star at Maysville High School. He lived in the same house he had lived in as a child and raised his own two children in. When I considered whether I would ever marry him, it was no small consideration to realize that this would be my opportunity to have the community to belong in that I had always longed for. The only way to become part of a small community that you are not born in is to marry into it, or buy into it, as some have done. I even liked his sweet gabled farmhouse and the farm surrounding it. It seemed like it could be the very life I had always really wanted.

However, that would have been an unrealistic view of life, too idealistic even for me. In spite of our feelings for one another, we both knew that there were too many glaring differences in temperament and philosophy to ever make a lasting partnership. Les was very fundamentalist in his religious view, even more than I was at that time. I had come a long way from that kind of approach since my college days. However, we continued to enjoy a wonderful friendship and were there for one another during a time when we both were in transition and searching for a new direction.

I loved being with him, but one of the things that annoyed me was that he left me alone for a week or more at a time without calling or visiting. Remembering back to when I first was enamored with David when we were so young, we thought we had to be together all the time. This just didn't feel like 'falling in love' the way I remembered it. Was it just because we were older now? During those times when I was left to reflect on the fantasy world I was creating, I would confide my doubts to Beverly. She was relieved to hear me expressing this, because she and Charlie both had serious misgivings about me forging a relationship with Leslie. One of the things that concerned them both was the rumors of some sexual misconduct Les had supposedly committed against his daughter. That was actually what had compelled his wife to leave when she did. I always dismissed those stories and Les refused to talk about it at all.

Leslie was very concerned that I not get pregnant. He did not want to be responsible for bringing another child into the world, as he was through with that part of his life. He did not like the idea of abortion and did not want to ever be faced with that decision. So I went to a doctor, explained my history, how I had just finished treatment for endometriosis, and I wondered what the chances were that I would ever have a child. The doctor said it was about fifty-fifty. On that day I took stock of my life. I considered the small chances that I would ever find anyone, Les or anyone else, who would want to start a family at almost forty. I made the decision to take that fifty-fifty chance. It may not have been a moral or courageous decision. It was made solely on my deep desire to be a mother. I did not have the courage to risk taking time to find someone who would want to be my partner in life, including helping raise a child. I was nearing forty and I did not know how long such a search might take. From what I had seen in these few months from my vantage point in Maysville, the prospects seemed rather bleak. I believe that in my heart, I truly believed that if the miracle really occurred, Leslie would have a change of heart and it would all work out. I did not think of it as being entrapment or deceptive because I did not know if I even could become pregnant.

Being involved with two men at the same time was not something I had ever dreamed of doing. It did not fit my self concept. Always before I would have wondered at the moral character of anyone who did these things, and probably would have been a bit judgmental. In years to come a pastor friend would ask me, "Were you very close to God at this time?" I can honestly say that I felt the presence of God next to me stronger than I ever had before. Not the judging God I had always heard about in church, but the Real God, who gives life and who wants for us all good things. The Ultimate Reality, who wants for us to live joyful abundant lives, who wants for us to fulfill our Divine purpose, who is as near to us as breath. Yes, I truly felt God near to me every step of the way. I did not consciously set about to make things happen the way they did. I am obviously not that intelligent but God was in charge, as always.

It was as if there was an angry, hurt part of me who had something to prove. David had left me with the belief that I was undesirable and unworthy. Not only that, but I felt he had cheated me out of the very thing I wanted most in life. Was there in my unconscious mind, a voice saying, "How dare you leave me alone? I'll show you".

The Universe has a way of making things happen just the way they should. As it turned out, another man entering the equation at just that critical moment was what was needed to make life unfold exactly right. Beverly introduced me to her cousin, Gary, an energetic talkative man, who called me 'gorgeous' the first time he saw me.

I became enamored with him right away and we began seeing each other a lot. Looking back on that time, I can see several things I would have recognized as 'red flags' which are the marks of a potentially abusive person. But I didn't know anything about those things then. One of those was Gary's immediate insistence that I not see anyone else but him even though we had only been seeing each other for a week or two. It was a very hard decision, but one evening I went over to visit Les and break the news to him.

When I told him I wouldn't be able to see him any more he was very accepting and gentle about it, almost as if he knew this would happen eventually and it wasn't that surprising. When I think back on that visit, I think what seemed like gentleness was probably great sadness. I cried deep shaking sobs all the way back home. I wished it would have been possible to continue our friendship even though I was getting to know Gary. If Gary had not been such a controlling, insecure person he could have allowed me to decide over time which one of them I would choose, as long as they both knew about the other, and it might not have been so wrenching. However, everything was in perfect order, I just didn't know it at the time.

Gary was very exciting to be with. During this period of my life I learned that the criticisms David had directed at me regarding my sexual attractiveness were grossly unfounded. Both of these men and others, affirmed me as a woman so completely that it was like being reborn.

After I had been seeing Gary regularly for about six weeks I realized that I had missed a period for the first time in many years. I got an EPT from a drug store and came up with a positive result for pregnancy. When first confronted with the results of my brash, almost unconscious decision, I could not immediately embrace the joy that it seems I should have at this long awaited moment. Instead I was suddenly aware that this really isn't the way I had wanted it to happen. I was terrified, and yet the excitement that the long awaited dream was about to happen was pushing its way into my awareness.

I went to a doctor in St. Joseph who I knew by reputation to be a kind man, and even a good Methodist. The test I had taken was soon verified to be correct. I told him my circumstances and history and said that I wasn't sure if I was really ready to be a single mother. He gave me the phone numbers of abortion clinics and said it was my decision, but as long as I came to him he would take care of us.

Beverly was the first person I told my news. Her impulse was to rejoice and be excited over the incredible news. However, she realized that I was still struggling with the decision of whether or not to abort. Beverly was fundamentalist in religious views and I have no doubt that she prayed fervently that I would have the courage to give birth. But what she said was, "No matter what you decide, I will be here for you." Beverly was true blue. There was never any question about giving up the child for adoption. In fact, to this day I cannot see how anyone could carry a child for nine months and then give it up to someone else. That is one thing I could not even think of. I told my sisters my news, and I told Charlie.

I will always remember the day I went to see Charlie. He was his friendly, exuberant self, sitting in his office. When I sat down and said, "I'm pregnant", Charlie inhaled a big breath and simultaneously pushed his chair back from the desk. It almost seemed as if for just a moment he wanted to be exasperated. But instead he said, "Well, that's a mixed blessing".

After all these years I will finally confess how it is that there was never one moments doubt that it was Leslie's child. It is just that Gary had a vasectomy. That really made things simple.

The decision I went through whether or not to bring this child into the world or to abort it, was very real. Even after all the years of wanting to have a child, finally being confronted with the reality that I most likely would be doing it alone, was truly frightening. I was still filled with doubts that David had planted about my ability to be a good mother. It was never a question of whether or not I wanted to have this child, but only a question of my own worthiness. I picked up the phone and dialed the number of the abortion clinic more than once, then would put down the phone in confusion. After doing this two or three times it became clear to me that I would never be able to live with myself if I did not have this child. Of course it was the correct decision for me. That is an undisputable, solid gold fact. But I will always be grateful that my freedom to make that decision was real. In years to come, my child, nor anyone else, would ever have to wonder if I really wanted to have her or not. I am grateful that I had a choice.

I was determined not to tell Leslie or Gary either one that I was pregnant until I had clearly made up my mind what I was going to do. I didn't want either one of them to influence my decision. It was going to be mine alone to make. I believe that was fair, since I was the only one who wanted her and who would be raising her alone.

Gary, knowing that it couldn't be his, was angry, and accused me of seeing Les even after I promised I wouldn't.

It wasn't that, it was just that I had only conceived about a day before I first met Gary. He was gone immediately in a huff. About six weeks later he was already married to another friend Beverly introduced him to, and he was being very abusive. Beverly tearfully described how he tied her up and kicked her in the stomach. She had no idea he was capable of such behavior.

Leslie steadfastly refused to believe it was his child. Who could blame him, since I was coy enough not to mention why I absolutely knew it was his, but he might have at least realized it could be. He was silent for almost an hour; we sat in the room not speaking. Finally he said, "I don't think you would be a very good wife because you would not be obedient." What a revelation. I calmly answered, "I think you're right". It may have been the first time I spoke my own truth without hesitation. This child was already empowering me.

Almost anyone would have pressed the issue, demanded a paternity test, and the accompanying child support. However, I am not most people. After mulling it over, I realized the gift I was being given. Anyone with courage and an independent spirit is a free Being. If this man did not want me or my child to be a part of his life, I certainly did not want to be in his. We were being set free. I did not have to give my child his name in exchange for child support. I did not have to continue to have contact with him all my life, possibly with another wife, in order to arrange visits, and all the other struggles and inconveniences that would legally go with forcing him to acknowledge us. He didn't love me and would only be relating to the child out of an overrated sense of duty. I did not need to be hindered by this extra burden and my child certainly did not need to deal with that conflict all her life. We were free.

As soon as both of them were gone, I could enter fully into the joyful anticipation of becoming a mother. And I did. My, how the tongues did wag; my, how I did not care. People naturally assumed that since I did not demand anything from a man and since I did not announce who the father was, that I didn't really know. Their world just wasn't ready for a woman like me. These are the times when you discover who your real friends are. I suppose I will never know everything Charlie did to smooth the way for me. There were people who were scandalized by my behavior and wanted to be judgmental. I know Charlie talked to them and redirected them in a pastoral way. I was totally oblivious to all of it. I was going to be a mother and that was all that mattered.

One of my friends at the church loaned me a lot of very nice maternity clothes and Kay had a wonderful baby shower for me at her house. Many of the women from the Methodist Church came and brought presents. I am certain that my family were all relieved to be happily far away. My friends at HeadStart took it in stride and it was just not that extraordinary for most of the Moms I worked with.

Probably the most touching thing of all was breaking this news to David's parents, who I remained in close contact with. I was so grateful that Diann, David's sister, came to visit from Louisiana, where they lived at the time. It was nine months after David's death and I just didn't know how I was going to tell his parents about it. Her visit came at just the right time. I told her about it and asked her if she would tell Mama and Papa Crabaugh, because I just didn't think I could. Just a few hours after she left my house Mama called. She was overcome with joy, and with great emotion she asked if I would let them be the child's Grandparents.

If anyone ever had any question if this birth was God's will, all one has to do is look at all the ways He has provided and blessed us along the way. The support and loving acceptance of the Crabaughs was one of the greatest gifts of our life. Didn't I say that one of the main reasons I even married David was his family?

I think there was a kind of competition between Mother and her sisters about whose children would be the most successful, or make them proud. Nothing embarrassed and brought her more shame than any misconduct of a sexual nature. Now the tally was complete. Every one of her daughters had embarrassed her by marrying the wrong person or becoming pregnant out of wedlock or both. Now every one of us had humiliated her. I dreaded telling Mother about my pregnancy more than I ever dreaded anything. In fact, finally, I really didn't. She guessed it. Early in the summer I was about three months along when I went to Cabool to visit them. I knew I would have to tell her about it, maybe that was the reason for the visit. But as long as she was in a congenial mood it seemed a shame to break it. I was putting it off. Charlene was living in Grandmother's old house down the road. I had gone there to visit and we were sitting in the kitchen talking about the problem at hand. Mother walked over to the house and entered the kitchen like a black cloud. She demanded darkly to know if I had something to tell her. I told her that I was pregnant and she wanted to know who, how, and anything else she could get out of me. I told her Les was a friend of mine and David's who we had known ever since we came to Maysville; that he didn't want to acknowledge that he was the father, that no, we were not getting married.

It took Mother many weeks, maybe up until the birth, to get past her anger even a little. I never did feel that she ever fully accepted her last Grandchild. One of my sisters reported to me that finally she had conceded, "If it was anyone else I would worry, but since it's Charlotte, I know everything will be alright". So this is the blessing I have taken with me. We never expected, or heard our Father make any comment about these things. However, I am certain that he was completely astounded at the number of irresponsible men there are in the world, and that his daughters all should have been so unfortunate as to each find one or more of them.

I had a sonogram early on and since I felt I had enough uncertainties and surprises, I wanted to know which my baby would be, and learned that I would have a daughter. I knew with certainty that this was the most remarkable child anyone had ever had, so her name had to be chosen with great care. Naming her was the first of many things that would fall to me alone. I had always loved my name because I had been named for my Father, so I wanted a name similar to my own. I got a book of baby names and began to go over it page by page. When I got to the Chars there it was, the name I was looking for. Charmaine, it sounded to me like the name of a happy, sprightly girl who would grow into a beautiful, intelligent woman. According to the book, the name means, 'a singer who makes people happy'. But in my mind it was a name as beautiful and powerful as my own. I thought I knew how Mary felt when the angel appeared to her and said, "You shall call His name Jesus". I felt as if an angel had spoken to me and said, "You shall call her name Charmaine".

Noelle was the other name I considered since it was a name I really liked and she would be born at Christmas time. Noelle means 'a song of joy'.

I consulted with other people just to get their reactions, not because they would really influence my choice of name. Charlie, thinking of the product named Charmin, said, "it sounds like toilet tissue". I dismissed him as the joker that he was. When I asked Grandma and Grandpa Crabaugh I was still uncertain if Charmaine or Noelle should be the first name or the middle name. Grandpa said it should definitely be Charmaine Noelle. He was right. That's surely what I would have decided anyway, but I thought I should let them feel that they had some input.

The fear that I had felt initially at the prospect of being a single mother transformed into an obsession to be the best mother it was in my power to be. Determined that this would be the healthiest baby, with every advantage it was in my power to give her, I did not touch a drop of alcohol or any kind of non-prescription drug from the day I first learned I was pregnant until she was weaned at about ten months. I consumed no pill of any kind except the vitamins the doctor ordered; not an aspirin, or Tylenol, or cold remedy or anything else. I ate well and have never felt better or more at peace that the months I was carrying her. I played classical music for her and read out loud to her even before she was born, a practice that continued unbroken until after she could read for herself.

Charlie continued to try and counsel me through all my misgivings, guilt and self doubts. After I became pregnant he admitted that he felt he was "...out of my depth", as he put it. So he referred me to a friend who was a counselor and hospital chaplain at Methodist Hospital in St. Joseph. I visited with him during the pregnancy and we became good friends, so that I continued to see him after I was no longer relating to him in the counseling capacity. That was the most appropriate relationship I had developed since David's death, except that he was also involved with one or two other women.

My good friend, and Charlie's wife, Kay, went with me to Lamaze classes as my coach. It was a little weird to have a woman as a coach when all the other Moms had the Dad with them, but we managed. I relied on Kay, who was always ready with advice and support.

On Christmas Eve, 1983 the first contractions began in the evening. At about 1:30 a.m. I called Kay. She said I should sleep through them if I could, so I tried. Christmas Day was a Sunday, but I didn't go to church. I was at the Harrison's when Moma and Papa Crabaugh came in the afternoon. They brought me a Christmas present, which was a little musical Christmas rocking horse that turned around while it played. From the time they started the night before, the contractions continued to get very intense, but they were never regular. Finally at about 3:00 pm the Crabaughs took me to the hospital in St. Joseph. I don't know if I seemed like a wuss for coming in so early, but the contractions were intense. The nurses had me walk around for a couple of hours, which didn't make them either stop or bring on labor. Kay came and stayed with me the entire time that I continued in labor until the morning of the 26th. All through the night I would wake up every few minutes or so and would wake Kay so that she could help me through it and record the time in the little notebook she had. The water broke sometime during the night, but still no baby. I hadn't refrained from pills for nine months just to blow it on drugs at the last minute, so I didn't want to be chemically induced. But finally, by Monday morning, having seen every doctor who works in the clinic with my doctor, and totally exhausted, I agreed it was time. They gave me an epidural and at 9:19 am December 26, 1983, Charmaine Noelle Crabaugh was born.

The remark that was heard most often was about how beautiful she was. She was 8 pounds, 10 ounces with a full head of hair, long lashes, dark brows, and long fingers right from the beginning. I was totally overcome with gratitude, relief and joy. I had envisioned how she would look hundreds of times, and yet here she was, even more perfect and beautiful than I dared hope. I prayed, "thank you" with tears of joy over and over. I told God, "I would have been completely happy with any child, one with imperfections would have been just fine. Yet you have given me the most beautiful, healthy, perfect child anyone has ever seen". It was one of the first lessons in finding that God's Grace knows no limits. He always gives so much more than we can hope or imagine.

JUST YOU AND ME, BABY

THE HEADLINE NEWS THE day Charmaine was born was the weather. They were saying it was the coldest winter in a century. It seems like they may have reported that a few times since, as well. Temperatures were well below zero for about a week during the time we were in the hospital. John York, a good friend who drove the van for HeadStart, came to take us home. John was a tall grandfatherly figure, who was also a Baptist preacher in a small rural church. He was good humored, and he and his wife, Barbara, who was a nurse, were very hospitable. They lived just a few miles from our house so we stayed with them for the first couple of days because even the oil in my car was frozen. The wheels wouldn't even turn. We just had to wait for it to thaw out. The pipes in the house had frozen and broken and all my house plants were dead.

When we finally got back and got things thawed out, the landlord, Mr. Fore, immediately gave notice that I had to move out in a month. He just didn't want to be known as the one who was giving shelter to that hussy with her illegitimate child. During that month I developed mastitis. My breasts were like rocks and very painful. When I went to the doctor I had to take Charmaine with me and he realized that I was doing everything alone. He said I would have to go stay with someone or else have someone stay with me. That was a problem because I didn't really want to do either. I didn't want anyone taking care of my baby but me. We had to go to Kansas City and have Grandma Crabaugh take care of us until I recovered. Donald was going into his last decline with cancer and she had her hands full. I can't remember for certainty, but I think the doctor gave me a choice about nursing. Either I could stop nursing permanently or keep nursing so that I would still have milk when the mastitis had passed. So of course, I kept nursing in spite of the pain because I was determined to do that.

When Charmaine was only about two weeks old we went to an office supply store in St. Joseph where I ordered a specially made item that has always been precious to me. I went in and told the girl at the desk that I wanted a desk name plate that said 'Charmaine's Mother'. That was to identify for me my most important task and purpose in life. She took the order and then looked at the baby sleeping in the baby carrier and asked, "Is this Charmaine?" I said, "It is", she said," You must be very proud of her". I said, "I am." I was always proud of her for no particular reason at all than just because she was mine. I think that I was never proud of her because she accomplished so much; but I believe she accomplished so much, at least in part, because I was proud of her. I put it on my desk at work when I returned and envisioned always having it on my desk wherever I might work after that. But I have to admit that often I lacked the audacity to do that. For most of these years it has been on my desk at home. Charlie thought it would have been more appropriate if someone had given it to me as a gift, but I didn't know anyone who was going to do that.

Digger Dawson, a real estate agent I knew from the Christian Church, helped me find a little house to rent in Maysville, just up the sloping yard from the Methodist

Church. The woman who owned it wanted to sell it, but she would let me rent it until someone wanted to buy it. It was a sweet little house, just our size. It was actually more comfortable than the big old drafty farmhouse. But it was such a chore packing up all the detritus from David and my lives for the last six years, without him there to help, and with an infant in hand. The Crabaugh's came to help and also Charlie and some other friends from the Methodist Church on a day at the end of January. John York was also a carpenter so I gave him many of David's tools and wood in exchange for refinishing some things for me. The little house we moved to had a shed in the back where the cats were banished to. It was sad to have to do that, but I had heard nightmares about accidents and diseases cats can cause an infant. Thinking back on it, I think that was a little hyper vigilant, but I was entering my cautious stage.

A kind, elderly woman, Mrs. Morrison, kept Charmaine during the day while I continued to work for HeadStart. I nursed her for the first ten months, until she began to get teeth. She never had even one mouthful of formula. I would get up in the night and pump breast milk to be used the next day. Most days I would take her home with me for lunch. I strongly believed in nursing a baby for a hundred reasons. It probably was the reason she was so incredibly healthy, not just as a baby, but all through her childhood.

During the summer HeadStart always shut down and we all were temporarily laid off, on unemployment. Then I had lots of time with Charmaine. We took bike rides with her sitting in a baby seat on the back with her singing a little tune as we rode along. We went to 'water babies' classes in St. Joseph. I got out my bassoon and tried to learn to play it again.

I was thinking very hard about what to do next because the Home Visitor job didn't pay enough to make a stable life. I wanted more than just a job; I wanted something meaningful that would make use of the potential I felt within myself and which would give my daughter reason to be proud of me. I realized that for Charmaine's sake, before she started school we needed to live somewhere else. Her life would not be easy with everyone in this little town aware that whoever her father was, it was not my husband. Even though I was at peace within myself, and understood all that had happened as God's plan, I didn't want to live within the illusion that other people would create about it and project onto us.

There were many friends and good caregivers that I left Charmaine with while I went to various towns applying for teaching positions. After a few years of ruminating on my failure as a music teacher, I thought I had maybe figured out how I could do it better. I actually convinced myself to try for it. But no one ever called me back after an interview and finally, in a conversation with one school principal it just hit me, "I don't want to do this". So I was back at square one. I thought about retraining as a doctor's assistant, librarian, or optometrist. How I would do any of those things never presented itself.

Traumatic events in a person's life are often the catalyst to asking deep questions about the meaning and purpose of life. Those questions had never been very far from my mind but when I met David I allowed his dreams and aspirations to take the place of my own. I began to try to see my purpose as that of trying to assist him in accomplishing his, as if his were more important. David's death would have been the logical time to begin this questioning again and would have done that except for my compelling desire to have a child, which caused me to push all those deeper questions to the background. Now with Charmaine's birth, those age old questions resurfaced. Pondering life's meaning was stimulated by desire to be the best mother I could, but even more than that, it was getting back to important questions I had long neglected.

Whenever I considered any of the things a person might do to make the world a better place it seemed to me that the answer to all human problems was a need to be connected to our Source, that is, to be connected to God and our own spiritual nature. I wanted to know how to help humanity get connected to God in order to find purpose, meaning and hope for their lives. It seemed to me that all the problems there are could be solved by loving our neighbor as ourselves and by seeking first the kingdom of God. This is the thinking that led me in the next direction my life took.

Charlie continued to offer me guidance and friendship. We had many thought-provoking conversations which most often turned to theological topics. I had always thought in theological terms and it was wonderful to have someone who was as invested in the subject as I was. Because of this and also because of the way I had handled the way my landlord had tried to manipulate me, Charlie began to see potential in me to be a minister. One day he said, "Why don't you go to St. Paul?" That was the United Methodist seminary in Kansas City where he had gone. He often talked fondly of the friends and professors he had met there. I was astonished at the suggestion and replied, "Why would I do that?" He said that there are many avenues of church work that one can discover there and began to tell me about them. I got materials and information about St. Paul and began to consider the possibility. Doing church work was exactly where I wanted to be. My mind went back to the day I had told my childhood friend, "I am going to be a preacher". And she had said, "You can't do that, you're a girl".

I finally got up the courage and called for an appointment to visit with the Dean of Students, Susan V. Among the things that are embedded in my memory from that time is that first conversation with Susan, who became a dear valuable friend. I carefully pointed out to her all the reasons why I could not be a seminary student. I didn't have any money; I had a small child, and had committed grievous sins in order to have her; and as my weakest argument I even worried that I probably couldn't do the academic work. Susan gently shot down every one of these obstacles with complete confidence. There was plenty of financial help if I didn't mind being in debt for a few years; lots of students had families, so there was plenty of good childcare available; and most surprising of all, God doesn't call those who have never made a mistake, only those who know they are forgiven.

A few days later, in the silence of the little house, sitting in the old swivel rocker that David used to sit in to roll joints and that I sat in to nurse my baby, I made the decision that would set the course for our lives. I would go to seminary. I still wasn't sure why, but I was convinced it was the right thing and that now was the right time. I didn't even give two weeks notice because the next term was starting in only a week.

There were sacrifices involved. I was to learn that

there are always sacrifices made when anyone decides to go to seminary, some seemed much greater than mine. In a whirlwind of activity I got help from church friends and moved almost all of my household belongings to Grandmas old house way down in Elk Creek. No one was living there now; it was empty and rent free. My Dad and brother-in-law helped take the things there and unload it. We were going to live in campus housing which was a small two room furnished apartment with only a very tiny kitchenette.

The most painful sacrifice was to find homes for my beloved cats. The people across the street, who had two small boys, adopted Ellie. It was heartbreaking to say goodbye to my old friend from twelve years ago, who had first come to David and me as we were leaving Los Angeles. I can no longer remember who kept Claudy while I located a permanent home for her. But she eventually went to live in Kansas City with Susan's assistant, Linda, who had two little girls.

One of the things I have wanted most in my life is a community to belong in. I have had a habit of making up an almost fairy tale story about small towns. From many quarters I have heard the nostalgic testimony of the beauty of small town life. I believe all this. It must be wonderful to belong in a town where everyone knows you, knew your parents and grandparents and your children. People rally around one another in times of joy or sorrow. I always wanted to be part of that. The painful lesson of this life has been that you have to be born into it, or buy your way into it or marry into it. I never encountered a small town where a person could move in and become an integral part without one of those conditions. Maysville was my first lesson in this. Many times I have wondered how life might have been different if David had lived and we had children and remained in Maysville; or if I had married Les and remained there. It is amazing how many years it took me to give up on the small town dream

Someone had a pickup truck that we put the things in which I was taking to St. Paul; the old rocker, the large bookcase, and lots of boxes of things. It was drizzling rain on Thanksgiving weekend, 1984 when we left Maysville with a few things in the pickup truck and headed for St. Paul School of Theology in Kansas City.

My journey to 'higher ground' had begun.

ST PAUL SCHOOL
OF THEOLOGY

WE MOVED INTO ADA Mead Hall on the St. Paul Campus on Thanksgiving weekend in 1984. We didn't know anyone yet and most of the residents of the building were gone for the weekend. Boxes with our belongings were stacked around in that disheveled manner that moving always creates. We were alone in a strange place and Charmaine felt it completely. She kept crying and wouldn't go to sleep. Even though I hadn't nursed her for a month or more and had no milk, I tried nursing her; comforted, she immediately fell asleep. It was the last time she ever needed that particular reassurance.

The next day we went to visit my sister, Jan. While we were there visiting Charmaine took her first step - from me to Aunt Jan. It has always seemed significant that the same day that I took this important independent step in life she also took her first step.

On Sunday evening the other students began to arrive and we found a sweet young woman named Marinell, who lived upstairs in our building, to take care of Charmaine while I was in classes. It was just the first experience of discovering the caring community that St. Paul was at that time. Marinell's husband was a seminary student from Texas. They and their son were packed into a small two bedroom apartment, where she also cared for three or four other small children of other students during the day.

Life for seminary students was often stressful. We learned to listen and help share one another's load. I always felt fortunate that in many ways I had it easier than many others did.

We soon got acquainted with the other students and their families in Ada Mead and sometimes had dinner and loud conversation in one another's rooms. Linda H, also a single mother, became a good friend. Charmaine and her daughter were close to the same age and enjoyed playing together. The young good-looking, Randy and his roommate, Bill, lived upstairs. Randy, who was eight or ten years younger than I, became very close for a brief time, as did Linda and Bill, who eventually married. However, just to be perfectly clear, Randy was very proud of maintaining his virginity. He even had a t-shirt made proclaiming it.

We all went out to eat occasionally. On at least one occasion, the light-hearted Randy carried Charmaine in his arms and announced to everyone in general, "This is my daughter". It is no wonder she was confused enough to call every man she saw, "Daddy". In her mind every male person was 'a daddy'.

When she was still very small, no more than two years old she asked me the inevitable question. She must have been waiting to acquire enough words to be able to form the question; because it was one of the first complete sentences I remember her saying. She asked, "Why don't we have a daddy?" My answer was possibly a bit heavier than it should have been. Maybe I wasn't prepared to answer it so soon. I replied that I had been married and my husband died before I had any baby. That a friend he and I had known, who was a farmer, became a very close friend to me and he was her father. Then she asked,

"Why doesn't he live with us?" This is the part I often wished I had been a little more compassionate about, but determined to be bluntly honest, I said, "He didn't want me for his wife, and he didn't want a little baby". She never asked about him again, and never brought up the question ever again. I think she would have gone her entire life without ever asking or discussing it if I hadn't eventually brought it up. It could have been like a blow to her budding self concept, but instead it was as if it seemed to her that he must not be a very good person if he didn't want to love us. Given the answer I had handed her that should not be any surprise.

A few months after we moved back to Kansas City Dixie came from Los Angeles to see her father who was very ill. She and Charmaine got to meet one another. It was the most wonderful thing to see them together and get to visit even though it was brief.

We went to Elk Creek to visit my parents in the summer. How strange to be there and see the dome again with my little daughter. Early in the morning we were just starting to wake up and the rooster crowed. Charmaine sat straight up and with eyes wide and a quick intake of air exclaimed, "Tu-ka-tu-la". Ever since, whenever I hear a rooster I think, "tu-ka-tu-la". The other thing that happened on that visit wasn't so funny. We were downstairs helping Grandma find something we might like to eat. Charmaine dropped a large one pound can on a big toe. Naturally she cried pitifully. The toenail turned black. I thought it would grow out eventually, but it never did. After a couple of years I began to realize that it wasn't going to just go away. Over the years I tried every treatment for fungus that there is; prescription and non-prescription. But it seems she will have a black toenail for life.

In the spring after the fall that we moved to Ada Mead some larger apartments in the building opened up. We moved upstairs to a two bedroom one and the view was wonderful. We could see across the campus and the sky toward downtown. It reminded me a little of the view from the residence hall when I had been a student at UMKC so long ago. On the fourth of July we could see the fireworks being displayed at Liberty Memorial.

I often thought, 'talk about a head start, my daughter is surely getting one, spending her toddler years among students of theology'. Because of changes in schedules and other things, we had to change caregivers a few times, but the caregivers she had were thoughtful, intelligent people who delighted in children. On one occasion I had a scare when someone came to get me from the class I was in because Charmaine had fallen and bumped her head. A student who was a nurse was nearby and she observed her and cared for her. She determined that it was not serious enough to take her to a doctor, but kept an eye on her for a few hours. I never worried about her safety or well being. It was a safe, nurturing place to be.

There were a good number of details to struggle with, such as how to get all my reading and class work done with an active toddler around. I actually never did get one hundred percent of my reading done, but I made good grades anyway. I remember one paper that I got a good grade on, but with the cryptic note, "did you do any reading for this?"

There were also the mundane tasks of keeping things going, like laundry and grocery shopping. I would lug the baskets of clothes down three flights of stairs to the washing machines in the basement, with Charmaine tagging along, sliding and crawling on the stairs as best she could. Sometimes she would get distracted and I would have to wait for her to adjust a toy or examine something found along the way, or just stop and talk. I was not always very patient, but it just didn't do to be in a hurry. I was grateful the laundry was in the building so we didn't have to go to a Laundromat. Bringing groceries in was even more of a marathon. I would leave her strapped in the car seat while I laboriously transported the bags of groceries inside the door. Then I would take her upstairs to our room and return for the bags of food. Without help, I didn't see any other way to do it. Many single moms don't have it so easy.

We had a hard and fast habit of reading every night before going to bed. That started the first day I brought her home from the hospital and continued until about the second grade, even though she could read for herself before that. In seminary, when we lived in Ada Mead, I was usually very tired, but we always read. One of her favorite books was 'The Amazing Bone' and also 'Strega Nona', who she called 'Strega Bona'. Most of the time she would beg me to read it again. I was so tired I would be very grumpy about reading it again, although I usually did. She would sit with her thumb in her mouth, twisting her hair with the other hand, absorbing the pictures while I read.

She never did learn to sleep in her own bed. I worried that I was being to lenient and checked every possible source for guidance in whether or not a child should be allowed to sleep with her parent. It is wonderful that whatever opinion you would like on the subject, you can find. So I picked the one that agreed with me and went with it. One expert said, "Let her sleep with you until she no longer wants to". I don't know when that would have happened. In junior high she just got too big and wouldn't stay on her side.

The quality and character of childcare I wanted for my child was a very clear image in my mind. During the second or third year it became necessary to find childcare away from the campus. That was rather frightening to me, and I took it very seriously. One staff person suggested, in a manner that seemed to indicate that they felt I was being a bit fussy, that I just take her to a daycare/preschool where some of the other students were taking their children. This particular place was very large, with over twenty toddlers in a room with two or three caregivers. I'm sure it met all the standards and that the caregivers were good, but I had an uneasy feeling about it. I just felt sure that Charmaine would find the noise and confusion of that many other children to be very stressful. As I have gotten to know her over the years I am very certain my intuition was right. I kept asking other students for recommendations.

Finally, Larry K., a third year student, who was student pastor at a neighborhood church not far from the campus told me about a woman in his church who cared for children in her home. I went over to meet her and almost cried with joy and relief. Once again, God was in control, orchestrating every detail. Phyllis was the most loving, motherly woman I could have ever imagined. She lived in a small bungalow type house with her husband and two young adult sons, all of whom were very large people. I often thought it must be hard for so many big people to inhabit such a small space, but they were congenial and frankly, didn't move around much. The house was cozy and clean with lots of soft objects around, including Phyllis' ample lap and a cat named Callie.

She kept two or three other children, who Charmaine became very good friends with. She loved going there every day. In fact, it hurt a little when she was so happy to be there she hardly noticed that I had gone. Phyllis had been a preschool teacher and she knew some things about teaching basic preschool skills. She was extremely helpful in getting my child potty trained during her second year. I rejoiced at that accomplishment almost as much as my own graduation when it came.

Charmaine became like a member of their family and even their next door neighbor, Ebbie. Ebbie was a sweet elderly little lady who delighted in the children at Phyllis' house. At Christmas she made a beautiful beaded ornament with a picture of Charmaine in the center. It became one of our most precious ornaments and may have been the one that began our custom of collecting a special Christmas ornament from every place we ever lived or visited. Twenty six Christmases and dozens of moves later we still remember the Edwards family and Ebbie when we get out that ornament and the wreath made of white yarn and colored balls that Phyllis made. You could say they have no earthly value, and you would be right, because their value is an indicator of the eternal treasures that have enriched our lives.

Phyllis' husband, Hal, and her oldest son, Howie and his girlfriend were very special also. Howie brought little gifts, such as the purple goose from a yard sale, and a tape of songs she liked. Once Charmaine even stayed a weekend with them when I had to go on a retreat with my class. After we left Kansas City we kept in touch every Christmas for many years, until Charmaine went away to college.

Susan V. had been quite right in telling me that I

could get a loan to go to school on. It was quick in arriving and covered tuition, housing and very sketchy living expenses. It was not uncommon for seminary students to be stretched financially, so we were not alone in that. Shortly after arriving at St. Paul I found a position on the staff of a large Christian Church in Leawood, on the Kansas side.

My job at the church was Director of Children's Programs. I was to recruit Sunday school teachers, make visits to new members and those we hadn't seen in awhile, help plan children's activities, and convene children's church while adults were having worship. It was not a good experience. I did not have much in common with the wealthy, middle and upper middle class people and I had no experience outside of my failed music teaching and HeadStart work. The senior pastor there could hardly contain his dismay that a person with my lack of confidence and experience was actually in seminary at all. The assistant pastor and Donna were more understanding and supportive. Donna was also a St. Paul student who became a good friend; she and the assistant pastor, like so many of the staff at St. Paul, could see my undeveloped gifts, graces, and general potential. I learned a lot from her and she helped me through my experience there. She was probably more helpful, in the background, than I even realized because she was well loved by the pastor and congregation. If she spoke a word in my behalf, that would have carried weight. Most of the dumb things and mistakes I made would not have happened if I could have been more relaxed, which would have been facilitated by the people having a more caring and light hearted attitude. I was there less than a year because the stress and anxiety from the tension and conflict were not worth it.

Dr. Marion Brown was one of the first professors who encouraged and supported me. She was a professor of Christian education at that time, so naturally I shared with her about my experience on the staff at the Christian Church. She assured me that I had good qualities for leadership and that the pastor and some of the congregation were being short sighted and judgmental for not appreciating and encouraging me. I was still insecure about being in seminary, and might have taken that experience as a sign that I was not meant for any ministry, but she said that particular church was just the wrong place for me. At that time I planned to go into Christian Education as my place of service. Even though I realized a 'call to the ministry', I still could not imagine myself as a pastor.

The culture shock of being shaken from my rural and small town roots and finding myself at St. Paul were greater than most realized. Here I was fresh from the dew covered fields, hardly acclimated to being a widow and a single mother, thrust back into the big city and into the extraordinary seminary culture.

Charmaine's first birthday was during Christmas break only a month after I had started at St. Paul. We went to visit Kay and Charlie, who now lived in Wichita, Kansas to celebrate after we had been to visit my family. During that visit I expressed my misgivings about being in ministry. Charlie had heard this self-doubting speech before and I think he was actually getting weary of it. He became uncharacteristically quiet for a few moments and then said something that has made a lasting impression on me. He said, "Well, Charlotte, if you can't see yourself as a pastor, there isn't anything anyone can say that will make any difference".

Only recently, after several years in ministry, have I come to realize what a great truth he had spoken. From 'A Course in Miracles' I have learned truths that are expressed in many places. Among them is that the ego is the self we create. If we believe that we are small and limited that is the self we will think we should be. But if we learn to become the Person who God created us to be, the power and things we can do are unlimited.

As the weeks and months went by one of the many things I began to become well acquainted with that I had no previous knowledge of were women pastors. Charlie had known many clergy women and recognized that I was one of them, but I had never met one, had never heard one preach, or talked to one, so I didn't know. As I got acquainted with them, watched and listened to them I began to realize that I had a lot in common with them; not the least of which just might be what we called 'a call to ministry'. It was more than just realizing, 'hey, I could do that'; it was realizing, 'I want to do that'. But way more compelling than any of that was the realization of all God had done and all the people He had used powerfully to get me to that place where it was possible for me to realize His 'call to the pastoral ministry'.

The first classes I ever had were electives that I took with students who had been there for three years and who were about to graduate. That is because I came in after the beginning of the year and the way the classes were structured at that time, I would begin with the beginning courses next fall when 'my class' got there. Everyone kept reassuring me; I would feel more at home then. One of my earliest experiences, which I will never forget, was a large woman in the class on Forgiveness saying, "Well the FIRST problem I have with the Lord's Prayer is,

"Our FATHER…." I was totally astounded and hung on every word after that. It seems they had had many discussions already about what to call God. Many people, this woman included, had some pretty bad history with an abusive father, and didn't want to associate God with that particular feeling. I understood perfectly, on a soul level that God is not male, any more than IT is female. But calling God IT is not acceptable because we have a personal feeling toward God that makes us want to make God a Being we can relate to close, like a parent. So the controversy was off and running and as far as I know, continues today. I was so relieved and grateful later when I discovered Paul Tillich, the theologian who named God The Ultimate Reality.

Among the currents of thought emerging in those days was the concept of feminine leadership. The women in seminary in the 1980's were on the cutting edge of the acceptance of clergy women in the church. The pendulum of change has to swing in order to gain momentum. So what I discovered there I often described to friends and family as 'a hotbed of feminism'. Women were becoming very assertive, and perhaps sometimes seemed unnecessarily so to those who didn't understand the struggle. Sometimes the tone of our discussions was disturbing to me and at times it was delightful. I have seen the younger women in recent years able to back off somewhat because of what we started.

Some of the women had bad experiences with the men in their lives and were hostile. I had to learn which ones to stay away from if I didn't want to be exposed to that conversation. There were a good number of lesbians and I only gradually learned which ones those were because it was far from my mind and it certainly wasn't being announced. It was something they had to keep secret because the church wasn't and still isn't ordaining homosexual clergy. I thought it was similar to the secret I had to keep about the circumstances of my child's birth. Because of this climate and also because of the hurt I was still smarting from I put the thought of finding a mate out of my mind as if it were not a thing that should be hoped for or even thought about. It was to be many years before I could accept that a loving companion would be a very good thing and by that time it was as if all the chances had passed.

Homosexuality was another topic that was discussed occasionally at St. Paul. It was generally understood that one should be as understanding and accepting of it as you would be of someone from a different culture than your own. I had had two good friends who were gay and since I had not ever discussed their sexual orientation with either of them, one male and one female, I had not ever thought about whether or not it was a choice In retrospect it seems a little uncaring not to be any more interested in something that was so much a part of each of them, but I didn't talk about sex to anyone. I was as accepting of gay persons as I was of anyone, but I still had difficulty understanding gayness. It was helpful to learn that it is not a choice, and that certainly made sense to me. But for years I grappled with why it occurs and what it means because it seems obvious that isn't what we are made for. At one point in a class discussion sometime during our third year, I simply pointed out that the people in the pews were not going to be as open toward it as we are in seminary, and that I was certainly not going to introduce the subject if I didn't have to. I intended to pick my battles cautiously. I guess I should have picked my seminary battles more cautiously because everyone in the class took that to mean that I was being hostile toward gays because I was not going to join in the battle to advance their cause. I would never in a hundred years have said something that I meant to be unkind toward any group of people. I did not mean that I was not at least trying to be open toward it, but everyone interpreted it that way. I was simply reminding them of a reality of life outside seminary. Some of our gay classmates were quite popular and there are probably some who are angry toward me to this day for that. As far as I'm concerned it was a huge misunderstanding.

The rarified atmosphere at St Paul was unlike anything I had ever experienced. It seemed that everything Charlie had told me was right. It was a good place to be. At that time the students and staff of St. Paul prided themselves on the caring community they had built as the hallmark of the seminary. Even though it sometimes fell short, it was the most belonging I had ever experienced. It seemed to me like the place I had been looking for to feel a part of.

Part of that feeling was created by the fact that we were invited to share our 'story' frequently. I told about David's death and Charmaine's birth often until I began to feel understood and affirmed in my journey. It was then that I began my lifelong habit of being very careful who I shared every detail with. Even in seminary not everyone was going to be open to accepting everything about my past, and not everyone wanted to be burdened with all those details. I began the habit of relating that she was born after my husband died, which was true as far as it went. Neither in seminary nor any of my places of ministry after, did anyone question me further, and most chose to believe that he was her father. I worried about this being deceptive until I had a conversation with a good friend a few years after seminary. He pointed out that there is a fine line between deception and discretion and that most people would not really want to know that about their pastor.

Once after a session of sharing stories of our life's journeys, one of my classmates asked Dr. Pherigo , "Why does God only call imperfect people to the ministry?" With his typical wide-eyed bemusement Dr. Pherigo quickly replied, "Because – that's all there is".

One story told by a classmate made me realize that truly not all men are the same. Charlie C. told how he had lived with a woman for awhile but they had split up, partly because he thought she might be seeing other men. About five years later she showed up unexpectedly on his doorstep with a small boy and announced that he was Charlie's son. Charlie embraced the child and reveled in being a father. He spent time with him whenever he could and tried to be a father to him. He felt blessed by having him for a son. I asked if he had ever had a paternity test, how he knew the boy was his. Charlie answered simply, "I knew he could be". That touched me deeply in light of my experience. I must not have been in a place where I was ready for another relationship; otherwise how could I possibly have let Charlie get away?

The subject matter of classes, discussions and reading was expanding my mind in all directions. I was having questions answered that I had wondered about for a long time. However, there were theological questions and problems that I had to dismiss and leave hanging, though they would reassert themselves later. I was so glad to be in this place where everyone was trying to learn to be caring and to grow closer to God

STUDENT PASTOR

EVEN THOUGH I ENTERED St. Paul at the end of 1984 I was not considered a first year student until the fall of 1985 because of the way classes were structured at that time. Second and third year students were required to have a place of ministry setting in some position in a church. This is also where the church recruited student pastors to pastor small struggling churches. There were not enough student pastorates for everyone who would like one, so on some level it became almost a competition. Once I had made up my mind that I would be a pastor, and also because of the negative experience on the staff of the large church, I did not ever want to experience a large city church again; not even on the staff. Because I was a single Mom I believed I needed to be in the city and not have to drive many miles to my church, and so I wouldn't be very far away from my small daughter during the day. So I was very intent on getting a student pastorate in the city.

All of us desiring to be a student pastor were interviewed by the district Board of Ordained Ministry, which we dubbed BOOM. It was the first of a long association, consisting of many ups and downs. My relationship with BOOM started out on a high note, as I was appointed to, what for me was, the most excellent student appointment possible. Wesley United Methodist Church in Kansas City was not much more than two miles from the campus. It had a wonderful, new parsonage for Charmaine and me to move into. The church had been built during a boom time in the 1920's, but with the expansion of the city and people moving to the suburbs, it had lost members consistently for many years, as had almost all inter city churches. These churches were beautiful structures, many of them quite magnificent, which had been left standing almost empty and barely functioning. The outstanding feature of this gray stone building on Peery Ave. was the dome ceiling on the sanctuary, giving it an appearance almost like an observatory. Some referred to it as 'the lighthouse'. It was a beautiful church with a large sanctuary beneath the domed ceiling and lots of beautiful polished mahogany woodwork and stained glass windows, even in the pastor's study. The sanctuary, which was made for a hundred and fifty or more, had barely twenty on a typical Sunday morning.

Gene Lowery, our preaching professor had said, "If you ever get over being nervous on Sunday morning, you should quit preaching". I had a long way to go those first few years. I had worked longer on that first sermon than I probably ever would work on a sermon again, but I was so nervous I was almost sick. It went very well that first Sunday; the people were very gracious and welcoming. They took Charmaine in as one of their own. But wonder of wonders, the second Sunday they came back; even though they had heard me once and knew what to expect. That was even more affirming than the first Sunday.

By now we had soaked up many lectures, reading, discussions and advice about what it takes to be a pastor. I think the most succinct, reassuring wisdom came from my good friend, Elsie, who said, "Just love them, they will love you back". In years to come I came to question if that really was enough, but it was the best starting point, and it was mostly true for student pastors.

The people of my first congregation, located in the blue-collar Sheffield neighborhood in northeast Kansas City, were possibly the most colorful characters of any church I ever had. Many of them came to Wesley out of a habit they had cultivated over a lifetime. They wouldn't know how, or have any inclination to enter another church. The old ones kept dying and most of the young ones asserted their independence to not come as soon as they could. However there were a few young persons who were the life blood of the congregation. We were mandated with finding a way to grow or face being closed by the denomination. We had many meetings to discuss what we could do to revitalize the church. In fact, it seems like it was about the only topic there was except for the genuine worship, especially during the high times of Easter and Christmas.

The Wesley Church was a popular place for couples to pick for their wedding, just because of the intriguing architecture, so I got used to consulting with couples and learning that weddings were not my favorite part of ministry. Worship on Sunday, or special occasions was the part I enjoyed most. The other most significant part for me was when I was able to be with someone and help them through a crisis. One such person was Diana, who was going through a bad time with her husband, the father of her infant son, about the same age as Charmaine. I tried to reassure and direct her during that time, which eventually led to divorce. It is very special to me that Diana has kept in touch with us all these years, everywhere we have moved, always sending Christmas and birthday cards to both of us.

One Sunday a year a special offering is taken to support students from other countries who are in United Methodist Schools in the US. I wanted the people of my church to feel connected to the work of the larger church and to introduce them to a person from another culture. So I invited a classmate who I greatly admired, John Innis, from Iberia, to come and speak to them that day. His story was a deeply moving one about the abuse he suffered in his own country when there was conflict there, and he was imprisoned and beaten when just a young boy. His dream was to go back there and do all he could to help the people of his country. I am very proud of that day and my association with John because he went back to Iberia and in only a few years after graduating from St. Paul, became Bishop of the church in Iberia. He was probably the most sincere person in my class and I am grateful to have known him.

The first person I met from my new congregation was the woman who was the head of the pastor-parish relations committee. It was her job to meet with the new pastor and tell her important things about the church and find out what I might need. That was how I was able to arrange for help in moving in. Mildred had an alcoholic husband and lived in a moldy cluttered house, all soft around the edges, as if it had grown up from out of the earth instead of ever having been built. I went with her to an Al-Anon meeting just to experience that group. They were what kept her going, even though her friends at church were sympathetic, they just couldn't share the depth of her struggle. Then there was Barney who had a gun and train shop close to the train tracks, Frank, who lived across the street from us, who was someone I didn't want to be alone in the same room with. But he was very friendly and took great delight in Charmaine. She liked Frank and would go out in the front yard when he was outside, to talk to him. Frank lived in the same house he had been born in. His wife had died a few years earlier and his children had scattered. The outside of the house was tidy and well kept, but no one was allowed inside. I had occasion to go over and knock on the door once. When he opened it and I caught a glimpse inside I realized why he didn't want anyone inside. There were newspapers and magazines piled up so high and packed in so completely that there was barely a path to walk between them from one room to the other. Several years after I left there I heard that Frank had been murdered in his house.

I loved the people of that congregation, maybe because they were the first, but more because they were so visibly broken and they knew they were. They didn't pretend to be anything they weren't. I loved their unpretentious quality. They welcomed me and affirmed me as their pastor. Being their pastor was a good beginning for me.

A funny incident happened during that year. We had a rummage sale during the summer and I took a few things to put in it. One was a tiny whimsical crocheted figure made to look like a little drummer boy that covered a small perfume bottle. I was happy that someone bought it. At Christmas I was surprised when unwrapping presents to discover that it had found its way back to me. Either God has a sense of humor or that little fellow was just meant to be with me.

It has been my fate to be cursed with a disposition that finds it impossible to accomplish a task unless there is a deadline staring me in the face. I have since learned that is only a result of an undisciplined mind, but whatever the reason, I started the routine of taking Charmaine to Grandma and Grandpa Crabaugh's every Saturday morning so that I could spend the day writing the Sunday Sermon. No matter how hard I tried, I could not get it done during the week. I could spend an hour or two a day studying the scripture and staring at a blank paper, but nothing would come until Saturday.

As a result of spending so much time with them Charmaine came to know them much better than she did my parents, who she only saw for a few hours two or three times a year. David's brother, Donald died two years after David, of the cancer he had been battling for at least ten years. Sometimes the five Crabaugh cousins would be there and since she was the youngest, the older girls delighted in pampering and spoiling her. I am grateful that they were there to be an extended family for us and to help so much when I was an overwhelmed seminary student and student pastor. When I would go back in the evening to get her and have dinner with them we would catch up on news about Kansas City, the family, and seminary life.

When the Wesley Church had first been built in the 1920's, one of the old style neighborhood houses served as the parsonage. Over the years it probably didn't get the regular maintenance that the church building did and the standards for district parsonages changed. It got to the point where even fixing it up wouldn't bring it up to code. This didn't bother many congregations, but this one, being right in the city, probably was convinced by their district superintendent that if they wanted to have a quality pastor and survive well, that they needed a new parsonage. Charmaine and I would have loved the little two story dwelling just down the street from the church, but a few years before we arrived they had purchased a new house a few blocks away. It was a wonderful parsonage, and one of the best houses we ever lived in. One of my seminary friends remarked, "Gee, you won't have much to look forward to after seminary, it will be a long time before you have a house this nice again." They were almost right.

The house had been built about six or eight years earlier and so was still very new. In compliance with parsonage requirements, it had three bedrooms and all appliances furnished. In excess of standards, it also had one and a half baths, a double car garage, and a full basement. It also had a nice fenced in back yard, where Charmaine loved to play. I dreamed of that house longingly many times after we had to leave it.

My brother-in-law, Ron, helped me move the furniture I had stored at Elk Creek in Grandma's old house. Just in time, too; some of it was starting to develop mold. Some of the people from the new congregation helped unload the truck and then go over to Ada Mead at St. Paul and get the things that were there. It was a huge shift from the cramped three room apartment to this grand house and it was easy for a small girl to get lost. The first day as I was unpacking, Charmaine called out anxiously, "Mom, Mom, where are you? I can't find you". On one of our first days there I heard her screaming in terror from the back yard. I dashed out to see a small green garter snake sticking its tiny head out and wiggling its tongue in fright. I don't know which of them was the most horrified, but Charmaine was definitely making the most noise.

We were both really happy that we would finally be able to have a cat. We went to a local veterinarian, who knew of kittens who needed a home, and got a little black one with white paws and a bib. Charmaine loved her almost too much, but she was a very docile, sweet kitty. She came into the kitchen carrying the kitty over her arm, and it was limp like a little rag doll. I laughed and said, "Look at her, we could call her Flopsy". An hour or so later Charmaine came back and said, "What was that Peter Rabbit's name?" After that the kitten's name became 'Peter Rabbit'. It seemed to me that my little three year old played with the kitten too rough. She wanted to force her to do things, which goes against the nature of a cat, and generally didn't seem to realize that she could feel pain. I tried to reason with her and scolded her often about it. Petey was not even a year old when she had kittens. At least one of them did not survive. Charmaine came up from the basement where they were and told me that one of them was lying on the floor praying. It had died with its little paws together in a way that made her think of praying. But the rest of them did very well and we took them to the same veterinarian we had got their mother from. I continued to be impatient and scold Charmaine continuously about her treatment of Petey. After awhile she began to develop a stutter. This was alarming to me and I racked my brain to figure what could possibly be bringing this about. Finally it dawned on me that the way I was reacting to her treatment of the kitty was causing her to be nervous and agitated. I decided that I was either going to have to shut up and never make another remark about it, or give Petey away. I knew I couldn't keep quiet, and even if I did, I would be worried about it. It was a very painful decision and Charmaine never understood or quite forgave me for it, but I found a home for Petey. Very soon after she was gone Charmaine's stutter went away.

One day returning to our house late in the afternoon I had a strong intuitive sense of a foreign presence there as I opened the door and started to come in. I felt cold and had a feeling almost like coming up against a wall. Almost immediately my eyes fell upon papers scattered on the floor and potato chips from the kitchen ground into the carpet. In the front room and in the bedroom drawers were turned over and the contents ransacked. My bassoon was the most valuable thing missing. A jewelry box David had made with trinkets I had kept from childhood and things he had bought and made for me was gone and the camera with undeveloped pictures of Charmaine's recent birthday party still in it. The thieves probably didn't get more than two or three hundred dollars for everything because they didn't know the value of the bassoon, or that the other things had almost no value. The sense of loss and being violated was extreme. After calling the police I called Elsie. She came over and tried to help me put things in perspective. The thieves had entered by cutting a screen in a window I had left up and came in the window. They must have been watching the house carefully to know when we were coming and going. Coming back we had startled them, and they fled out the front door. It was frightening for Charmaine and me both. She often asked about 'the bad guys'. I was called to the police station once to identify what they thought might be my bassoon. However, it was very mysterious that I never did get to even see the instrument. They said there had been a mistake and I left with my hopes dashed. The insurance money was not enough to cover the cost of replacing it and there were so many other things we needed at that time the bassoon was never replaced. I grieved the loss of all those things for years. It was a good lesson in non-attachment, although I didn't recognize it at the time.

During the two years we lived in that first parsonage on

Ninth Street Charmaine attended a Montessori Preschool on Independence Ave. that was partway between the seminary and our house. It was a wonderful experience for her and I am confident it gave her a great start. She loved her teachers and the other students. I remember her asking me why we couldn't have green beans like they had at school. It was the last opportunity she had for several years to be with a diversity of children of other ethnic groups.

Among the memories of living in our first parsonage are our favorite TV programs, MacGuyver, Wheel of Fortune, Charmaine loved "Banna, Banna"; Magnum, "Why don't you get a Daddy like Magnum?". She would get every chair, wagon, book and toy from her room, make a huge circle in the front room, and give me very little help putting it all back. I was a much too indulgent mother.

Charmaine had an invisible friend she named Biddy Monster. I think it was derivative of the nickname I gave her, 'Bitsy'. Biddy Monster was often doing things no well behaved child should do. One day Charmaine breathlessly informed me that Biddy Monster was dancing right out in the middle of the street. I shook my head and said, "Well, that's very dangerous, I sure hope she doesn't get run over". She came back a little later and told me that Biddy had returned to the yard.

About halfway through the year the District Superintendent began to say that some changes were going to be made in the alignment of the charges. A 'Charge' is the church or churches that a pastor is appointed to. They were discussing putting the Wesley church on a charge with another nearby inner city church, so that they would have the same pastor. Of course, this had already been decided by the cabinet before it was brought up to me and the congregation, but they went through the motions of pretending to let us discuss it and decide to allow it. This would mean that I would have to move to another student pastorate because the two churches would no longer have a student pastor but would have a full time pastor.

This was very upsetting to me, not only because I was just getting to know and love the people, but because of my resolve to not have to move very often. Here I was starting out, after only one year, having to move already. The other awful thing about it was having to leave the beautiful parsonage. As it turned out, the church I was being sent to had an old inadequate parsonage and it was being rented out. It was decided that Wesley's incoming pastor would use the parsonage of the other church that was being added to the charge and we could stay in the Wesley parsonage for another year. It was an unusual arrangement and I am eternally grateful to the Wesley congregation for allowing us to stay rent free.

The Wesley church had to close in the next decade and the building was sold to a Pentecostal denomination. It has always been curious to me that there were a handful of parishioners who continued to go to the building that had once been the United Methodist Church, even after the style of worship changed so dramatically with a different denomination.

The first major hurdle in the ordination process was passed in the spring between my two student appointments. The United Methodist Church has changed greatly in the last several years, so this is all history, but in those days there was a two part ordination process. After two years of seminary and one year of serving a church a candidate for ministry could be ordained a deacon. After seminary and serving a church full time for two years we were fully ordained as elders. It was all very confusing to everyone except clergy.

Applying for the ordination process was every bit as strenuous as any seminary class we had. There were pages of questions about our personal lives as well as our beliefs about God, the Church, and every aspect of spirituality and religion that you could imagine. It took many days and a lot of serious thought to complete the questions as thoroughly as possible, to the very best of my ability. In addition, there were several interviews by district and conference boards of ordained ministry. All of these were very intense, and required through preparation. It was a time of great stress and anxiety. Not everyone who went before the board was approved. Some had weaknesses pointed out to work on and come back the next year. The candidates who had this experience were usually tearful or angry in spite of the board's efforts to be as pastoral and supportive of each person as possible. We were asked many of the same questions we had written answers to, and others as they thought necessary. One question a pastor on the district board asked me, which I will never forget, was: "Are there any skeletons in your closet?" This put me on the defensive somewhat because I supposed that the story surrounding my daughter's birth had reached them, and there was no telling what kind of commentary accompanied it. I replied that there was nothing God had not forgiven me for. This seemed to satisfy them and may even have impressed some.

There were actually two levels to ordination. At the institutional level one is called a probationary member of the Annual Conference, the governing body of the church. A probationary member was considered clergy, but could not vote on certain issues. At the Sacramental level an ordinand was a Deacon. I don't remember any distinctions of that office except that we could not serve communion anywhere but the charge we were appointed to. As a Deacon we had not entered the covenant agreement that is such an important part of the Elders orders.

My parents came to the campus of Central Methodist College in Fayetteville for my ordination as a deacon. The church there is a magnificent structure, and the grandiose, magisterial ceremony probably seemed a bit overblown to their less pretentious Baptist sensibilities. Neither of them liked crowds and they had never been to Fayetteville before, so it meant a great deal to me that they came. I never could explain adequately the two part ordination process to them. One ordination is as good as two to them, so they did not make it back for the even more ponderous occasion, which I considered 'the real thing', two years later.

I can still feel the pressure of Bishop Handy's large hands on my head as he intoned in his deep voice the words, "Charlotte Wright Crabaugh, take thou authority to preach the gospel, administer the sacraments and order the life of the church….. ". I wonder what it was like for my Dad, who always called African Americans 'darkies', to watch as our large dark skinned Bishop, walked to each of the fifteen or so if us and, one by one granted us authority to be pastors.

ARLEY

THE SECOND CHURCH I was appointed to as a student pastor was the Arley Church near Kearney. It was a rural church a few miles outside of Kansas City. The people there were more regular middle and upper middle class folks. They were very gracious, but there were some misgivings about having a woman pastor, which was going to become a theme everywhere I was to serve. As far as I was aware, almost all the doubts disappeared after my first Sunday there. Many of the people were well educated and there were several professional people there, including a reporter for the Kansas City Star. Many of them had very nice new homes. But being a rural area, there were also several farmers and people whose families had been there for generations. The church was enjoying a growth spurt for the very reason that the inner city churches were suffering – because of people moving out to the suburbs and areas surrounding the city. They had recently added a new fellowship hall and kitchen with classrooms in the basement, with construction being done entirely by people of the church. They were professional architects and construction people, so the work was excellent.

In many respects Charmaine's Sunday school experience there was the highest quality that she was ever to enjoy. The teacher, Miss Richele, was an unmarried woman and being a Sunday school teacher was an important part of her identity. She was very defensive and protective of her position. She was also very good, always coming up with seasonal crafts for the children. One day on the way home from church I asked Charmaine what the lesson had been about. She said, "A woman came and poured 'fume on Jesus' feet because they stunk". I believe the very proper Miss R would have been as surprised at that interpretation of Mary Magdeline anointing Jesus feet as I was.

It was an enjoyable year at Arley. I was glad to drive out to the country two or three times a week. I have good memories of pleasant church dinners, fellowship events and funerals and weddings.

I became good friends with Don and Betty H, who lived right behind the church. Busy, outgoing Betty helped me in getting acquainted with parishioners and showing me around. After I graduated from St. Paul and went to other places Charmaine and I visited with them at their cabin on Tablerock Lake in south Missouri. We had fun swimming and boating on the lake. Don was a master builder and had built their house in Arley as well as the cabin on the lake and much of the new addition on the church. The Hartels were pillars of the church who kept it strong.

The two churches I served as a student were certainly different. In the years to come, their fates would be different, also. The Arley Church has continued to grow and become quite vital.

I continued to have serious self doubts about being the pastor of a church. What I was learning about United Methodist expectations for ministers sometimes did not fit who I knew myself to be. I knew I did not want to be an administrator, like the manager of a business, and proselytizing was something that has always and will always leave me cold.

In all fairness, Methodists don't do what you would call proselytizing but even any kind of evangelism felt difficult to me. However when it came to the parts of ministry which were strictly being with people, bringing the message and leading worship, being with people in crisis, encouraging, praying, sharing faith in all the ways there are, I knew I had found my place. I had to struggle with feelings of inadequacy in the area I felt weak in. As an observation, I did not notice, not did it seem likely, that those CEO/ business leader types were doing any struggling with their inadequacy as spiritual leaders. I could imagine lay people with the talent and inclination for it being trained to take care of the business end of the church, but I envisioned myself as a spiritual leader. In years to come I was in for a rude awakening.

Sometimes my misgivings would become so strong that I would feel almost ill. At such times I would think, "I don't want to do these parts of ministry that seem so important. I'm on the wrong path; I should leave and do something else". But always, I would let it pass and believe that God would not have called me to this place only to fail.

This is the struggle that had been with me from the beginning and would continue to haunt me. I could have been a music teacher, I could have been a wife, and probably other things, but I didn't yet know how to accept myself just the way God made me. I was still trying to make myself in some other image. So I reinvented my ego many times over to fit the role I imagined I should fit while all the time my soul, my inner self, the part God created, was screaming to be heard. It wasn't that

I shouldn't be in the ministry; it was that I should have imagined ministry the way God, and my own soul, meant for it to be. All the parishioners I was ever to pastor would have benefited greatly if I had been able to do that.

In seminary a certain portion of a class was given over to developing the spiritual disciplines. We were encouraged to have a 'spiritual friend' and to learn to give and receive some kind of spiritual direction. We made a 'rule' for ourselves to follow to encourage us to grow closer to God. However, these endeavors were not a big part of our seminary experience. Most of it was purely academic learning from Christian theologians who were recognized by the Church. A wholehearted attempt was made to integrate the Wesleyan quadrilateral of scripture, tradition, reason and experience into our education. The approach to spiritual experience in seminary and in the churches never did seem to be adequate to me. I was always seeking a deeper and more constant awareness of God's presence than I was able to experience. I always thought it was an inadequacy on my part and believed I needed to put more effort into spiritual disciplines, even though I didn't know how I could do that.

I created the belief that I was destined for rural and small town churches. I had always preferred the country, and it just felt more comfortable to me. In spite of the fact that the United Methodist ministry is called an 'itinerating ministry', a real tip-off that you must not expect to settle in anywhere, I chose to ignore that and continued to dream of being in one church for the rest of my life. I never would let go of that dream, no matter how many times I was moved.

Graduation Day did finally arrive, much to the relief and joy of all of us. With all the pomp and ceremony that the United Methodist version of High Church can muster, which is considerable. We donned red capes to match the black mortar board hats that we had all worn at various colleges some years before and filed in alphabetical order behind the United Methodist and school banners. We listened to one of the theologians whose work we had read and walked up one by one to receive our Master of Divinity degrees. I sat between Charles C, who under other circumstances I might have fallen in love with and maybe even married, and Liz Coleman, who wanted me to help her attach the angel wings she had under her robe. I have always felt badly that I did not; but after all, it was such a solemn occasion.

May 14, 1988 was a sunny, very windy day in Kansas City. All the pictures of my Mom and Dad and Charmaine, Charlie and Kay and all my seminary friends show us with wind blown hair crowning our smiling faces.

CONWAY / NIANGUA

For the last month before graduation my classmates and I had our first experience with the appointive process. Each year in the spring the Cabinet, which is all the District Superintendents and the Bishop, meet to decide the fate of all the churches and the clergy in the conference. When I was in seminary I was in the Missouri West Conference which was the west side of Missouri. Since then it has been restructured to be the Missouri Conference, which is the entire state. As the most recent pastors to enter the system, we were the last ones to be appointed. We all waited breathlessly as one by one we were called by various District Superintendents with the news of where we were to be appointed. I had decided that I would like to return to south Missouri to be near my parents and somewhere in the Springfield area. So I received a call from the District Superintendent in that area, saying I would be appointed to the Conway/ Niangua Charge if I would accept it. We didn't have to accept the first one we were offered, but if we didn't we had to accept the second one. It was always a good idea to accept the first, and I didn't have any reason not to. It was in the area I said I would like to be in.

A few days after that call I was having a loud celebration with several classmates at my parsonage when I received the second call from him. It was hard to hear over the commotion, and I'm sure he must have wondered what all was going on. What he told me was that several of the church folks were displeased about being sent a woman pastor; some had even said they would leave if a woman came. He said if I didn't want to go under those circumstances, I didn't have to, but that I could decide. I suppose that put the DS in a kind of tight spot, he was supposed to be the liaison between the clergy and laity, but I saw it as some sort of test. I was afraid that if I wasn't willing to accept the challenge the Bishop and cabinet would hold it against me. So I said that wouldn't stop me from accepting it. I actually think that DS was disappointed. He didn't want to have to face the people again and go through what he was sure would be a year of conflict. He talked the people into trying it for at least a year.

The small parsonage where Charmaine and I lived for the next two years was in the town of Conway. I think the population was around 1200 at that time and Niangua about 700. It was a small tidy house right next door to the church so that the yards ran together. There was a large tree in the back where Mr. McShane, who mowed for us, hung a tire swing for Charmaine, which she really loved. I think it had been built by builders in the congregation in recent years. It met the specifications for parsonages set out by the conference except for square footage. It was too small for the dining room table, buffet, and chairs, which I had inherited from David's grandparents, so they were stored in the empty rooms in the church next door. It was smaller than the house we had come from, but it was just the right size for us and we were comfortable in it. I was so astonished when we arrived on moving day, to find milk, eggs and bacon in the refrigerator. The women of every United Methodist Church I have ever known take great pride in presenting the parsonage to the new pastor as neat and clean as a new penny. That is not always easy because the designated conference 'moving day' is only one day for the pastor who is leaving to get out and the pastor who is coming to get in. They always have to work around that. In this case, the outgoing pastor, who had three boys, moved out a few days ahead and they were able to get the carpets cleaned.

There was a pretty little fruit tree beside the house at the back door. It had beautiful blooms in the spring and then produced some small fruit I didn't recognize, a little like hard plums. I asked Jake and Mary Lula Miller about it and was told that it was called boar's head plum. Mary Lula said they weren't much good for anything except jelly. Being a country girl, raised in the culture of growing, harvesting, canning and picking blackberries, I had to try them. She was right, they made wonderful jelly and I have often wished I could go back and get some more of them. I used that experience of making jelly from those dreadful plums for a devotional article which appeared in the Marshfield Mail on June 1, 1989. Even though, years later, as I write this, my theology has moved away from what it was then, the words still speak to me. It went like this:

THOUGHT FOR THE WEEK – At first we didn't know what the little green berries growing on the tree by the back door were. Someone told us they were 'wild boar' plums; "they make real good jelly, but they're not good for much else." As they got ripe and started falling off the tree I kept trying to find something promising about them; but I just couldn't. They were hard, small, with a big seed in the middle, and very bitter. I didn't see how they could be good for anything but compost.

As I think back on it now, my gathering some of those plums into a large bowl, and taking them inside was a little like what God does with us when He reaches out and fashions the followers of Christ into the Church. The first thing I did was to baptize them, as a sign that they had been salvaged, and also to cleanse them. I pressed them down hard all together to make juice. The seeds and tough skins were left behind. Then they were placed on the heat with lots of sugar and some pectin. Not unlike God's grace, joining believers together in faith, leaving behind all petty differences and breaking down the walls that would divide us. Refined by the fire of the Holy Spirit, made new by God's love and strengthened by the faith that binds us together, ordinary sinners become the Church of Jesus Christ in the world.

We are just like small, hard, bitter fruit; people who are flawed, weak and broken, with no qualities worthy to redeem. Yet the power of God is great enough to transform us into new beings. It is not we who are great or do good things, but rather the love of God and the power of the Holy Spirit working in us that do great things. We who follow Christ are not perfect, but we are forgiven. My, what sweet good jelly those awful plums made!

Nianuga was about eight miles over on a county road. The graveled streets were like unpaved country roads. The old houses were far apart, leaving spacious yards or weedy lots. I don't remember if the streets were even named, if so, no one used the names, referring instead to the old Jones place, or where the grocery store used to be, or even where the old oak was that got hit by lightning. It wasn't intended for strangers to find their way around easily but with a population of 375 there wasn't room to be lost very long. The sturdy frame structure with a steeple, that was

St. Marks United Methodist Church, was tucked way back at the far edge of the houses. Their old parsonage, which had become uninhabitable, was sitting next door to the church. It was torn down the second year I was there.

When I first arrived I went to various places in the tiny hamlet to introduce myself to the community, as I had been told was a really good thing to do. There wasn't anything there except the post office, a gas station with a store, and Days Lumber yard. J.L. Day and his wife, Juanita, were some of the most gracious people I have known. They were friendly and supportive always. However, as I was going to learn in my years in ministry, even the people who supported me had to be cautious. I was temporary but their lives were in that community. They had always been there, and their relationships with their neighbors would have to continue long after I was gone. In every church there were persons who appreciated having me as their pastor and who were good friends, but who did not stick their neck out in my behalf when I was not present.

At the post office I introduced myself in a friendly manner, anticipating a little conversation, and acknowledgement, as I was accustomed to. The postal clerk behind the desk did not show any sign of having heard me except to hand me the mail with a wooden expression, with no word spoken. When I mentioned this to my friends they were not in the least surprised. It seems that other people in town, outside of my church were mostly some fundamental Pentecostal sect who thought women clergy were the work of the devil. This probably helps to explain the extreme reaction some of the church members had to hearing they would have a woman pastor.

I never met the people who left the church because I came until someone introduced us at a community gathering several months later. It was a polite and maybe even necessary gesture; still I think all of us would just as soon not have been introduced.

My spirits were somewhat dampened by the time I stopped at the gas station store so I didn't actually introduce myself, just enjoyed a brief exchange, knowing that later they would learn who the woman with the little girl in a red car was.

I have lived all over the state of Missouri, in towns of varying sizes and I can without blinking give Niangua my personal prize for being the most unfriendly, narrow-minded town in the state. The word Niangua is an Indian word meaning 'bear'; and it was.

Both of these churches were bitter toward the control the UM denomination placed over them. Rather than being grateful that they were never without a pastor because of the appointive system, they chose to be resentful that they never got to have a say in who was sent. Their grudge against the denomination for ordaining women was just the tip of the iceberg. We had a wonderful new UM Hymnal out that had been many years in the planning, which they refused to consider purchasing and using; preferring their old time worn ones. The Conway Church did come around to buying the new ones and we used them while I was there. However Niangua would hardly even allow a conversation about it, pointing out every old favorite hymn they could scratch up that wasn't in it. There were only about two or three of those. The hymnal they had always used was not even any Methodist one; it was from a Pentecostal publishing house. Having two hymnals to work with made the planning of worship more complicated. That was soon relieved by Junior Rader, the song leader, who insisted on picking the hymns at Niangua. It was a point of importance to me to have a worship service that was tied together by a theme, or main point of the day. But I had to let that go at Niangua.

Neither church had been using a printed bulletin with the order of worship and the hymns in it. They thought of it as an unnecessary expense, and possibly a waste of my time. But I persisted, and we used them while I was there. They were not accustomed to having the pastor wear a robe, so I felt it would be one less barrier between us if I would not wear it. This was a disappointment to my ego, as I was rather proud of wearing it. Looking back, I think giving up that bit of arrogance was a good thing. I only wore it for services of communion, baptism, weddings and funerals.

Their differences with the denomination whose name they bore never ceased to amaze me. Most of the parishioners, especially at Niangua did not agree with infant baptism. The UM doctrine accepts every form of baptism as long as water is used. We may prefer that it be done in infancy, because of John Wesley's explanation of prevenient grace that is with us even before we know it; but if one preferred to be baptized as an adult, or didn't wish to baptize an infant, that was acceptable. Ums don't believe it endangers the child's mortal soul, as some do. We would sprinkle, pour or dunk at any age. Personally, I think UMs are very easy to get along with. I preached a sermon on baptism, in which I explained the rationale behind our beliefs about it. I must have done a pretty fair job because after the service Gary D approached, and said that now he at least understood why we do it, but he still didn't agree. That is because all the sacraments are tied directly to the emotions. There is nothing really rational about any of them, strictly speaking. It either speaks to your heart or it means nothing.

The first Sunday at Conway must have gone smoothly and been uneventful because I don't remember it. However when I arrived at Niangua my authority was put to the test. Someone brought up an issue that needed to have some discussion and a vote. I don't remember what it was now, but I made it clear that we were there for worship and that the matter would have to be saved for a church meeting. After that we had a good worship service. At Niangua, if I was ever detained for even a few minutes, as sometimes happened on communion Sundays, Junior Rader would get the service started without me. In fact, I believe they relished this. This church didn't really want to have a pastor.

They resisted my leadership at every opportunity. There is a strict code of ethics in the United Methodist Church that the pastors are taught. That is, if you wish to have a wedding in a UM church you must first go to the pastor. If you want some other pastor to perform the ceremony you tell the pastor so that he/she can invite the outside pastor to perform it. In this way you acknowledge the authority of the pastor in charge. I am certain that I and others had explained this to the people of that church more than once. However, they refused to let go of their own control of the church. They would not acknowledge that the pastor appointed by the bishop and cabinet had anything to do with them. It was their church and they would do things their way. This is the way it is done in some denominations and that is good for them, however, if you are going to pretend to be a United Methodist Church you really need to play by their rules, and these people would not. So it was very painful, and a great wedge between us, when I returned from vacation the first year to learn that a previous pastor had returned and held a wedding at the church. Most of the congregation had been present and it was an important event in their life. No one had mentioned that it was planned for when I was away and no one would have told me about it except that one pure-hearted unsuspecting soul, who knew nothing about the subterfuge, let it slip.

Much of my anger was directed at that pastor, who was of the old school and was what is termed a 'local' pastor. That means that he was not seminary educated and was not an ordained elder, and not as constrained by the appointive system as I was. He didn't feel it was necessary to obey the rules. He was one of the reasons that church was the mess of confusion that it was. Someone might take me to task for insinuating that local pastors are not seminary trained. The reason I have this prejudice is that I do not consider a few weeks for five summers, which they complete for 'the course of study', the same as three years of ones life. I don't think the seminary does either, because they don't spend the rest of their lives paying for it as those of us with a degree do.

That was not the only time that pastor interfered with my ministry at that church. I had to learn to bite my tongue and bide my time.

The only young person at the Conway Church was Joni, who played the organ for church. She was a gentle country girl just a year or two out of high school, with a pleasant smile, and a Rubenesque figure. Charmaine was usually the only child there but Joni would nurture her and any other children who might show up, by reading the Sunday school lesson and coloring or making some craft to augment the lesson while the adults met for their class. After church she and her parents would take Charmaine home with them while I went to the Niangua church and I would pick her up on the way home. I took Charmaine with me a few times so the people there would know her and she was well acquainted with the D's from Niangua who kept her at times when I had to be away.

After my first Sunday, while talking to the DS, I mentioned that we had dinner with the D's. He was surprised, and said I had been in 'the lion's den'. I took that to mean that they were the most outspoken about not wanting a woman pastor. They were an example of the persons who were kind to us and good friends, while always probably preferring that I was there as a friend, not their pastor. They had a farm where they raised beef cattle. Charmaine loved riding around in the pickup to deliver hay to the cattle and sometimes discover new calves. She talked about being a farmer when she grew up, but she would not have beef cattle, just milk cows. I think it was hard for her to learn that the Dills would kill their cattle for meat. There was also a couple in Conway, the Schultzs, who had a dairy farm. When we were there for dinner Charmaine would drink close to a quart of the good fresh milk.

Jake and Mary Lula M lived in a most unique house a few miles outside of Conway. They became very important friends to us. Jake wore a patch over one eye, and when asked about it, he relayed the story of how Mary Lula had accidentally shot him when they were out hunting. A raccoon had run into a hollow log. Jake was looking into the log at the same time that Mary Lula shot into it; thus blasting his eye. I don't know how the gentle Mary Lula ever recovered. It had to have been even more terrible for her than it was for him. They were the most congenial couple, I never heard either one say a cross word to the other or about the other.

Jake had designed and built the house, which was not traditional in any way. Even though it started out on the ground, the top floors resembled a tree house, the way the rooms and passageways were connected. It had a green house off the kitchen and was heated with a large wood burning stove. They were as unique as their house, and were entertaining on a variety of subjects. Jake was extremely opinionated; so much so that if a person didn't see things the way he did, especially a minister, he would cut off all relationship with them. So there were a lot of times that I did not feel free to express my true thoughts about things with him. Our friendship would not have lasted as long as it did if I had. Gentle Mary Lula was completely addicted to Jake and seemed to understand her purpose in life to be to agree with him at all times.

There was a stream across the road and beyond a meadow from their house. In the summer we went there to explore and wade in the cool clear water with them. A large protruding stick jabbed into Charmaine's leg and we had to stop everything to rush her to the doctor. The injury wasn't too serious and I don't think it dampened her memories of the fun we had there. They also had a pond she got to go fishing in, something she had begged me to do. So I was grateful to them for letting her finally get to go fishing.

Our next door neighbors had a granddaughter Charmaine's age. Whenever she came to visit, she and Charmaine played together. They were both learning to ride a bicycle with training wheels. It was such a great day when I finally took them off and Charmaine rode off on her own for the first time. After that we would take rides together on the streets of Conway on our bicycles.

When a family down the street from us had some little kittens to give away we took that as a sign that we were to try our hand at adopting a kitty again. The small yellow tomcat became good friends with a little gray cat who lived nearby. The people of the church didn't want us to have a cat in the house, so rather than give them any more reason to be upset with us we tried to keep him in the garage. He and his little friend were often there sleeping in a pile together. He disappeared mysteriously after a few months and we never had a clue as to what happened to him. That was upsetting and we and his little gray friend grieved. When Charmaine was in kindergarten we went to the animal shelter in Lebanon and found Abby. She was a long-haired gray cat with a light yellow stripe down the middle of her face and on one side, with white paws and stomach. She was a very sweet kitty, less than a year old when we got her, who purred as soon as she was petted. We had a difficult time discovering what her name was. We tried out several that didn't stick and finally one day Charmaine made up a name. She said, "Let's call her Abelda". I don't know where that came from, except the imagination of a five year old girl. I said, "Okay, but lets shorten it to Abby". That became her name for the next fifteen years. She moved with me six times and was my friend and companion longer even than David had been.

The first year we were in Conway Charmaine turned five on her birthday in December. Having been coached by an old HeadStart teacher and entertained by students of theology, she had probably mastered more skills than many of those entering kindergarten that year. However the rule is that no child enters kindergarten until they are five. So that year she went to a preschool in Marshfield, which was the closest. It was a very good preschool, run by a young woman in her home. It had all the space and equipment that was required for licensing and she was very conscientious about caring for the children. Charmaine was the oldest one there, but she enjoyed playing with the others. I would drive her over to Marshfield, about eight miles, every day and return to get her in the afternoon.

The second year we were there Charmaine entered Kindergarten at Ezard Elementary School in Conway. She had been anticipating riding the big yellow school bus for a long time. So even though we lived no more than a mile from the school, she did not want me to drive her there, but was very excited to climb the steps and sit down in the bus that stopped right at our front door. I went out with her and spoke to the congenial bus driver. I asked him if there would be someone to meet the bus and show her where to go. He said, "Her teacher will be there and if she isn't I will take her in myself". Thus reassured, I watched her small legs take the huge step into the bus. I waved to her smiling cherubic face and I then went inside and cried the rest of the day because my little baby was not a baby anymore.

Charmaine loved school from the beginning. She had a great year with Mrs. Lyons, her teacher, and all the other kindergarteners. There was a fun program at the end of the year in which each student presented a different letter, learned from Astro, the phonics character. There was a graduation, in which all the students wore a red robe and a red mortar board hat with a tassel. Our friends, Jake and Mary Lula, came and brought her a graduation present and took pictures of her in her red robe. She would have been in first grade at Conway the next year, but we moved that summer to Sedalia.

Sometimes I would entertain Charmaine with stories of my fiends and things we used to do in college. She had met Dixie on a visit we made to Los Angeles just before she started kindergarten. Every Christmas we had the excitement of a big box of presents from Dixie in Los Angeles. She sent Charmaine wonderful toys, which she always loved. Dixie was like another aunt to her and Charmaine was well aware that I had first met this wonderful friend in that magical place called college. She began to realize that when she was grown she would get to go to college, also. One day as we were driving past farms there in Laclede County, a conversation ensued that has become crystallized in my memory. She asked where she would go to college and I replied, "You can go anywhere you want to, but you will have to get scholarships because I won't have enough money to pay for it." That was followed by questions about what a scholarship is. I told her she would have to make very good grades to get them. I believe that was a very definitive moment for her. In that moment she decided and made it her intention to be the best student and get those scholarships. In the years to come she manifested that intention many times over. That was only the beginning of my learning that this incredible spirit God had sent to be with me as my daughter could do anything she decided to do. She was a strong-willed child and most of the time I did not try to contain it, but only marveled at it.

One of my seminary classmates was appointed to a rural church about ten miles east of Conway. I hadn't really known him until we were out of school and moved just a few miles apart but we became good friends during that year. He was moved at the end of the first year because his congregation had even more difficulty with him than mine had with me. Phil was a serious, scholarly man. He was divorced and his teenage children came to stay with him. The conservative, fundamental rural Missourians thought he was too liberal. He was a kind, friendly person but he wasn't exactly the back-slapping jovial image they had in mind for a pastor. But it was good for me to have someone as fresh from seminary as I was to talk with. A few times Phil and his two children and Charmaine and I would go to Springfield to a movie or some other event.

The churches were difficult but life is made of the little things. While we lived in Conway we were close enough to my parents on the north forty in Elk Creek to drive there on a Sunday afternoon. We would stop at the local hamburger joint before starting out and drive on some of the most beautiful winding Ozarks roads to their house. Sometimes we just went to Marshfield for a Happy Meal at McDonalds. Bennett Springs State Park in Lebanon was close and we went there to see the fish hatcheries. We were close enough to Charlene and Ron in Springfield to see them often. Charmaine enjoyed seeing her Springfield cousins and spending time with them. We had everyone, my parents, Charlene and her children, and even Phil, at our house for Thanksgiving. I was glad that we were nearby when Charlene's life fell apart around her and Ron was sent to prison for child abuse. At times it seemed to be the whole reason we were there at that time.

There were also persons at the Conway Church who didn't attend the whole time I was there as pastor and there were some who didn't want me there, even though they were civil to me. So when it came time to have some kind of farewell for me Jake and Mary Lula had it at their house and all the people who were my friends came. Jake asked me what my favorite food was and I told him pizza so they ordered several large pizzas and we had a very good time.

In recent years I have developed an understanding of the thinking of people that makes them fearful of accepting any new idea or belief that was not held by their parents or grandparents. The fear these people had of clergy women and the misunderstanding so many have of homosexuality does not allow the freedom of God's amazing grace to manifest in our world. Fear is the antithesis of love and in our fear we are shutting ourselves off from the grace of God. I too, had fears that were keeping me from living fully. If I had not had perhaps I could have helped them conquer theirs. I have wondered if it could be possible that many of the things that are happening in our world are God's way of helping us wake up and realize that we let the things of earth divide us and separate us from one another and also from God. Gender, sexual orientation, age, and even personality are all earthly manifestations that have nothing to do with the spiritual beings that God made us, and who we truly are. When we allow these things to come between us we are closing the door to the richest of God's blessings.

I believed it was very important for me to stay in the same place for those two years no matter how difficult and even futile it seemed because I was a probationary member of conference. We had to be in full time ministry for two years before we could be made a full member and ordained an elder. I thought that moving would give them a lot of questions to throw at me and maybe even question my pastoral capability. The boards of ordained ministry didn't want to hear about your troubles, no matter how real they might be. They only want to hear about your successes. My success was that I hung in for two years. At least one couple who had not attended at Niangua the first year I was there, was upset when I was returned a second year, because they had understood the DS to say I would only be there one year. That's not what he said, and anyway they belonged in some other denomination.

At Annual Conference in 1990 I was ordained an Elder in Full Connection along with several of my peers. This time Kay and Charlie came from Wichita for the occasion and also Mama and Papa Crabaugh, who brought Charmaine with them. Before the service, at the same resplendent church where I had been ordained a Deacon, when everyone was trying to find a good seat Charlie said to Charmaine, "Charmaine, you are going to be SO bored". But he could not deter her; she had a part in the service and was excited to see what was going to happen. Each of us who were being ordained Elder came forward separately and had other elders and persons who had been supportive or were important in our journey to come and lay hands on us along with Bishop Handy. Charmaine came with Charlie and put her hand on my shoulder since she could not reach my head. No hand that touched and blessed me on that occasion meant more than that small one. That was probably the last year they allowed family members to come forward for the laying on of hands but it meant everything to me that she was able to be a part of it. It is possible that I might not have even answered a call to the ministry if I had not been her Mother. So yes, she belonged there.

Charlotte and Charmaine Crabaugh, Christmas at Goodwill Chapel, Sedalia, 1992

SEDALIA

THE CHARGE I WAS appointed to in Sedalia was three small rural churches just outside of the city limits. Goodwill Chapel was the one that owned and maintained the parsonage, and there was New Bethel and Pleasant Hill. I would go to New Bethel for Sunday worship at 9:00, Pleasant Hill at 10:00, and Goodwill Chapel at 11:00. Fortunately, they were not too many miles apart.

New Bethel was on highway 65 a few miles outside the city limits. The original structure had burned in the early sixties, so the brick and white building with a needle shaped steeple, was relatively new. The sanctuary and foyer was the only room above ground, with seating for less than one hundred. There was a full basement which could be divided by folding screens for classrooms, though there weren't any at that time. The only time we divided for classrooms was for vacation Bible school in the summer. The congregation was the most diverse of the three, with a few persons of every age. There were very few children and teens. Many had been raised in the church, like Carol, who played the organ and did just about everything else to keep it going strong. There were business people and educators among the thirty or so attendees.

The Pleasant Hill congregation was the most elderly, with about a dozen persons on a typical Sunday. They were mostly farming or retired railroad workers who had been there since childhood or at least since they had first married fifty or more years prior. However in spite of that it was also the one where Charmaine and one other little girl, Nicky, had a Sunday school class with Nicky's Grandmother, Betty Hickam, teaching them in the ancient moldy basement. Occasionally they were joined by Ben, Leroy V's son. That is the same Leroy V who was a well known country singer in the fifties. He never sang for us because he was a member of the union, and we couldn't afford him. But he joined his voice with ours for the congregational hymns. He had also been raised in that church.

I would drop Charmaine off at the Hickam's on my way to New Bethel. They would have Sunday school while I was having church at New Bethel. Then I would go to Pleasant Hill for the service. Charmaine and Nicky were the acolytes, who lit the candles. After that service Charmaine and I would go to Goodwill Chapel. So Charmaine had Sunday school and two worship services. The smallest of the three, Pleasant Hill was actually her main church. It was the classic 'little brown church in the vale', except that it was white. Located on a rise among the rolling hills, from the pulpit, I could look out across the valley through the tall clear glass windows. There was something about that place that lifted my eyes and made me look toward the future.

Goodwill Chapel was what is described as a 'family church' because it consisted of mainly two families with a few friends thrown in. Probably for that reason it had more young couples than the other two. The grown children chose to continue coming to the church they had been raised in. They had children and the church had some possibility of growing their own future. They were not really willing to admit it, but they were fearful of new people coming in and making changes, which of course, is part of what getting new people means. They did put out some feelers in that direction though, making more outreach effort than the other two churches combined. We canvassed the entire neighborhood, of new houses built near the new elementary school, talking to our neighbors and handing out flyers inviting them to join us. We also erected a large sign out on the main road pointing to the church so people could find it easily, as it was a little off the beaten track. These activities earned us an award for evangelism at Annual Conference that year, but not any new members or even guests.

Goodwill Chapel was the largest building, with several classrooms on the same floor with the sanctuary in the white frame structure. It had a lovely square steeple built in with the front door at the bottom of it. Goodwill was the one that was closest to town, right at the edge, but on a secluded road. That location seemed to invite vandalism. They had built in a storage space under the platform in the sanctuary to store the microphones and sound equipment because they had been stolen before. One night I was awakened by a sheriff's deputy at my door, who said there was trouble at Goodwill Chapel and I needed to go with him to check it out. I had to get a sleeping Charmaine out of bed and bundle her out into the cold night air and into the car. We followed him to the church where we found someone had broken out the basement windows by ramming a large vehicle, probably a truck, into them, sending broken glass all over the basement floor and bending the iron bars enough to get in. There wasn't anything of great value to steal, but they took an old Bible that had a lot of church history in it and brass trays and communion chalice. They defaced a concrete area outside the kitchen door with satanic symbols, using paint and mustard taken from our refrigerator. One of the neighbors had heard the crash and called the sheriff. The deputy even sent a dog through the building before we entered, but no one was there when we arrived. This was very upsetting to the people of the church and there was much discussion about how to prevent it happening again. After repairs were made to the kitchen I believe a security alarm was installed.

Christmas was the time when tradition and nostalgia really took over. All three churches had their own Christmas Program or Service, which were scheduled carefully so that I could be at each one. They each decorated a large tree in the sanctuary. I thoroughly enjoyed every one of them, and usually didn't have any more a part than any one else did though I contributed a song at each one. This was the time when each church's individual personality really came out. They each had a very large turnout for their program.

Pleasant Hill had high twenty foot ceilings and every year they put up a magnificent tree from Leroy VanDyke's land that reached to the rafters. They produced a variety show of monumental proportions, with children, grandchildren, and neighbors who I had never met any other time, coming to perform. At the end was an appearance by Santa Claus and bags of candy for everyone.

Gooodwill Chapel had some kind of production, like a play, with Helen M, a retired teacher and the energy behind just about everything, getting it all together. We had refreshments in the basement after it was over, with everyone in a very warm, congenial mood.

New Bethel had a more liturgical sort of Christmas

Service, with scripture readings and special songs to fit the occasion.

We made a visit to Sedalia to see the parsonage and meet with some of the people a few weeks before we moved. It was a very different situation than we were coming from. They had a woman pastor for a few years already and liked her very much. In fact that was going to be the problem. They didn't want to see her go, so I was going to have to go through a period of their missing the outgoing pastor. This was one of the common problems of ministry that had actually been addressed in seminary. It was a bit of a relief to find that something that I was going to have to deal with was something that we had actually discussed.

The pastor who was leaving was married with grown children and grandchildren. Her husband was her right-hand man, a little like an associate. He helped with worship services and even went with her to visit parishioners. They were great friends with people of the congregations. It had been a little like a two-for-one deal. Now they were getting a single woman with a child and of course things would not be the same. There was some worry about if I could do what they were accustomed to at all.

Mary was a local pastor and so was ordained a Deacon. I was to be ordained an Elder at Conference. The ego, in collusion with the United Methodist hierarchy set me up for some feather ruffling, When Mary assured me that she was sure I would 'do just fine' in *her* churches it sure felt like patronizing to me. Was there some reason an elder wouldn't 'do just fine' following a deacon? Actually there was - that would be because of the interference of that former pastor; a problem I was familiar with.

She was constantly coming back to visit church people. But the last straw was when she began to counsel with and perform a marriage for a couple from one of the churches, which had all been arranged before I came. These things might seem benign to an outsider, but to me it was interference while I was trying to establish myself as their pastor. After discussing it with another clergy woman friend I made a visit to her and requested that she refrain from doing pastoral duties in my churches without consulting me first.

The parsonage was almost as grand as the first one we had in Kansas City. This one didn't have some of the excess, such as only one bathroom, and a smaller garage, but it was plenty for us. The usual ranch style, it had large rooms and varnished wood floors. It was located right on the outer edge of Sedalia just before the open fields start. The lot on one side of us was brush and trees and just behind us was a field where cattle grazed. From my desk inside I could look out across fields and rolling hills. There was a large yard which I was expected to keep mowed. So I went to the local Wal-Mart and bought a lawn mower. It was in a box as 'some assembly' was required. I actually got it put together and it ran just fine. However, the day I was out in the garage with pliers and screwdrivers, the instruction sheet, and numerous nuts, bolts and screws spread out before me, I faced a very unfamiliar, frustrating task. After an hour or so, Charmaine came around and in a perplexed voice said, "I wish you would stop doing that, you're making my stomach hurt". I knew immediately she was referring to my constant stream of outbursts, not befitting a minister at all, which was upsetting to her. I thought it was astute of my six year old child to be able to connect the source of her physical discomfort to what was happening.

The lawn was quite large and I have never been a physically robust person. I tried for awhile to keep up with the mowing but it was exhausting and took me hours. Finally, an extremely kind neighbor began mowing it for me on his riding mower. He wasn't a member of my churches, in fact, he was a Catholic. I would have just thought I wasn't up to that much mowing and shrugged it off except that the same neighbor told me that a few years earlier when they had a young man who was a seminary student, someone from the church came and mowed for him. Interesting.

The United Methodist Church was just becoming used to having women clergy. A lot of the discussion in seminary had been feminist; emphasizing that women could do jobs that had traditionally been men's. They didn't want to concede that there would have to be some changes in the way things are set up. It seemed like everything was a test. The churches didn't think they had to change anything to accommodate a woman in the position. If she couldn't mow her own lawn, she should hire it done. There were occasionally little jobs around the house that many men would know how to do, which I didn't, such as leaky plumbing, and so on. So maybe the trustees were called on more than they would be if there was a man in the house. I felt sure that the churches believed they were cheated by having a single mother for a pastor. It was true that a woman had to do her job ten times better than a man before anyone would admit that she could even do it as well.

The people of these three churches stepped up to be surrogate grandparents and caretakers better than any of the churches I had. On Grandparents day at school the Ks, or Helen M would go to Charmaine's class; even though I would have passed for a Grandmother anyway. I took a trip to Alaska with a group of women from the Conference in 1991, and Charmaine stayed with Sam and Marion A for the ten days I was gone. Sam was a smiling, good-natured railroad engineer. He was gone for several days at a time, but when he was there he would show Charmaine around the farm where they had cattle, dogs and cats. Marion was a sweet gentle lady who spent a lot of time playing games with her. Charmaine probably got more attention during that time than she usually did.

A month or two before I left on the trip we acquired another cat. Charmaine had complained about Abby not being friendly. She said, "This cat doesn't like me". I tried to tell her that she was still trying to make kitty do what she wanted her to and cats just don't like to be told what to do. I tried to convince her that another cat would be the same way. But she wore me down. We responded to an ad in the paper for free kittens. I still remember reaching into a baby playpen and picking up little DJ where she was with her mother and a couple of siblings that were left. She was black except for sprinklings of gold and a calico tummy; what some call a tortoise shell cat. Charmaine had named the kitten DJ, for DJ on the TV show 'Family Affair', before we even went to look for a kitten. She was a lively, feisty kitty. Abby resented her of course, and for awhile there was tension, but eventually they made an uneasy peace, although they never liked each other much. Over the years DJ became an outright grouch but we loved her.

The As were gracious enough to let DJ come along to their house while Charmaine was staying with them. She kept them entertained as they all had fun playing kitten games with her.

The trip to Alaska was a Volunteers in Mission (VIM) sponsored by the Missouri West Conference for United Methodist Women. Most of the other thirty five travelers were seniors. At forty four I was the second youngest one. However, at that age my hair was almost as white as any of them. A woman we met on the train from Denali Park to Anchorage looked at me pensively and remarked, "Young face, old hair, great wisdom". I thought it was a wonderful thing to say, and I treasured the comment. There were two goals for our trip; first, to help construct a church in Wasilla, and second, to learn as much as we could about the people, sociology and history of Alaska. Some days were spent at the University of Alaska in Anchorage. We heard lectures on the history and culture of the native Alaskans, as well as current conditions and needs for mission work. We spent the rest of the time in Wasilla helping with the construction project, except for a few days enjoying Denali Park.

We were all astonished at the vibrant colors and enormous size vegetables and flowers attain in the constant daylight of Alaskan summers. It was never completely dark the entire time we were there, although some reported that it almost was around four or five a.m. We had great fun rafting a river and stopping often to take in local crafts and collect objects to take to folks back home. I bought Charmaine an Eskimo doll with fur parka and mukluks.

As with all VIM trips, we were encouraged to bond with the members of the team, which we did throughout the days, but especially in the devotional time each evening. I enjoyed the friendship of the other women and for several years after our trip we had an annual reunion.

One of the most significant aspects of the trip was also very private. Driving on the Denali Highway, we looked far up the rocky hillsides beside the water and saw in the upper distance, tiny specks of white moving among the rocks. I strained my eyes to see the Dahl sheep grazing and ascending the rocky precipice. Later when we were able to see them much closer I could see their horns and elongated faces, and distinguish the mothers from the kids. It was the first time I had seen the real physical image of that dream I had treasured for so many years. It seemed like a message to me, as if the sheep were speaking to me, to help me remember, and keep seeking the meaning of the dream. I was inspired to purchase a figurine of a Dahl sheep on rocks, which I have cherished, not only as a memento of the trip, but also of that dream.

Things went much better at the three Sedalia churches than they had at Conway and Niangua. However I always felt an undercurrent of dissatisfaction with me and a sense of loss of their past minister. Sedalia was a much more enlivening place to be in and we enjoyed living there. There were movies, and restaurants and shopping. Smith-Cotton is the high school there and one day Charmaine asked me, "Will I go to Smith-Cotton when I am in high school?" Since she was only in first grade, I knew that was probably not possible. Sadly, I had to tell her that because I was a pastor in the United Methodist Church the future was not laid out so clearly for us as it was for other people.

We arrived in Sedalia in June of 1990. During that summer finishing touches were being put on the new school, Parkview Elementary that Charmaine was to attend. I thought it was a bonus for her to have a brand new school to start out in.

Charmaine enjoyed her first, second and third grades there at Parkview and excelled. She had an especially fine art teacher who brought out the best in the little artists. She had poems in the "Young Authors" book that Sedalia schools publishes each year. The mystique of the big yellow school bus had worn off already during the year at Conway and she never was very interested in riding one again; a feeling that intensified with each passing year regardless of where we lived. It wouldn't have mattered even if she had wanted to or needed to ride it because the rule was that no one within two miles of school could ride the bus. We lived one and three quarters miles from the school so if I couldn't have taken her each day and picked her up she would have been expected to walk all that on a road with no sidewalks.

Pets were always a large part of our life. I think that every spring there was a new pet experiment. The hamsters that came and went have become a blur in my memory. There were three or four of them during the elementary and junior high years. But I do remember the beautiful lavender beta fish we had for almost five years. As we were driving home from the pet shop Charmaine said, "His name is What". Observing that it was an unusual name, I wondered why she would call her fish 'What'. She explained that he kept swimming around in the bag and looking out as if he was confused, saying, "What? What?"

Charmaine was convinced that she should have a dog. I had serious misgivings about that because I had never had one except for Fang, who was really David's dog. I

knew I didn't know how to train one or make one behave.
They were big and sloppy and just a lot of trouble. But as
usual, I finally gave in. We went to the animal shelter and
found an adorable, playful little black terrier who earned
the name 'Wags' by the incessant wagging of her little
tail. No one could help but love her; she was irresistible.
The cats were terrified of her, and that was a problem. We
had to have her tied up outside most of the time, which
made me sad for her. I would let her in in the evening
to watch TV with Charmaine, but she was so rowdy it
was challenging. After several months I realized I just
couldn't train her and her presence was very disturbing
to me. I talked to one of my support group friends about
the problem. She had fallen in love with Wags so she was
very happy to take her. That was a lot easier than taking
her back to the shelter or trying to find a home for her
with strangers. We went over and visited her several times
and she was very happy in her new home with another
dog to play with.

The last pet we adopted before we left Sedalia was a
little black Netherland dwarf bunny, named Aretha. She
was the sweetest little creature we have ever seen. We
got her a special rabbit hutch that we kept in the kitchen
by the back door. Charmaine liked to have her out, and
snuggle with her. To this day I still have pillow cases and
a few other items that she nibbled on. She liked to pick
something up in her mouth and toss it with a quick twist
of her head, which entertained us enormously. Charmaine
loved her 'Bun-Bun' more than any pet, and we had her
until she was in college.

There was one thing that Charmaine begged for that
was truly impossible to get, and that was a horse. I am
grateful that we were never placed in a parsonage with

a horse stable, or she would not ever have been able to understand why we didn't have one.

One of our favorite spots in Sedalia was Liberty Park. The jewel in the center of the park was a clean quiet fishing lake with a curved bridge crossing to an island. We loved to go to the island and watch the busy squirrels from a concrete bench after enjoying a lunch of hamburgers or sandwiches brought from home. We even got a cheap little fishing pole so Charmaine could finally try her hand at fishing. I always wondered what we would do if she caught anything, but she didn't. The gymnasium where she first learned some basketball was at the edge of the park and just down the street was the pool where she had some swimming lessons. I always thought she had inherited the body structure of an athlete from her father, but I guess she didn't have the environmental influence to nourish it.

Seeing that she wasn't going to become the star athlete of any school, I thought that surely she would blossom as a great musician. She talked about playing an instrument in band when she got old enough and she gave some thought to deciding which instrument she would play. I tried to steer her toward flute, since the towns we were going to be in most likely wouldn't have a string program or orchestra. I knew that some piano lessons would be most useful, whatever other instrument she decided on so I urged her to take piano lessons from our good friend, Carol, who was the organist at New Bethel. Charmaine did extremely well, even memorizing pieces spontaneously, which amazed me. But I had to fight with her to get her to practice, and as soon as she had finished the first book she was done. She felt that she had fulfilled her obligation to take piano lessons, but that was all she would do. Many years later, I still have the little piano I got for her to learn to play. Scholarship was always her area of expertise. She excelled in every area of academic work, always getting high nineties in every area of the MAP (Missouri Aptitude Profile) tests.

Going to the State Fair in Sedalia became a ritual for us for several years, even after we moved. Our friend, Leroy sang at the Budweiser pavilion every year and we also enjoyed looking at the arts and crafts and the endless variety of rabbits, chickens and other animals. But of course, Charmaine's favorite was the rides.

During the summers we began a ritual that continued through her elementary years, of her playing t-ball and me going to watch two or three evenings a week. After a couple of seasons I came to the realization that the bleachers are built facing the setting sun because the sun is either in the parents eyes or the pitchers'. I have some photographs that illustrate much of the experience; Charmaine, in her orange team t-shirt, in rather bored poses in the outfield. Her coach told me that on one occasion she had missed going for a ball because she was holding a firefly in her glove and didn't want to let it go. I was grateful that her coach could see the humor in it.

I was never very good at extending myself socially, which was probably my greatest handicap as a pastor. So as I sat there alone watching her play I wished fervently for someone to be there to watch her with me, as the other parents did. I am sure she could have been more of an athlete if she had someone to play with her at home, as most of the other children did. I had very little experience of any sport and was lucky to even know how the game was played, to be able to enjoy watching it, but I had always thought it would be fun and wanted Charmaine to have that experience. So thinking these things made me think of her father more and more often. He would have been so great at teaching her how to hit and throw and catch.

When school pictures came in the second grade year I looked at her picture and realized that there was no way anyone looking at that photograph could deny her parentage. Her features and expression were like looking at a miniature Leslie. I brought it up in the support group I met with once a week and with their encouragement, I wrote to Leslie and enclosed the picture. I knew he was remarried, but I also knew he and his new wife were separated. So I guess the spinner of fantasies in me was starting to think about how great it would have been if we could have been a family. It would not have been great but it had been long enough that I was starting to forget that reality. In the letter I asked him if he ever thought of us, as if he really knew he was her father, and was just pretending he wasn't. I just told him we were doing well and this school picture had particularly made me think of him.

After a few weeks I began to think he was not going to respond but finally the answer came. He apologized and asked for my forgiveness, saying he had been wrong. That alone was enough to make me think very warmly of him again. We began to communicate regularly. He wanted to meet Charmaine, so we went to a McDonald's restaurant not far from Maysville and had lunch with him one Saturday. Charmaine had not been enthusiastic about meeting him, and did not say much at all except one word responses to questions. My thoughts went back to that day I had answered her question, "Why don't we have a Daddy?" I realized it would take a great deal to cause her to make a place in her heart for this man, who she had shut out all these years. I never had any intention of asking him for anything, any more than I ever did. My feelings were very complicated. I still wanted the only thing I ever had, just recognition, or some sign of caring. Maybe I felt a little guilty about keeping them from one another all this time, even if it was his own fault. I was surprised when he wanted to agree to an arrangement that was entirely his idea. He would send us two hundred dollars a month for child support, without having to go through any court and legal transactions, if in return I would send him a letter telling him about what she was doing. He was a good man, for whom duty and responsibility were very important. He was also very suspicious of my motives. So I began that habit and kept not only his letters, which never said much, but also a copy of the letters I sent to him. One of my friends suggested that over time maybe we could come together again. That was not a wise suggestion, and not one anyone who knew both of us would have made, but it gave me some kind of hope. At the same time, I believe he had some hope that in time she would warm to him and acknowledge him as her father.

Even as I was leaving seminary one of my very caring professors had told me that one of my greatest needs would be for support and that I must always be careful to cultivate a support system. As the years progressed that came to be almost a cruel joke. True as it was, it was almost impossible for a single person within the itinerant structure of the UM Church. As soon as I would find and establish some rapport with a nearby pastor friend, I would be moved. It was not easy for me to reach out time after time and make this connection. Perhaps it has been part of the lessons my soul has been sent here to learn in this lifetime. While I was in Sedalia I discovered the most wonderful support group that I have had in this life.

It started when Mary Jo B, a local counselor, offered a class on "Discovering the Inner Child". That was a period of time when 'the inner child' was the self-help psychological trend. I took the class and found in Mary Jo and other members of the group, a warm caring mentor and friends. After the initial class was finished she offered us the opportunity to continue on a weekly basis as a support group just for sharing the hassles of every day life. There were eight or ten of us, almost all were mothers ranging in ages from thirties through fifties. I became good friends with them and we sometimes had gatherings at one another's homes and met the children who we shared so much about. The purpose was to have other women to share the things we experienced as problems and offer another perspective. We laughed, cried and gritched about husbands, children, neighbors, jobs, and anything that came up. I trusted them and felt safer talking there than anywhere I had ever been. It was a blessing that none of them were either clergy persons or Methodists. I felt no constraints in sharing every feeling and self doubt I had about being a pastor, as well as the injustices I often felt, real or imagined. Mary Jo encouraged us to look at ourselves honestly and fearlessly. It was a time of great psychological growth. We received a lot of tools for coping with each of our individual struggles but it was the friendship that was the source of strength. Mary Jo often said, "It is the love that heals".

It was an important period of growth, of becoming more than I had been. I thought back to that powerful dream and realized it was that sure footed beast, ascending the rocky cliff to higher ground, one foot hold at a time, as the water rose and slapped at his feet. I will never forget them. I have often wished I could meet with them again to see where they are on their journeys now, the adults their children grew to be, and to share about mine.

When Kay and Charlie had moved from Maysville even before I started to seminary, I had mourned aloud how different everything would be without them and how I would miss them. Charlie had been very nonchalant, saying "Oh it's just another phase of our friendship, now we can visit one another and have the excitement of that." That was true for a few years. But the year we moved to Sedalia it all changed. Charlie was always very ambitious within the hierarchical structure of the church. He was looking forward to the power and prestige of being a district superintendent one day. But I did not enjoy the hierarchy at all. It was a kind of game, like the corporate world, that men were more inclined to enjoy. He could see that I could have been extremely good at it if that had been my disposition, and he tried to interest me in the politics of the church.

When we arrived for the visit they seemed to have forgotten that we were coming and were not at home when we arrived. When we finally all got together everything was good for awhile. Charmaine and their daughter, Lizzie, always had fun together. Charlie's questions about my new churches seemed slanted toward the expectation that I would surely be able to make a great congregation out of them and people would flock to them and create an exciting large church. This annoyed me because it didn't seem like he was hearing my real concerns at all. It all came to a head while we were visiting the Space Center in Hutchison. He and his son were both egging me in a way that I found humiliating. I lashed out at him and left the building. We all went home in different vehicles. Charmaine and I left the next morning and I never spoke to Charlie again. I felt very badly about it and wrote him a letter of apology, but he never responded. I came to the conclusion that he had decided to dispense with any friends who weren't going to help him in his climb up the ladder of success in the church because he also cut ties with another friend we had in common, who he had known since seminary. A more benevolent interpretation of his laying aside of these old friendships is to say that in his mind he had simply outgrown us. He felt he was destined for the high road and we were less ambitious and maybe less qualified than the people he wished to surround himself with. In my new understanding of the Law of Attraction perhaps he was right. It all depends on what you wish to be attracted to.

I deeply regretted the loss of our friendship and always have thought fondly of the good times we had, which often bring smiles and laughter to Charmaine and me.

I had lost one friend, but the following summer I reconnected with even older ones. For our vacation Charmaine and I went to Wappapello State Park in south central Missouri, not too far from Willow Springs. We rented one of the cabins there for a few nights and explored the area around the park. The reason I had chosen that area was so that I would have the opportunity to drive to Hutton Valley, where my childhood friends, Frances and Velma, lived and look them up. I drove into the tiny hamlet, which consists of a few scattered old houses, and saw their last name on a mailbox. We went up to the door and knocked, not knowing exactly what to expect. Their Mother, older, but still the same, came hesitantly to the door. I told her I was Charlotte Wright; she looked closely at me and exclaimed, "Why, you sure are!" Velma, who lived just down the road a few miles, was there very shortly and we had a wonderful reunion. Frances was working so I came back on another day to see her. On that day we walked the mile or so to Velma's house and ate lunch with her and her husband. It was just like old times, walking the rocky dirt road with Frances and trying to catch up on a lifetime of events in one day. They didn't express the surprise I had thought they would at finding out I was a Methodist minister. I was really pleased to learn that their brother, Roger, was a Baptist preacher. Charmaine was exactly the same age we had been when we first met. But both of them had grown children and were grandmothers. We exchanged addresses and phone numbers, but Sedalia was a little far away to visit. So I didn't see them again for a few years.

I might have stayed in Sedalia for a long time but for the peculiarities of the United Methodist itinerancy. One request I had always made from the beginning, was to be placed where the chances of having to be moved quickly were not so great. It never did any good for me to ask that. Maybe it was a common request, but it was always ignored. When I was placed in the Sedalia churches I went on something they called 'equitable salary'. That was an arrangement in which the Conference paid part of the pastor's salary from a special fund set up to help small churches which couldn't support a fulltime pastor without some help. A Charge was only allowed five years to receive that assistance before they would be assigned a part time pastor. The hope was that with a full time pastor they would become strong enough to be able to pay the full salary themselves, and the assistance was decreased a little each year. These churches had already been receiving the assistance for three years when I was appointed there. It seems that if they truly expected the churches to become strong and stand on their own, they would have known it was important to keep the same pastor for all five years. If they could have gained membership and strength enough to carry the salary themselves in the first two years I was there, I could have stayed. It was like a test for the minister. The Conference guidelines for salary also mandated that an elder receive a certain salary. They would not allow an elder to receive any less than the base set out for elders.

There are several things that begin to dawn on my awareness, at first, and for a few years, only on a feeling level. The United Methodist Church has put into place some carefully thought out guidelines which they believe are essential for success in the worldly plane in which we must operate. But they have let those rules obscure the more Real Truths of the Eternal, which we are here to serve. Those who have come to power in the denomination consider the earthly rules before they do the spiritual truths, and tell themselves it is how the Holy Spirit works.

I would have been moved at the end of the first two years except that there was one couple at Goodwill Chapel who sympathized with my desire to stay, and who felt so strongly that I should stay, that they actually chipped in the entire amount of the salary that the churches were short of that was needed to meet the demands of the Conference. They believed things were going well and that their church was gaining momentum. They honestly believed it was not a good time to change pastors, but their appeal to the Conference did no good. So they came up with the extra amount themselves, in spite of the fact that there were some who would have been glad to see me leave. They did not do this only for me personally, but because they believed it was the best for their church. So I was able to stay for three years. They were not a wealthy family and it may have been wrong of me to even allow them to do it. They were humble and quiet in the strength of their convictions, so did not try to use their support for any manipulation, although if that had ever come up I would have been in a tough position. Such friendship and support is rare, and I have always been in awe of such magnanimous spirit and grateful beyond words.

It is the small moments of spiritual connection that nourish the soul. One Sunday I had talked about rainbows. Earl S, the treasurer at New Bethel called one evening a few days later and in a more animated way than was usual for him inquired if I had seen the rainbow. We hurried outside and there was a resplendent rainbow stretched across the horizon. My heart was warmed as much by gratitude for a friend who knew to share this beauty, as by the rainbow itself.

The people of the three churches hadn't always worked together well, but they came together to help us move. With much laughter and joking they made light of the work, helping me finish packing and loading the truck. One of my support group friends also came and helped Charmaine and I pack boxes before moving day. I remember having strawberry shortcake out on the patio of our new parsonage with Sam and Marion after everything was all unloaded. A week later Patty K came and made a chicken dinner with Charmaine's help while I worked across the street at my new church office.

The friends we were given, the love they shared, these are the blessings and the memories I have of my years in the ministry.

SWEET SPRINGS

THE FIRST TIME I saw Sweet Springs I had to fight off depression like a demon. This was a long time before I learned the affirmation,' I will look for the good in every situation'. My impression of this forgotten town of about 1500 was that it looked like it had been bombed. I cried all the way back home to Sedalia, thinking to myself, 'I just can't live there'. Later another minister who had also served there told me that he thought pastors were sent there for punishment, though I never knew what I was being punished for.

After I met some of the people and saw the parsonage I felt somewhat reassured. This may have been the best parsonage we ever lived in, with a nice patio just out the double glass doors from the TV room, a two car garage, full basement, and two sinks in the large bathroom. It had all the other traits that most parsonages had: three bedrooms, carpet, central air, all appliances furnished. The DS had told them I liked flowers and gardening so one of the women had planted some flowers in front of the house, which was a very nice prelude. There was a spacious grassy yard with maple trees in the front and Irises in back. I actually did mow this lawn myself, a monumental task which always left me exhausted and very red-faced.

The day I moved into the Sweet Springs parsonage no one from that church came to greet me or to help unload the truck. It was done entirely by my friends from Sedalia. However, after the truck was all unloaded and they had left, the man who was the chairman of the trustees at Sweet Springs came by. He brought some kind of dish his wife had made, which was a friendly gesture. He asked that I not put any holes in the walls for hanging up pictures. He explained how one could snap the heads off of needles and use them to hang small pictures. It seemed almost surreal, his coming by after ten at night and giving me instructions on how to hang pictures. Someone had to have notified him that the truck was unloaded and no one was there but me and Charmaine. It was very late, I had had a very long hard day of moving. I was not about to be hanging anything on the walls that night. Yet he felt it urgent to tell me immediately not to deface the parsonage. I felt completely desolate, homesick for Sedalia, and almost in despair about the future.

The pastor who had served the church before me had been removed from the ministry by the Bishop before the appointments changed so they had been without a pastor for a few months, which is not supposed to happen in the United Methodist Church. He had been a successful pastor of large and mid sized churches in the Kansas City area and had been sent to Sweet Springs when he and his wife divorced. He was being punished for adultery in that situation. In the less than a year that he was there, the church had been mesmerized by his charisma and style of preaching. They thought his being there was the most fortunate stroke of good luck they had ever had. I quickly learned that no one knows a pastor better than the pastor who follows him. The people of the congregation were still reeling from the events that caused the previous pastor to be removed and his ordination rescinded. From them I learned all of the following, whether true or not. He had a teenage son who he left alone in Sweet Springs much of the time while he went into the city. A woman who was the secretary of his former church, who he was not married to, lived with him in the parsonage on weekends. His son was on the football team and the pastor would bring his girlfriend to the games with him where they would behave in ways not becoming to mature adults. He brought her to church with him and she was there with him to greet the parishioners as they left the church. He had a large dog that was left alone in the house and destroyed the tile in the kitchen, which had to be replaced before I came.

Bishop Handy was outraged by his blatant flaunting of the moral code the church endorsed and caused his ordination to be revoked. The people were confused and hurt because they had genuinely liked the man. They were all disappointed but there was at least one woman who thought it was unfair of the Bishop to discipline him so harshly. So I was set down in the midst of this to bring about some kind of peace and carry on the business of the church.

There were actually three churches on this charge. One of them, St. Paul, was a tiny African-American congregation also in Sweet Springs. The other was the Church in Concordia a few miles north. Every Sunday after the service in Sweet Springs Charmaine and I drove to Concordia for the service there. One Sunday a month there was a service at St. Paul after the one in Concordia.

With only ten members the St. Paul UM Church was almost too small to call a congregation. I was always sorry that they didn't feel like joining with the other church in town, but they felt a separate sense of identity and wanted to keep their little church open as long as they could. As long as they could pay even a little of the pastor's salary and a little of the apportionments the Bishop and cabinet would let them. They were all members of the same family. Since some of them lived in Marshall they often attended church there on the other Sundays.

It was unusual for a small Missouri town to have any black citizens at all. To understand their presence in the community one had to learn a bit of the town's history. Sometime in the 1800's there had been a mineral springs there. People came from all over the country to experience the healing properties of the water; thus the name – Sweet Springs. A resort or spa had been built which was a booming business. There had also been a bottling company which had bottled the water and sold it all over the country. Black servants had served the clients and vacationers who came to the springs. The black people remaining there were descendents of those who had worked at the resort or bottling company. They remained after the springs dried up in the early part of the 1900's. Both the blacks and the whites seemed comfortable with the relationship between them, which was so deeply engrained. Some of the civil rights ideas had reached them, but neither side of the racial equation seemed to have any idea that there was inequality, which as an outsider was sometimes glaring to me.

The entire energy behind the little group of believers at the St. Paul Church was a gentle pure spirit named Ann Wheeler. Ann was a small determined woman who was the one who filled out every form required of the Conference, attended every meeting which the church was expected to be at, opened the church doors on Sunday, and if there was any cleaning done she did that, too. She was sympathetic to my struggles, as I was to hers. She was a good friend. Ann was probably in her fifties and had worked very hard all her life, hardly knowing what a day of rest was and had experienced many disappointments. The other attendees were most usually her husband and brothers, with often a sister, friend, and some of her children, not as regularly. There was a piano in the simple one room frame structure but we didn't have a pianist or even a guitar player for accompaniment. I often thought with regret of the many piano lessons I had taken and wondered where my training as a musician had gone. But I tried to play as many notes of the music as I could so that we could sing some. It was surprising the hymns they were not familiar with, and the ones they knew that I didn't. Every time I met with them I felt inadequate to the task and wished there was something I could do to enliven the worship.

Every year in the summer or fall Ann and the St. Paul church would host a 'homecoming'. Scores of African-American friends and relatives from all over the area would arrive at the little church with pots and baskets of the best soul food I ever tasted. Large wooden tables laden with savory dishes of every kind would appear in the church yard. After eating we would gather in the sweltering church for singing and black preaching by one of Ann's sisters who was a preacher. Charmaine and Ann's Grandaughter, Vanessa, amused themselves among the crowd. I wouldn't be surprised if those events have become pleasant memories of their childhood in Sweet Springs.

Concordia and Sweet Springs were both predominately German Lutheran towns, with large Lutheran churches. However, it was most pronounced in Condordia.. There is a large private Lutheran prep school there and the magnificent Lutheran church would be an imposing edifice in a city of any size. In tiny Concordia it had almost God-like aura. Anything that was not Lutheran or at least of German origin was considered inferior. It was the only time I ever felt real gratitude for the German last name that I had married into. The Lutheran pastor did not participate in ministerial alliance meetings and on Easter Sunday when we rolled into town to conduct Easter sunrise services with the other churches at the little lake just outside of town the Lutherans were also gathering to greet the risen Christ at their church. Christ, being omnipresent, was surely at both the services, but I just thought it was a shame He needed to be.

The members of the Concordia UM Church were also of German lineage. Besides having German names they had other characteristics we like to attribute to the Aryan race. The atmosphere of the church as a whole was solemn, but most of the people were friendly and welcoming to me and Charmaine. There were usually not more than twenty worshipers on a Sunday. There was one family, and one person in particular who was outright hostile to me, and that was the treasurer, who wrote out my checks and sent whatever was necessary to the Conference. She resented my presence, and only God knows why. I have no doubt that He has forgiven her because He understands. Because the other persons in the congregation knew her and had known her probably since childhood, and would know her long after I was gone, she was never admonished for her hostility. But I felt their caring and their love as much as they dared to extend it.

The church was struggling for survival perhaps more than any church I ever served. During the time I was there a couple who had been members for many years left when the man decided to enter the ministry of another denomination. It was a loss for the church but I thought it was a wise move on his part if he was called to the ministry. There was no activity of any kind except Sunday morning worship. A couple of times a year I would stay after for some kind of business meeting and once a year they would host a chili supper fund raiser.

The most interesting thing about the Concordia church was something they didn't really like to talk about. A very famous healer, Katherine Kuhlman, had lived in Concordia as a child. Apparently her father had been the town drunk. The people of the town didn't believe the stories of her healing simply because they remembered her as a child. A busload of followers and the charismatic leader, Bennie Henn, came to town to make a film of her life and get some footage of the church. It was the first time I had ever heard her story. It was said that she had attended the UM church and it was where she had first 'been saved'. Charmaine was with me the day they came and Bennie said she was about the age Katherine had been when she was there, so he wanted to take some shots of Charmaine sitting in the sanctuary. It was an exciting day, but we never did get to see the film. Mr. Henn said the church could capitalize on the history and that with a little publicity people might come from all over to be where she had gone as a child. But the people I talked to were not interested and didn't want to claim any part of her.

All of these churches were depressed because they were living in the past and nothing could ever be the same as it had once been. It pulled me down and I became depressed during the time I was there. I wanted to leave after two or maybe even one year but the DS made me stay, because by that time I was being evaluated for being 'ineffective' and I had to stay until the evaluation process was finished.

The year we moved to Sweet Springs was 1993, the year of the great flood all over the Midwest. Charmaine and I had been looking forward to a Volunteers In Mission trip for several months so during that first summer we went to Montana to help at a Blackfoot Indian Reservation. The leader of the trip was Lee Whiteside, a clergy friend of mine who was the Director of the Office of Creative Ministries. I had met him through the Rural Church Alliance and from serving on the board of the OCM. I admired him greatly for his gentle unassuming manner and his wisdom. On this trip I also met his wife, Beverly, and discovered that I had known her in college at UMKC when she had another name. We had a wonderful time visiting and getting reacquainted on the trip.

We helped in constructing a small building on the reservation which was to serve as a rough kitchen. After it was constructed we stayed for a few days to experience the Blackfoot retreat at which many came from all over the country. Charmaine and I experienced a sweat lodge with the other women. We all gathered in the circle in the evenings to pass the peace pipe and hear the leaders speak and we took turns helping prepare meals.

However, just as the retreat phase was beginning Lee had to return to Missouri to coordinate the disaster relief efforts as a result of the flooding, which was extremely severe. After he left the cohesiveness of the group deteriorated and we found it difficult to work things out with some of the group members. We were glad to return home and begin our new life in Sweet Springs.

. Charmaine was in the fourth grade in Sweet Springs the first year and it was a rather hard adjustment. After the first week or two I asked her if she liked school and she replied, "Everything except recess". But she was very brave and determined. One day she cried because she didn't want to go. I felt like crying too when she got out of the car at school. I wanted to tell her that she didn't have to go if she didn't want to.

Things began to improve soon though. She made friends with Vanessa, from the St. Paul Church and Vanessa's cousin, Tiffany, became a best friend. By the end of the year her class elected her to receive the citizenship award. I was very proud because it was a hard road from the beginning to that successful end. The police officers in Sweet Springs endeared themselves to us during the three years we were there. I suppose officers in the small town had a variety of situations come up to keep life interesting and among them was writing out a report on a missing bunny. We had corralled Aretha inside a small roll of wire fencing that we had attached to the ground with some metal sticks. She loved to sit out in the yard under the shade of the trees and nibble the grass. But occasionally she would lean on the wire causing it to bend enough for her to scramble over it. As soon as we discovered that she was missing, Charmaine and I became frantic, walking all over the neighborhood, peering under cars and into peoples back yards looking for her. As it turned out the two or three times she escaped she was only next door at Hayfee's house. Hayfee was a sprightly eighty year old Lutheran woman who brought us some goodies when we first moved in to welcome us to the neighborhood. After searching everywhere we could think of without a trace, in desperation we called the police to report a missing bunny in hopes she could be located before a dog found her. A woman officer came out to get the information. She was very considerate and concerned. I was always impressed that the police would take time to offer assistance in finding a little girl's rabbit. Maybe the police were my favorite part of Sweet Springs, especially in contrast to some we knew later. A while after the officer had gone we located Aretha under Hayfee's car or in the shrubs next to her house.

We developed a habit of going into Sedalia, only thirty miles away, just for something to do. Often we would go to the Wal-Mart and amuse ourselves looking at the toys and clothes. Charmaine couldn't just look without begging for a toy. About half the time I would be able to resist her pleading, but often she would come away with a new treasure.

Sweet Springs was in the vicinity of Whiteman Air Force Base, about as far to the southwest as Sedalia was to the southeast. Whiteman is where the B-2 stealth bomber was housed. One quiet Sunday afternoon we were taking a stroll along the residential streets of Sweet Springs. It was quiet; there was not a person, car or even a dog in sight. Suddenly in the sky above us there was a huge black triangular shape. Soundless, it seemed almost to hover there. Fans of X-Files and Star Trek, our first reaction was that it was surely a space ship and that everyone else had already been taken. Fortunately we remembered hearing about the B-2 and deducted that this was it. The enormous object was a formidable sight. We watched it ascend and float away until it was a speck in the sky.

Each summer girl's softball teams formed. I discovered early on the first year, before I was acquainted with the lay of the land that it did no good to request a place for Charmaine on the team the members of our church were in. It was a closed society with the players hand picked, based on family income or social standing. It is true that I never went to anyone and asked questions, but it seemed clear that they wanted to maintain their clique and I supposed that a single mom did not fit the requirements, regardless of her position in the community. I expect that if Charmaine had been a stellar athlete they would have found a way to make an exception. As it was, the high society team came out in their designer t-shirts and first class gear. Even though the girls had been tutored not to make comments or act snobbish, they just couldn't help it. The team Charmaine played on was coached by Tiffany's Mom. Mary S, also a single mother, was a large, energetic black woman who had lived in Sweet Springs all her life. She knew the rules and accepted them with more grace than I felt. The team consisted of girls from families with few financial resources and problems that they didn't always try to hide. They rounded up bats and balls and gloves that were often ragged hand-me-downs.

They played teams from other towns, and won a few and lost a few. But every year we had to endure a game or two played with the divas. Charmaine's team, the Blue Angels, wore navy blue t-shirts donated by the TA truck stop where one of the mothers worked, with their advertising on them. It was probably only a matter of self image, of not believing in themselves; or is it possible that having fathers who know the game well, to coach them, actually helped. In any case, they were always soundly beaten by the more sophisticated team. In spite of my feeling that it was an unjust arrangement, I was sincerely grateful that Charmaine had unpretentious teammates to associate with. I am certain that she enjoyed the time spent with them at practices and games a great deal more than she would have with the elite group.

At school Charmaine was in the gifted program and Academic Bowl, which was a competition with other schools. It was during these years that Charmaine devised a little game she liked to play when we were riding in the car. She would say, "Ask me something. Anything." It was like Jeopardy. She thought she could answer any question I could throw at her. She was probably right; especially since at such times I was feeling pretty tired. I just wanted to turn off my mind and having to think up questions was an effort. I would tire of it pretty quickly and say I was tired. This was disappointing to her and I began to notice that more and more she began to withdraw and be uncommunicative. Among all the negative things that happened during the time in Sweet Springs was that it was the time my daughter began to enter the pre-adolescent stage and I began to feel as if I was losing her. How many times I would like to go back, to draw her out and find out what she was thinking. So I began my habit of a running monologue, thinking that if I kept talking, she would chime in eventually. She didn't for many years.

It was during her sixth grade year that Charmaine came home one day and announced with finality, "I'm a vegetarian". She has not eaten one bite of meat since that day. I had to scramble to find meals that would fulfill what we in this country have come to believe is a 'balanced' diet, without meat. Fortunately, I already knew that vegetarianism is a very healthy way to eat. My father was a vegetarian. So she didn't really have to fight with me about it, I just had to learn how to do it right. I'm not sure at all that I did it very well, but she never had any illness or bad effects from it that I could identify. She never had liked meat very much, but I believe the decision was prompted more by her love of animals than anything else. Over the years she has become an articulate, well educated vegetarian. In high school she wrote a paper outlining why she is, that was quite compelling.

There were a few children at the Sweet Springs Church and they had a Sunday school class in the little house that was where the church office was. It had been the church parsonage before the new house across the street had been purchased. It was next to the church building, separated only by a grassy lot. Their teacher, Diana Willis, was the widow of a man who had died while serving as the pastor there. It was such a tragedy and the people had gathered around her with such caring that she had never left, even though it had been several years since his death. Personally, I might have advised her to leave and go to the city and start a new life. But I understood the need to be where people had known her husband, and he had been very greatly respected.

The first year I was there we organized a confirmation class. By making it for an age range from fourth grade through high school we were able to create a class of six students. Charmaine was the youngest and the oldest was a high school student, the daughter of the high school superintendent. She was a remarkable girl with a lot of leadership potential, but who had a natural humility that enabled her to enjoy learning with the younger students. The rest of the class was fifth grade. I enjoyed that class probably more than anything during my time as pastor there. On Easter Sunday the oldest one was baptized and all were confirmed.

I always took Charmaine to school each day but one morning the car wouldn't start. I tried to think of someone who I could call who could give her a ride to school. Everyone either went to work in another town and had already left, or were too old to drive. The one person I could think of who was the most likely to be able to do it was a woman who did a little bit of everything at the church, including custodial work. But when I called her to explain my dilemma she was annoyed. She took Charmaine, but it was so unpleasant to be made to feel like I was putting her out. Any other church I have ever served would have had any number of persons who would have been happy and willing to come to my assistance in a pinch, but here I was on my own. It was like being stranded in a desert.

The Cursillo (kur-see`-o) movement was going strong in those years. It is best understood as a renewal movement within the Church. It was my great delight to become involved in it while I was in Sweet Springs. While infusing me with the spirit of joy and hope it may have been the energy and inspiration that kept me going.

It is astonishing that in the midst of such stagnation one would find such a blessing. There were three couples in the Sweet Springs Church who had been drawn into the Cursillo movement. They first described it to me as a weekend retreat, from Thursday evening to Sunday afternoon that was a bit like summer camp for adults for the purpose of deepening spiritual experience and understanding. Cursillo is a Spanish word for 'short course'. It was a short course in Christianity. Cursillo was a very vibrant, energetic, intense experience. The more well known, Walk to Emmaus, was derived from it but I always considered Walk to Emmaus a watered down version. It lacked the intensity of Cursillo, which is exactly why some preferred it. I always thought it was regrettable that so many powerful parts of the weekend experience were eliminated or changed as to be ineffective in comparison to Cursillo.

Large churches in Kansas City which were part of the movement took turns hosting the event. They were churches which had facilities for showers and enough space for about sixty persons to stay for three nights. Some people were skeptical about Cursillo because there was a bit of secrecy about it. It was necessary to have a certain amount of trust in the sponsors who invite you and tell you about it. You needed to understand that the good things they told you were true and that details were withheld because the fewer expectations you had the more effective the experience would be. The weekend unfolds a little like a play complete with antagonists and redemption. If it is done well it is a wonderful parable on the Christian life. It is so much more than sitting and listening to Rollos (short talk) regardless of how inspiring and wonderful they are.

For me one of the best things about it was being with many clergy friends from the conference and having a light hearted good time as well as meeting new friends from the churches who participated. On the last day, many people who have been through a Cursillo weekend come and there is a magnificent rollicking celebration. There were then opportunities to go to each Cursillo weekend after that to help as a facilitator. I went to many of them and gave Rollos and helped in several capacities in the next few years. It became an important part of my life for which I am always grateful.

Three of the four couples who were in Cursillo left the church while I was there. One was a dentist who moved to Kansas City where there were more opportunities for his children. One was the local druggist who had owned the town's drug store his entire adult life, and had come into it through his wife's family. Sweet Springs was dying and the drug store was the last business left. It too, eventually failed and they had to find opportunity elsewhere. The other was a hog farmer with a very large operation. While they certainly experienced economic challenges, the reason for leaving the church was that they had teenage children who wanted to be in a church where there were activities for the youth. Who can blame them? I believe I would have done the same in their place. But as pastor, I couldn't express that opinion.

At a leadership event that I attended the highly respected speaker said, "If you are ever in a church where the people do not want to grow or change, you should leave." Now there's an idea I would have loved. I wanted to leave before I got there, but I was trapped in the denomination's system. Every pastor who had been there felt the same way. These people wanted someone to put things back the way they used to be and that's all they wanted. If that was not possible then they just needed someone to be with them while they died a gentle death; a chaplain pastor. I was that. Without pressures from the conference demanding that I conjure up more members instead of losing them I would have understood that as my mission and been okay with it.

Each year pastor and laity are each given the opportunity to say whether they want the pastor moved or not. After my first year in Sweet Springs and Concordia was the first time I did not ask to stay. I simply said, "I'll stay or I'll go, which ever you think is best". Of course I was left there. Sometime during the second year the DS came to visit and he expressed the opinion that I was 'ineffective' as a pastor. He had been my DS in Sedalia also and was responsible for my being placed in Sweet Springs. I never understood why he didn't have more questions about how a pastor could go from leading a church that was awarded an evangelism award at Conference, to being 'ineffective' in a dying church.

I always thought his reasons for this assessment were based on personality traits that he thought a pastor needed, that I didn't have. I had come out of the starting gate from St. Paul's with as much enthusiasm as anyone, but over time, being in churches that frankly, didn't need a full time pastor, had dulled my exuberance. This DS had characterized me as 'laid back' and I suppose he did not mean that in a good way. It was stunning that these churches had not grown in numbers or spirit for many years regardless of who was pastor, but I was elected to take the fall for it.

In the years since these events I have learned something about The Universal Laws, which are God's laws. I look at the District Superintendent's judgment and at my defensiveness through the lens of what we would have done differently if we had known those Laws. He might have visualized me as being energized and able to fulfill the promise I set out into the ministry with. I might have visualized myself as an effective minister able to bring new life to those congregations; and therefore would have become that image that God placed within me. Instead the DS was attacking what he saw me as, rather than believing in the Spirit that God had placed within me. I was able to draw enough from my own belief to keep going, but I was not helped, and probably hindered by his lack of belief in me. Mainstream Christian Churches do not teach, and seem not to understand the power of visualization and the knowledge that we are Divine Beings, able to do whatever we can imagine.

I had never felt so scrutinized and picked apart for real or imagined flaws. I left there very defensive and a bit more withdrawn than when I had come.

He arranged for me to have consultations with a counselor the Church hired to help pastors make career decisions. I am convinced that he did not do this to help me improve because he did not convey that he cared enough about me to want me to; but rather to cover all the bases so that the Church could not be charged with not giving me a chance. The stated goal of our consultations was to decide if I was to remain in the ministry or not. If I was not, then what direction would I take; if I was, then what could I change to become effective. Since by then I was clinically depressed and on anti-depressants, I was also sent to a psychological counselor. The Church paid for these specialists both of which I enjoyed visiting with. I learned some things about my values, beliefs and aptitudes, as well as being bolstered by the psychologist who was very understanding and supportive. However, at the end of it all I knew I was called to the ministry and there was nothing else I wanted to do.

That DS was very ill with pancreatic cancer and shortly after the appointments had been made the third year he died. At that time the heavens smiled upon me and my friend, Lee Whiteside was appointed to finish out his term as DS.

Shortly after he became our DS the treasurer at Sweet Springs came to me with this news: "We have enough money to pay the utilities or your salary, but not both." I was so relieved to have Lee to go to with this situation. He was able to obtain funds from the Conference to get us through the year and the following year the churches had a student pastor. The meetings with him and the church leaders during that crisis was gut wrenching. I had to endure criticism from persons in the church as if I were to blame for the church's problems.

I never did get over missing Sedalia and my friends there, the entire time I was in Sweet Springs. One Sunday morning I was actually weeping as I was preparing to go to church. On impulse I called my friend, Carol, the pianist at New Bethel and talked to her for a few minutes. It helped to recall that not far away there were people who regarded me with kindness and respect.

It was while I was in Sweet Springs that I discovered 'Sun' magazine. It was so refreshing to read something that was not from Cokesbury, the UM publishing house. It was more than a breath of fresh air; it was a lifeline to reality. The writing in that magazine is by real people living real lives; and there are no ads. Every month there is an interview with someone on an issue of relevance to the changing world and life in our society. In March 1994 there was an interview with Kenneth and Gloria Wapnick about the <u>Course in Miracles</u>. This was the first time I had ever heard of it. I knew I had to read it. I thought it sounded like the missing link I was looking for. For a long time spirituality as practiced in the Methodist Church had begun to be inadequate for me and I had begun looking for deeper meaning.

I have learned that the Universe is unfolding exactly as it is meant to. Maybe this is another way of saying, "All things work together for good for those who believe". It was no accident that I was placed in the churches that I was. It was exactly those experiences I needed to have to learn the lessons I came here to learn. It was no accident that I discovered Sun Magazine and that it contained an interview about a book that was to transform my way of thinking and lead me on to higher ground. It was a few more years before I actually had that book in my possession and began to read it but I never forgot about it. It was like a beacon beckoning from the future.

I am writing this in retrospect, several years after it all happened. I have complained a lot about Sweet Springs, and it was very difficult being there. However, as always, the best things are just small moments: Charmaine's birthday party at the house with a few good friends; they made balloons with faces; a vegetarian dinner with Lee and Bev and Charmaine before a church meeting; the beautiful irises in the back when the sun shone through them making them iridescent; the sweet little dog, Mac, who we just couldn't keep. We had two fish in the church office for awhile. I named them Paul and Silas and told Charmaine they were the apostles who started new churches after Jesus ascension. She made a little cartoon picture, in which the fish were looking out of the fishbowl, asking, "How am I supposed to start a church in here?" It was a commentary on my feeling about being there. Charmaine would often come to the office while I was working on church stuff and play with the copier and typewriter and colored markers. I still have some of her creations.

I have always enjoyed Halloween. I guess because

dressing up like something you're not and wearing a mask and going out among people who won't recognize you is a little like being invisible. It is very freeing. So I enjoyed getting Charmaine dressed up, also. She didn't like wearing a mask so we would just paint her face or put on heavy makeup. One year she was a black crayon in a costume I made.

One of the first things I had done after seminary when I had my first full time appointment was to buy a new car. It was a bright red Ford Escort. Just a few months after I had it all paid for we had a bad accident on highway 71 between Sweet Springs and Concordia. It was an icy night in the winter and the car spun around twice on a slick bridge and stopped headed the right direction. I thought we were going to pull out of it okay, but before I could get going again someone came up behind us and hit us hard. The insurance company called it a total so I had to buy another one. For several weeks we saw our bumper lying out on the shoulder, with the sticker that said, 'live simply that others may simply live'. Charmaine and I still disagree to this day about exactly how the accident happened; a perfect example of how different persons experiencing the same event will remember it differently.

I went to a dealer in Warrensburg and found sitting on the lot, a Mercury Tracer similar to the type I had wrecked except for the color. I didn't even know they made cars that color. It was primary purple. The young woman who was our salesperson said it was 'a ladies car'. I thought it was beautiful and it had all the other qualities I was looking for so that was our new car. At Easter one of my parishioners said it looked liked an Easter egg.

As my District Superintendent, Lee Whiteside met

with the cabinet on my behalf to find a new appointment for me. He may have had to use his considerable powers of persuasion to convince them that I was a good pastor, after the accusations of 'ineffective' that had been leveled at me. I had gone through all the consultations they had required of me and had been given a stamp of approval by the counselors I had worked with. At first they were going to appoint me to another church in that district, which was further north on the Missouri River. But when he learned that there was an opening in Weston, where he had once served, Lee went back to the bargaining table and secured that appointment for me. It was the best appointment I ever had while in the United Methodist ministry.

Even moving out was problematic because I had no help at all. I always underestimated how much work, and how long packing was going to take. Movers came from Marshall with a moving truck and had to help finish packing, which made it cost a bit more for the church I was going to. My sister, Jan came and helped me clean the house as everything was moved out.

I left on a sour note and felt that I shook the dust from my feet. But it was with great joy and anticipation that I approached Weston. North of Kansas City and south of St. Joseph, it was the very town that David and I had visited so many years earlier when his brother, Donald lived there. I remembered thinking then how I would love to live in that lovely, quaint town, almost like a storybook setting. I could hardly believe it was actually happening; we were going to a town I had really dreamed of living in.

I had been crucified, died and resurrected.

WESTON

THE ORIGINAL SETTLERS TO Weston in the 1800's would be astonished and I hope gratified to see that the present day citizens have so carefully preserved and restored their old anti bellum homes and buildings. The United Methodist Church building stands at the top of Main Street where it was originally constructed immediately before and after the civil war; with construction coming to a halt during the war. The parsonage that housed pastors and their families in those early days and for many years is one block over on Spring Street within the shadow of the church. A simple two-story white brick house, it was one of those that seemed to emanate a storybook quality many years ago when David and I first visited the town. Long before we moved there it had been sold to persons who had spent thousands of dollars restoring and modernizing it. When I was appointed to Weston it was owned by a couple from the church. The old parsonage appears frequently on the Christmas Homes Tour, where visitors can appreciate the quaint homey ambiance. I had hoped briefly that maybe the historic old church had such a home for their pastor, but those hopes were soon dashed.

Blackhawk Street was just down a slope and across the backyard from the old parsonage. It was a beautiful quiet, 'no outlet' street of old restored homes, some of which also appeared on the Homes Tour, all except for the little green cracker box house which had been constructed in the 1950's as the church parsonage. I think the present day city planners would not have allowed it to be built there because it did not adhere to the strict guidelines to protect historic authenticity which have been adopted since then. I have no doubt that it was a great blessing and a relief to pastors when it was first constructed. The original parsonage was drafty and inconvenient even after restoration. This one was at least insulated and had an attached garage. It met the minimum standards for UM parsonages, but the problem was that it exuded an air of benign neglect. The house at 616 Blackhawk had probably been quite comfortable when my friend, Lee and his family had lived there, but that may have been the last time anyone had paid much attention to it.

When I first saw the house it was still being occupied by the outgoing pastor who was also a single mother. There was great hostility between her and the congregation so it was a bit of an uneasy meeting between us. I tried to overlook the clutter that was so deep I could not get a really good look at some of the rooms. She would not allow me to see the garage, so I could only guess what must be lurking there. She had three prepubescent boys who had been uncontrolled much of the time. I was to hear many stories about her and her children in the weeks to come, similar to my first days in Sweet Springs.

Her boys had broken a corner of the large picture window in the front of the house and cracked the window in the front door. There were thistles among the weeds growing around the front of the house and the paint on the trim all around was peeling. In the kitchen there was a large burned spot in the linoleum which was the result of a hot pan being dropped there. One of the bedroom doors had a fist-sized hole in it.

There were many loving warm hearted people in the congregation but my perception was that none of them were on the trustees committee. Over the years the people had adopted a hands off attitude toward the parsonage. The pastor before the one just leaving told me that before his wife would move in the church had to fix the kitchen cabinets, which at that time didn't even have doors on them. He and his family had stayed in a motel for the first few days they were there. He had built an extra room on the back of the house about twenty feet by eight feet across. It was a wonderful room with all glass on the entire side that was added. He had done it all himself with some help from friends. I have never heard of a church allowing the pastor to alter the parsonage in such a way, but they seemed to be unconcerned. It had been meant as an enclosed back porch where people could gather. He feely admitted that it wasn't meant to be permanent. It only had concrete blocks under the floorboards and there was no source of heat or air conditioning. I used it for storage until it was torn off by a volunteer group after the church decided to try to improve the house while I was there.

After seeing the house I went back and declared that I would not live there. Lee very calmly asked where I planned to live. But he did talk to the DS in that district and he nudged them so that they fixed the broken windows before we moved. Later someone removed the damaged door, since the room wasn't going to be used as a bedroom while we were there. Even though there were several clean up, fix up days devoted to the parsonage the trim remained unpainted the entire time I lived there. Eventually what to do about the parsonage became a battleground.

One of the first persons I met from Weston was Mary Edna N, who I met at Annual Conference just before I moved there. She was to become a very good friend and advocate before it was all over. When we first met, she said more than once with relief in her voice, "I'm so glad you're here". Those words were like balm to my bruised spirit. I was to hear it many times after I arrived at the church. The church had been through a bruising experience also and for the first three years we were to find great joy and healing in being pastor and church together.

As I began to get acquainted with the town and congregants that first year I found myself whispering under my breath, "I have died and gone to heaven". Those were joyful years when everything just seemed to flow. I loved everyone I met and may have been at the highest level of awareness I ever had been.

My father died while we were in Weston and the people of the church were extremely thoughtful. A different person brought dinner to us for a week. They also surprised me on clergy appreciation week almost every year, sending cards and gifts of appreciation. At Christmas each year they took up a collection for my gift and I never ceased to be amazed at their generosity.

My life seemed to be a study in the half full glass: I could have a husband, but not a child or I could have a child, but not a husband; I could have a good parsonage, but not a good church; or I could have a good church and a lousy parsonage. I just couldn't seem to have it all at once.

Charmaine had reached the puberty age of junior high when we came to Weston and she immediately began to assert her individuality. The last Sunday we were in Sweet Springs she wore a dress to church. The first Sunday in

Weston it was jeans. I don't think anyone in Weston ever saw her wear a skirt or dress. The days when I could dress her up like a doll were gone. And that was just the tip of the iceberg. She never liked the house in Weston. She liked to stand on the iron railing on the front step with her arms stretched to the poles holding up the roof over the steps, give it a good shake, and declare, "I could pull this whole house down." I would dryly respond, "Please don't".

About two weeks after we moved Charmaine went to church camp at Camp Galilee, the camp she was familiar with in south Missouri. Camp was one of the strong points of the Methodist church, and it was good for her to go. She had not yet accepted living in the house and had not unpacked a single box of her belongings. They were sitting stacked up in the middle of her bedroom though the rest of the house was completely unpacked. I had urged her to get them unpacked before she left for camp and I even said I would unpack them while she was gone if she didn't. I knew she didn't want me messing with her things, so I thought that would work. She didn't believe I would carry out my promise and left them. When she returned they were all neatly put away in the closet and she went ballistic.

It was a mistake I regretted for a long time. I had overstepped the bounds. She unleashed all the pent up anger that only a teenager can feel. I don't think she actually said, "I hate you." on that occasion, but I felt it. She expressed the opinion that I didn't care about her and didn't know what she thought about anything. The lesson I had intended, that I will do what I say, didn't seem to be worth the resentment it unearthed.

When school started it was a difficult adjustment, as

usual. It took many weeks before Charmaine began to make friends and feel comfortable in the new surroundings. I have always felt a warm place in my heart for the first friend, Jesse, who began to show up and go places with her. They went their separate ways after the first year, but I was so glad to have someone there to befriend her in those early days. The second year she became pretty tight with Sarah, who was a year ahead of her in school. They spent a lot of time together and when Charmaine got frogs, Sarah did too. By the time she got to high school she was well established and had lots of friends.

In spite of her growing teenage angst, she still preferred sleeping with me, as she always had, to sleeping in that bedroom. Finally, it wasn't that she had grown so big, it was just that she began to sleep diagonally and take up most of the space, when I said I couldn't get a good night's sleep with her there. Then she began bringing in all her bedding and making a bed on the floor beside mine. She did this almost all through high school.

Though she continued to maintain the highest grades and take great pride in scholastic accomplishments, among them being named to 'Who's Who Among American High School Students' three years in a row, she became very uncommunicative and at times sullen toward me. Like all parents of teenagers, I tried not to make too much of it, but it hurt me a great deal. On more than one occasion I remarked to our neighbor and good friend, Sue, "I wanted a little baby very much, but I never really wanted a teenager". It was supposed to be a joke. Actually, if I thought that far ahead I believe I thought that by that time I would have a mate. I wouldn't have believed that I would remain single. It was a thought I could not have endured at the time.

I have always maintained that Charmaine and I got off easy by not having to deal with dual custody arguments or all the tensions that would have been present if we had a husband and father who was not understanding and supportive in the hundred ways that might have been possible if different choices had been made in our lives. However, I also realize how very much more stable we each would have been with a strong understanding wise father figure there with us. I know that every child needs a father and I am sorry that Charmaine did not have one in those crucial years.

In retrospect I sometimes wonder if maybe the Church should not have enlisted single mothers to pastor churches. It could be a conflicted position to be in. I always made it clear that my child came first. In truth, I think that should be true of male clergy as well, but I never knew one who didn't have a wife beside him to help. There were times when I thought people weren't asking me for help when they needed it and that hurt almost as much as my daughter saying I didn't care about her.

Our little family of pets was still with us. Abby we had since kindergarten in Conway, DJ and Aretha, the rabbit, from Sedalia. Charmaine seemed to be always on the lookout for new and unusual pets. I like animals, too so maybe it was an excuse for me to have pets that my own parents would not have allowed when I was a child. In addition to hamsters, we also had hermit crabs, fish, and frogs. The frogs were ordered as tadpoles from a 'Grow-a-frog' kit. Three little tadpoles were shipped to us and we watched them grow legs and lose their tails. When they were fully grown one of them died, leaving two, which Charmaine named Pat and Morrison. On this day as I sit writing it is thirteen years later. Abby, DJ and Aretha are long since gone, and Charmaine has flown the nest, but Pat and Morrison are still here with me. They swim groggily in a tank just across the room from where I sit and write. This is a testimony to several things; first, that I am not like other people, in case there was any doubt. Second that frogs live a long time – fifty years the last time I researched it. A few years and a few moves back I started calling them 'the immortal frogs'. I once wondered aloud why I have kept them through six moves all these years and a friend answered, "It is a connection to Charmaine". That must be it; they aren't much company although they do still sing their little trilling frog song occasionally. They have provided entertainment for the several cats who have known them.

Sometime I must make a list of all the things I would never have done or seen if I had not been Charmaine's mother. Somewhere on the list would be taking a cruise to the Bahamas and a vacation to Orlando and to New Orleans. She liked to fill out the cards found at malls and the State Fair which promise a 'free cruise' to the Bahamas. I thought it was amusing, since nothing is free and I didn't see the harm in it. She happened to be present when I answered the call saying we had 'won' so it was harder to duck out of it. We had a big discussion in which I got to explain that the only thing free was the actual cruise and a few nights at a posh hotel in Orlando. There was the travel to get there and back and all the incidentals. She wanted to go so badly, and my imagination was stirred, so in the end I decided we could make it possible.

We flew to Orlando in January of 1999 for a memorable trip. The beach was almost empty and I found it comfortable to have a sweater on. We saw some of the sights, such as Ripley's Believe It or Not, Universal

Studios, the Biggest McDonald's, to name a few. There was the adventure of riding with me while I tried to find my way around the unfamiliar city in a rental car. We went out a few miles to Cape Kennedy to see NASA and saw orange groves on the way. Either before or after the cruise we had the dolphin experience. We got to step into a roped off area of the water which the dolphins would swim into. They stayed motionless while we stroked their smooth sleek heads. The dolphins seemed to enjoy it as much as we did. It was a heart-warming experience to share with the ocean creatures.

I took pills for seasickness several hours before boarding the cruise ship, as recommended for people who get carsick, but it did no good. I was feeling queasy even before the boat pulled out of the dock. I enjoyed parts of the trip, but for the most part I was in the cabin feeling really awful while Charmaine went all over the boat making friends with the staff. We floated all night and spent the day in the Bahamas, then came back and spent the second night on the boat going back. The only part we saw was the tourist section where souvenirs are sold. We ate some authentic Bahamian food and bought some souvenirs to add to my Christmas tree collection and some other things. It was a really fun trip to share together and I've always been glad we went.

The second part of our winning was a trip to New Orleans. This time we made it a road trip. I am so grateful we got to see that beautiful city several years before Katrina. That tragedy touched us more personally than it would have if we had not seen it. We stayed in a great hotel not far from Canal Street. We walked the French Quarter, visited the Aquarium of the Americas, and rode street cars to the big zoo.

par's

On the way home we encountered a little black kitten someone had abandoned or lost at a rest area in Arkansas. He was a friendly kitten, trying bravely to get handouts from the visitors. An attendant there said he had been there a few days. Charmaine could not bear to leave the kitten, and I have to admit my heart went out to him, also. I argued that we couldn't keep him because our two big old cats wouldn't want him around. Charmaine pleaded that we could just find him a home. Of course, we found him a home. That was how we found Ernie, or he found us. We did make some attempts to find someone to take him when we got back but by then we had become very fond of him.

Ernie was a street-wise, smooth operator. The older cats did not welcome the newcomer, as I had predicted so he set off to find more welcoming surroundings and practice the skills he had been learning at the rest area. After he was missing for a day we embarked on a search to try to find him. He had been visiting the stores all along Main Street. Every shop we went into, the people knew him. They would say, "Oh, yeah, he was just here a while ago". Sometimes he had gotten a handout. He had made friends all up and down the street, but was just a step ahead of us. Finally someone gave me a tip that he had been spotted in the home of a man just up the hill behind us. I called to ask him and he said, "Oh you mean this wild cat?" So I went to reclaim Ernie and visited with the man, who was a lapsed member of my church.

Ernie was a lively, spunky little tomcat; we enjoyed him greatly and 'the girls' soon made peace with him, or at least he chiseled out a place for himself. I was grateful that Blackhawk Street was quiet, with the only traffic being the people who lived there. They soon learned to watch for the little black streak crossing. Instead of returning to Main Street, he discovered the little creek in the other direction and explored along it almost daily in every season.

Doug and Sue B across the street were probably the best neighbors we ever had. Doug had pity on me and always kept the lawn mowed. I think he thought of it as a service to the church, but it was my responsibility so I was very grateful. Sue had a wonderful herb garden and they both loved puttering around in their yard which was full of lovely flowers and shrubbery. They had a little black and white dog and a cat named Mr. B. One day a large golden dog mostly German shepherd, appeared on our street, seemingly out of nowhere. He was friendly and went up and down the street, trying out every household. He seemed to like our street so I dubbed him Captain Blackhawk. Doug and Sue tried to find out if anyone had reported him missing but after several days they decided to keep him. Doug wasn't much for fancy names and called him simply Big Dog. Doug taught Big Dog a few tricks; he would say," Would you rather live in Platte City or be dead?" And Big Dog would fall over motionless on the ground.

One of the pillars of our church was a highly successful building contractor, who I will give the name of Matt. He had trained as a minister at Oral Roberts Univ. but decided he might do more good in the world as a layperson with a lot of money, and he was probably right. He had come to Weston with his family a few years before we came there and was very influential in the community. Sometimes it seemed like he considered it his mission to annoy me and other church leaders, but overall he helped in a positive way.

Matt organized several trips to Guatemala for a mission project to build buildings in remote impoverished communities. He made it possible for Charmaine to go with them on one of these trips and she wrote a lengthy report on the experience for our newsletter when they returned. It was a marvelous trip, the first of many that she would take out of the country.

In her high school years Charmaine wanted to get a job to have money for things and to have something to do in the summer. The jobs she wanted were mostly in The City and since we only had one car it really wasn't possible. So she found work at the shops in town. She worked for awhile in an antique store that had an old fashioned fountain in the back, making sodas, shakes and fountain drinks. Another one was at Plum Pudding, a tea room run by some of my parishioners.

My daughter dragged her feet about getting a driver's license. I think that was in rebellion because she couldn't have her own car. One Christmas I gave her a little wooden toy convertible. It was really cute but she was not amused. We went for driving lessons frequently and she took the driver's test. I shall never cease to be amazed that a student with a straight A average could find a way not to pass the written driver's test. After that was accomplished there was the driving hurdle. I think I wanted her to get it more than she did because I was tired of driving her to track meets, ball games and oboe lessons in Liberty. She didn't like for me to tell her how to do things and I never wished for a Dad for her as much as I did then. Parallel parking was the worst. I could whip in a space as easy as going forward, but I couldn't explain how to do it for anything. We almost came to blows over that.

It really was hard for her to be one of the few in her

class who didn't have her own car. When she was named 'student of the month' the prize was a special parking space up close to the door designated for the student of the month. That was especially exasperating

Betty D, a parishioner of my mother's generation, became Charmaine's surrogate Grandmother. She was a kind, thoughtful, wise woman who listened to Charmaine and gave her attention when she needed it. I believe God placed her there and she was influential in guiding Charmaine through some critical times. We both felt her love and empathy often. Sometimes I would need to be gone for a Cursillo event or some other church business for a day or even overnight. Charmaine would stay with Betty and they would play board games and talk. It was worth it to be in Weston just to find a friend like Betty and several others who have always remained close.

One of the things I am most proud of that I helped put into motion while in the Weston church was a weekly prayer group. It was Betty who came to me with the idea. She was concerned about many trends and conditions not only in our town but in the world. She had a strong conviction in the power of prayer. So we began meeting each Saturday morning in the homes of the women who attended for prayer and some kind of refreshments. We had never specified just women but that is what it turned out to be. No quality control expert has ever been able to specify the effects of prayer but each of the women came with their concerns and we prayed and were changed by it. The group is still going after more than ten years.

After years of languishing I was finally in a real church, one I might have actually chosen if I could have. There was a newsletter, and actual news to put in it. There were lots of things going on; in fact, I sometimes wished there weren't so many meetings. I held a confirmation class three of the five years I was pastor there. I called my pastor's column Charlotte's Website, just because it was catchy, not because I even knew what a website was in those early days of the first pc's. Looking back at those old newsletters, my column was really pretty good; interesting, sometimes downright entertaining, and inspiring. Every month Carla S, Julie P and I would meet in the kitchen at the Benner House, which Julie and John owned, and plan the next newsletter. They were the steam behind it. The Suttons's printed it off, I was a contributing writer. I thoroughly enjoyed our newsletter meetings, at which we would eat some of Julie's wonderful cookies and plan who would write which articles, all the while enjoying the ambiance of the wonderful old Victorian house which was the oldest of Weston's Bed & Breakfasts.

The church hired a youth director at about the same time I arrived. Aric was a student at St. Paul and it was a bonus to me to have a seminary student around to share conversation and seminary stories with. He kept the youth busy with activities and inspiring gatherings and fundraisers. He was an important part of the church and I was sorry when they felt they couldn't afford the salary anymore and he had to leave after less than a year. After that Gerald and Kelly S took over as youth leaders. We went on some outings with the youth including an enlivening float trip to south Missouri.

The fourth of July fireworks at the football field was one of the memorable things about living in Weston. We would walk the few blocks to the school because it was much more pleasant than trying to find a parking place. They had a bountiful display of fireworks each year, but before they started there were sky divers who descended out of the clear air onto an X marked in the field. It was spectacular. On the way home the air was fogged and smoky with the sulfur smoke which still lingered the next morning.

An aerobics class was already part of the church activities when I arrived there. It met three times a week in the church basement, led by Colleen, who became a very good friend. She also had one of the more interesting stores on Main Street, full of antiques and retro clothing. The class usually had somewhere between six and ten participants but it was not strongly supported by the church, I suppose because it didn't seen to bring in any new members. I benefited greatly from it and was sorry when Colleen couldn't continue to lead it. After that I started going to the YMCA in Atchison, about a thirty minute drive, for aerobics three times a week. It became a welcome respite to get away from town for a few hours, and the closest thing to a support group that I had.

This church was full of energetic people who loved to be involved. There was always a lot going on. The United Methodist Women, UMW was always doing a special project or fund raiser. That group was such a contrast to other UMW's I had been familiar with that it took my breath away. One of the first meetings I attended was to plan for Applefest, which the church helped the town enact each year. The women were pure professionals. Several were business women and their organization and expertise exceeded anything I had been part of before.

With two apple orchards on the outskirts of town, Applefest was a really big deal. Thousands of people flock to the tourist town the first weekend in October for an old time celebration of crafts, music, apple-butter making and lots of wonderful food. The activity was on Main St. so the church was right in the thick of it. Each church in town had a booth and each sold a specialty item made from apples. Ours was apple pies and I was happy to contribute my own expert pie making skill. There was some good natured competition with the Christian Church which was justifiably proud of their apple dumplings.

Thousands of people came to town for this event, creating lots of traffic, even though Main Street was roped off. Living only one block over from Main Street, we experienced cars parking on every square spot of ground on Blackhawk Street. There were fines for parking uninvited in people's yards or blocking driveways, not that I wanted to get out anyway. I could have made a little money by charging five dollars for parking in the yard, but thought better of it.

The first big activity that began right away was fund raising for tuck pointing the outside of the church building. It went well because people were enthusiastic about raising money for their beloved old building. The first year fund raising continued along with much discussion of other renovations needed.

There were a good number of persons who were sympathetic to the need for a new parsonage. After study groups and meetings and votes taken, the parsonage was also put on the list of building needs but there was always another group that was opposed to any discussion about it. I often pointed out that the parsonage did not compare well to other parsonages in the Conference. There were some points at which it did not meet the new parsonage specifications that had been put in place since it was constructed, such as the square footage. It was unfortunate that I placed myself in the middle of that battle. If I had it to do over I would get some supporters and turn it over to them, and try to appear as neutral as possible. However I made no secret of the fact that it was far below the standard of any parsonage I had lived in so far and they were in churches of much smaller congregations. I always felt I was presenting the facts in a very diplomatic way but it was just an issue I should have been removed from.

There were two former pastors of the church who still remained as part of the congregation, a testimony to the pull this community can have on persons. They and persons who had been part of larger churches in other places were among those who were supportive of getting a new parsonage. I will always remember the comment of a woman who was a rather crusty member of trustees. She seemed to believe that I was arguing parsonage improvements on my own behalf as she remarked, "Well, you're doing rather well for a single mother". I guess that was supposed to mean that I shouldn't put myself in the category of other pastors, but rather of many single mothers who have to work very hard and often have to live in much worse places. I thought it showed some prejudice against me as a woman in ministry. If it were a male minister making the same observations perhaps they would pay more attention.

Discussions about the parsonage became quite heated. The Pastor/Parish Relations Committee had to weigh in on it with recommendations as well as the Trustees and then a Parsonage Building Committee was formed to make further studies and make recommendations. Everyone was always concerned to bring every single move to a vote so that no one would feel anything had been railroaded through. This made the whole process very sluggish and time consuming. In November of 1998 Bob

S, an extremely credible and knowledgeable gentleman, a retired stockbroker with a lot of life experience, wrote a compelling argument for the construction of a new parsonage. He outlined in detail the improvements needed, explaining that trying to improve the old house would be more costly in the long run as it would still be an old house even with improvements. I did not see how anyone who read his report and who knew this reasonable, no-nonsense man could fail to see the necessity of a new house. However, the congregation voted overwhelmingly to renovate the existing house rather than build or buy a new one. After that they did some work in the bathroom and tore off the temporary room that had been tacked on to the back. That left less storage space, but the controversy kept going and the rest of the recommendations were not carried out. I had to carry the things I had been storing in the extra room up to the attic space over the garage because there was no where else to put them. It was an enormous amount of work to get the Christmas decorations up and down the little pull down ladder for the next five Christmases.

The tuck pointing of the church building was carried out and completed in November of 1998 and installing of new heating and air conditioning was begun soon after. All this caused great upheaval, as all remodeling does, but of course it was with joyful celebration that it was all behind us.

While inspecting the building before the tuck pointing began, a hive of honeybees was discovered living in the outside wall. After consulting with experts about what to do about the bees it was determined that it was best to just let them alone. I wrote a funny story for my pastor's column about the bees, explaining their presence and why we would just let them bee. I never got much feedback on my columns, so I don't know about anyone else, but I enjoyed it a great deal.

In spite of all the building activity we continued to keep alert to our responsibility to continue to be in mission to the needs of the world outside our building. It was always important to me that we not get engrossed in our own maintenance and forget the reason for being a church. We went to a church in Kansas City, which was in mission to the homeless, and took a turn serving a meal there about once a year. During Advent we collected bears that were taken to nursing homes or to HeadStart or places that served homeless children. It was fun to see more bears in the sanctuary each Sunday. We made it a point that they would sit in the pews during Advent and be hugged and 'filled with love' for those who would receive them. It was one of my favorite projects.

In a town that was not growing and had seven other churches, having a new member join was usually a big event. It was normal to expect two or three in a year. In the five years that I was pastor in Weston we received 37 new members, 12 of them in 1998 alone. That was phenomenal, if I may say so. I was so pleased to be there when all this growing was happening. However, the tensions and conflict over the parsonage issue finally brought out the very worst in me and perhaps in others, as well.

Meanwhile the church had raised money and renovated the entire basement of the church which is kitchen and fellowship hall. It was a mammoth project which I helped get started by finding a man in Kansas City who is in the business of helping non-profit groups raise money. He had some great ideas which we implemented and the campaign was off and running. The church had three phases of fund raising and renovating. Phase one was the tuck pointing. Phase two was the kitchen and fellowship hall. Phase three was the parsonage.

The completed kitchen was a stunning success. The women of the church swelled with pride. People from other churches and all over the community were suitably impressed. We had received donations from far and wide, including members who had moved away and now lived in other places. On a plaque in the basement are the names of these donors which also includes my parents who had been to Weston to visit. My own name is on another plaque naming those who worked to accomplish the renovation.

A year after the church kitchen was renovated the monumental step was taken to make over the parsonage kitchen as well. The reason for doing this was not for the comfort or convenience of the pastor but only to make the parsonage saleable. No one ever did acknowledge the rudeness of blatantly saying 'this is to make it saleable' without ever acknowledging how unlivable it was in its present condition.

Dave F, a fine cabinet maker who owned a cabinet shop came and installed some beautiful cabinets, the best I have ever had. I got to pick out the kind of wood, handles, and counter top I wanted. It was a pay off of sorts for enduring all the arguing about the parsonage. There was also a new tile floor and my neighbor, Doug, was an expert wall paperer so he and Sue came and put up the wall paper with apples which I had also picked out. The finished project was a real joy and I reveled in the new kitchen I had when it was all finished.

THE END OF THE
YELLOW BRICK ROAD

THE NEW MEMBERS WHO were added to us almost all became very involved in the activities of the church and they added a richness to our experience that cannot be denied. They were mainly people who moved in from Kansas City except for a few who had grown up in Weston and had come home for retirement. It was wealthy people who came to Weston because Platte County was an expensive county to live in. I was there at a transitional time. The new people came with ideas and habits from the city churches they were used to. I had never wanted to be pastor or even a member of a big city church. There are many things about them that do not suit my temperament. The early days when I was a small town pastor seemed to be ending; almost like my daughter becoming a teenager, I felt myself thinking, "Hey, growing is a good thing, we're supposed to, but I never wanted to be pastor of a big city church."

Suggestions and criticisms began to gnaw at my deep-seated insecurities and I started to act defensively. I began to lose confidence in myself and that is fatal for a leader. If I had known the things I now know; i.e. "Human beings create their experiences by the activity of their thinking. Everything in the manifest realm has its beginning in thought."(Law of Mind Action/Law of Attraction) I would have known I could create the outcome I desired and that

I did not have to be a victim. It is one of the lessons I came to this world to learn. Now, thanks to my friends in the Methodist Church who placed me in a place where I could learn it simply by asking the Universe, "Why did this happen to me?" Now I know.

It wasn't just our own church that was experiencing changes. The United Methodist denomination as a whole was in the midst of a long decline in membership, as were most mainstream Christian churches, which continues even as I write. They began to cast about for what to do to turn this around. One of the trends that grew out of this was a reinventing of our style of worship. It was the consensus that the music needed to be more upbeat, with a praise band and singing short snappy choruses instead of using our hymnal and the lofty theological hymns we grew up on. Many churches across the country no longer had an adequate pianist or organist anymore. This was not the case at Weston. We were fortunate to still have Percy and Mary, who had played piano and organ together for decades and they were a team we were very proud of. They even presented a concert of secular music and duets once every year. However, during the time I was there Percy's strength began to fail and gradually she was no longer able to play the organ for church. That left just Mary at the piano.

There was division across the denomination about the changes in worship that were being pushed, which included more than just the music. The older people were perfectly happy with the style of worship they were accustomed to so in order to implement the changes two services were recommended, a traditional and a contemporary. That did not seem feasible for smaller congregations like ours so we tried various ways to enliven worship. We began to incorporate the choruses into our traditional service as a way to start the transition. Mary was an excellent pianist and could play just about anything put before her, but everyone has their own style and when Mary played the new choruses it didn't seem a lot different than many of the songs we could sing from our hymnal, just more trouble for everyone. I had doubled as song leader in every church I had served (with the notable exception of Niangua). But now among the new members there emerged a lay person who believed she could lead the new choruses better than I was doing.

This began a long and tiresome tug-of-war with Kay (not her real name. I had also directed the choir the first year I was there but when Kay came she wanted to do it and I happily handed it over to her. It was fine to have someone else take over that task, but Kay wanted to do more and more. I rather enjoyed doing the children's time we had each Sunday morning, but I guess Kay thought she could do it better. She did come up with some cute ideas, but her theology was questionable. I often had to grit my teeth to keep from jumping up and correcting her.

Kay was a talented energetic business woman. I enjoyed going to her coffee shop after church on Sundays with a few others and stopping there at other times. I truly admired her outgoing concern for others but I think her talents were in the business world.

In time Kay began to imagine that she was called to the ministry. She planned to attend the summer sessions that the first pastor I had followed back in Sedalia had done. In order to enter the candidacy for ministry she had to have the recommendation of her congregation and her pastor. I talked with her about it and had observed her for awhile but I did not really feel I could recommend her. Even people who wouldn't really have wanted her for a pastor voted for her to enter the candidacy. I guess they thought that a little bit of training would fix her personality.

Kay became a real thorn in my side. We tried to be friends, but she annoyed me more and more. She was pushy and I had the feeling that she truly believed she was more suited to ministry than I was. Her husband, Mr. H, was at least as critical of me, from the sidelines. He probably thought I didn't realize it, and if I was as lacking in intuition as he, possibly I wouldn't have.

I began to cast about for an alternate to pastoral ministry. The most obvious thing for me was hospital chaplaincy. Since I had never taken the Clinical Pastoral Education (CPE), which had been optional in seminary I decided it was time to find out if that was a viable route for me. I enrolled in the nine month course and drove to Heartland Hospital in St. Joseph, about a thirty minute drive, one day a week.

The CPE training is much more than just academic or practical skills for being a chaplain. It is like psychological therapy as well. It was a huge experience for me, increasing understanding and appreciation of my own self as well as skills for communicating and relating to others. It too, helped move me to higher ground spiritually. I met new friends among the staff there and in the process came to the realization that I would not be comfortable working in a hospital environment.

I was either stubborn or tenacious or maybe desperate, but I continued for a while to try to become the pastor everyone wanted me to be.

One of the major committees in the United Methodist structure is the Pastor/Parish Relations committee, which we refer to as PPR. In my mind I always referred to it as the Pastoral Police Regime. I had hated meeting with that committee in every church I had ever served. Its stated purpose was for pastoral support; to act as a liaison between the pastor and congregation; to ensure the lines of communication were always open so that the needs of the pastor could be met without he/she having to guess who to approach about any problems that would come up and the congregation could relate concerns regarding the pastor to a committee member, and therefore not have to confront the pastor. It was their responsibility to fill out a form each year with questions about pastoral leadership. They got to say what their needs and desires in pastoral leadership were and to rank their pastor. They were the ones to say whether or not the church wanted the pastor to return for the next appointive year. This committee never functioned as the governing hierarchy of the Church may have meant for it to. In my experience, Pastoral Police was truly a more accurate name for it.

There were two kinds of members on PPR. The ones the pastor went to and begged to be on it because she needed supporters who would speak on her behalf, and the persons who loved to be there to 'keep an eye' on the pastor. The latter kind was there to criticize and undermine the pastor's leadership at every opportunity and would have paid for the privilege of being there if they had needed to. By the time I arrived in Weston I was savvy to the workings of this committee and how distorted it could become. For the first three years I politicked around at Charge Conference time and got my friends and supporters on the committee. But by the fourth and fifth years new members who I was often unsure of were coming along who needed a place to serve in the business of the church and supporters who were willing to endure PPR were becoming thin. At one point a chairman, who I had felt relieved to have serve there caved to the negativity swirling around and resigned, leaving me to the mercy of Tess (not her real name), who conveyed to me the feeling that she believed that I was unsuited to ministry. A pastor in a system like this lives a life very much like any other politician.

Among our new members was a powerful businessman who I will call Buzz. He had built a large business in Kansas City and, looking to his retirement years, had come to the country to retire. He had grown children by a first marriage, but he and his second wife had a preschool age son. They had an idealistic dream of raising him in a small town atmosphere, and chose Weston. They purchased many acres of prime Platte County real estate and built a spacious extravagant home on it in the wooded countryside nearby. They were frequently gracious and generous hosts to church gatherings at their grandiose dwelling.

Buzz was accustomed to being listened to and having things go his way. Nothing in my experience had prepared me to 'lead' a personality like this. I always listened to him and almost always allowed him to implement his ideas, usually with some suggestions of my own. He had come to Christianity late in life, and like most recent converts, was very enthusiastic. He was more fundamentalist in his beliefs than I or most of the congregation. For most Methodists spirituality is a deep quiet river; for Buzz it was more like a thunderstorm.

One of the things Buzz wanted to lead was a Bible

study. Perhaps I should not have allowed it to erode my confidence, but it did. I interpreted it as his rejection of me as a spiritual leader in addition to not seeing me as an administrator, either. He had not asked me to lead any study and did not ask me to assist in leading this one. The people who flocked to join it further reinforced my insecurity. In retrospect, I see that I did not have to experience it as a put down, but I could not see any other way to view it. In spite of that, I kept up a supportive and positive façade about it before the congregation.

The following year I led a Bible study using the same curriculum. The people who attended the one I led were people I considered friends and felt camaraderie with except for one. I was certain that the woman who had become the PPR chair, Tess, was attending the group for the sole purpose of checking up on me. She didn't want to trust reports from my 'friends' that I was any good at teaching a class. I could have relaxed into teaching the class if she had not been present. Her presence grated on me because we had an established dislike for one another, which we smiled civilly and ignored like an elephant in the room.

After sharing around the table about our life journeys, when it was Tess's turn she smiled smugly at those of us who had related humble beginnings in modest, but loving environments, and said, "Well, I guess I have had a privileged life." It was all I could do to refrain from turning to her and asking how she could think that her wealthy, cold self-centered parents were in any way a 'privilege' greater than the loving homespun close knit families any of the rest of us had described.

One of the things I had learned as far back as my HeadStart days was keeping a day planner. I kept it with me constantly and referred to it many times a day. I was confident of my ability to write down times of meetings and other relevant information. However, the more activity increased at the church the more I became increasingly challenged in this regard. Sometimes people would arrange a meeting with me or tell me about someone needing a visit, as I was greeting everyone leaving church on Sunday morning. I felt certain I would remember these and it was a real palm to the forehead reaction when I forgot. After forgetting a few of these I began trying various things, like urging them to give it to me in writing, or keeping a pencil and paper with me. I remember saying, "If you don't write it down, it's like you didn't tell me." But I was beginning to get a bit depressed again and so I kept slipping up.

One day Buzz came to me with a suggestion. He provided a time management course for all his employees and he felt certain that I could benefit from it. He was willing to pay for it if I would go, once a week for about two months. I had been facing more and more negativity from all sides so I thought it would just give him more fuel if I refused so I agreed to go. I drove to the city at the appointed time each week and visited with him about it frequently.

There are certain habits of 21st century western civilization that just grate on my rebel spirit. Chief among these is keeping lists; any list. It is probably the reason I couldn't stick with Weight Watchers. The idea of writing down every thing I ate was very disagreeable to me. Perhaps it was my Cherokee Great-Grandmother asserting herself, but whatever it was, it seemed to me that living the regimented life that the time management expert was recommending was a kind of prison. There is probably room for an entire volume here, but it will have to wait. There is surely some middle ground between being a completely unorganized person who will never accomplish anything, and a person who is driven by schedules and lists to the point of never pausing to look up at the sky. I could not think of writing down my activity at fifteen minute internals all day every day or any of the other lists and accountability tools that were presented. I believe that if this is what is required of me then I am truly in the wrong place doing the wrong thing. I went into the ministry because I was drawn to the spiritual side of life. Many times someone has said to me, "But the church is a business". Yes, it is. I think that may in fact be one reason it has lost touch with the soul, the inner self, which is where true wisdom originates.

After putting me through the time management course and seeing no dramatic change in my habits I guess Buzz truly gave up on me. In my defense, I can honestly say that I accomplished every task and met every need of people that I could realize and did it on a timely basis. I have never understood what else the business minded people of the church actually expected of me. It was obviously something I wasn't being, that they thought I should be and not something I wasn't doing. He always remained on cordial, even friendly terms but behind the scenes he was working against me. Buzz was pals with his former pastor in Kansas City, who shortly became a DS in another district. He would go and commiserate with him about the changes he was trying to make in our church. He got a lot of ideas from him. We had two different DS's while I was there. The first one was a dapper crowd pleaser sort of fellow who everyone liked, but I found out later he wasn't my friend. The second one I had known in the Conference by being on some committees with him and other contacts through the years. I considered him a friend and ally. This one had not been our DS very long when Buzz contacted him and requested that he come for an informal meeting at his house. I no longer remember clearly but it was supposed to be a meeting to discuss the future of the church in an open forum with some invited church leaders to be there. It was not even announced in church. For some reason I was not supposed to feel threatened by this. To have the DS invited out to discuss your church with a lay person who has power in the form of money is threatening any way you look at it. So we visited and decided to form a visioning committee. That's the only thing I know of for sure that came of it.

It was just at about this time that Charmaine came up with another request that seemed impossibly far-fetched at the time. She had received a flyer announcing a "Shakespeare In Italy' study abroad program for high school students, sponsored by the University of Dallas for the summer of 2001. The cost for the program was $3,900. The students would study Shakespeare's plays and the culture of the Italian Renaissance while touring the places being studied: Rome, Florence and Venice. They would study the art, architecture, theology, philosophy, and history of the renaissance. It was a three-week trip, which would earn her 3 college credits.

My first response was to say that we didn't have that kind of money lying around. She said the sponsors had ideas that would help raise the money. I answered that if she could raise it, I would let her go, never dreaming that it would actually be possible. My daughter is the most incredible dreamer and manifester of dreams that I have ever known. She continues to amaze me in the things she is able to make happen. The fund raising ideas consisted of asking people for money. The information sent out suggested business and community leaders so she sent out the form letter to many places in Kansas City and the surrounding area. She got a few responses from those in Weston, and as it turned out, those few were so generous that was all she needed. Always the philanthropist, Buzz came up with most of the money and other donors filled in the rest. It just takes my breath away to realize that my daughter seemed to understand "Ask and you shall receive," much better than I did. I am still learning.

It was her second trip out of the country and it really fueled her passion for traveling, which she has continued. During her college years and beyond she was to travel to many continents and visit many countries that I never dreamed of.

Most United Methodist pastors would agree that it is a definite blow to a pastor's ministry to have a person in the position of chairman of the PPR who is hostile to the pastor. That person has more power than any one person should have in the church. Tess was a new member, new also to the polity of United Methodism. She and Buzz began a conspiracy that I could never counter in spite of the fact that I had some strong supporters on the PPR and most of the congregation was happy with me as their pastor.

During the PPR meeting in February of 2001 in which the committee was to fill out the questionnaire from the Conference regarding pastoral qualities I was asked to leave while they discussed it. For the next two hours they discussed whatever it was and I am grateful that I never have to know. My friend, Betty D was dismayed and almost in tears when I returned. Tess had managed to convince the majority of the committee that I needed to make major changes in myself or be replaced. I remember feelings more clearly than any actual decisions or conversations. What I remember is the complete and utter despair I felt that night.

That was probably when she said they had decided that I should hand in a report of how I spent my time. I countered with a request that she tell me what exactly she thought I needed to accomplish that was not getting done but she never, ever answered that question even though I repeated it many times during the course of that and other discussions. In consultation with my DS, he affirmed that I did not need to respond to that request. However, I did agree to use one of my newsletter columns for that purpose, which I did. She did not find my newsletter response to be adequate. It was clear that she and Buzz and a handful of others were out for blood.

For most of the time that I had been in the ministry I had returned time after time to the question of leaving it. From the time I had been in Sweet Springs and the DS had asserted that I was 'ineffective' the question had never completely left me. When things were going well I enjoyed being a pastor but in times like this I knew that I simply could not endure the stress. When I questioned myself about it I would always scream internally, "But where will I go, what will I do?" Never would I be able to find a life as comfortable and sustaining materially as the pastorate had been. It was terrifying to think of leaving and have nothing to fall back on. If it was just myself, and I didn't have to think of providing for Charmaine, I would have left long ago. In time I was to find out just how real those fears were to become.

In the United Methodist Church appointments are set annually by the bishop and cabinet. In the spring of 2001 our District Superintendent notified me that the cabinet would appoint me to serve in Weston for the coming year. It was always a relief to be reappointed but my relief this time was muted. I knew emphatically that I was not going to leave Weston for a year no matter what I had to do because Charmaine was coming up on her senior year and there was little doubt that she would be the valedictorian of her class. I was not going to do anything that would take that honor, which she had worked so hard for, from her. She had probably been working on that ever since the day when she was five years old and I had told her she would need to get scholarships to go to college. She had let no moss grow in her path ever since.

Chances are good that she would have received the scholarships regardless of where she went her last year, but it would have been a sad lonely year. I even entertained the thought, for about five minutes, of going to another appointment and letting her stay with friends in Weston for the last year. That too, would have been a sad lonely year for both of us. She would be going away to college soon enough; I wanted to spend the last year with her. The stresses and challenges of pastoral ministry in the last two years had taken all the joy out of it and I had completely lost my confidence. I still didn't have the answer to the consuming question, "Where will I go? What will I do?" But I had decided it would not be this, here.

On March 11, 2001 I made this announcement at the close of worship. "For a very long time I have struggled with a very difficult decision. It is necessary to tell you, on this day, the outcome. Even though I have been assured that I would be reappointed to serve Weston in the coming year, I have requested to be placed on voluntary leave of absence. Weston UMC will be appointed a new pastor.

It is with sadness that I make this decision. I care very much about this church and I have made a lot of friends here. I will miss many things about serving as your pastor. But I believe this is best for me and for the church.

I will not be appointed to another church, but will be doing something else. Charmaine will be finishing up high school next year at West Platte. While I don't yet know what that 'something else' will be, I have finally decided to let God be in charge. There is great relief in turning one's life over to God. The first thing I have learned is you have to let go of what has been before you can take hold of what will be. That has been the hard part. We will have three more months to say and do all the things needed to make a good ending to my time here, and prepare for a good new beginning. I believe God has great things in store for all of us."

After the service while I was in my office Mr. H came in and with a huge gleeful smile and a self-satisfied attitude congratulated me on "The best decision I had ever made". He was just so pleased it was enough to make me want to stab him through the heart, because that is what I felt had just happened to me. In that moment I was suffering great pain and here was this man in a celebratory mood rejoicing in my suffering. It is difficult not to hate a person like that, who obviously did not have an ounce of human kindness or sensitivity in him. In the years since it has become another pearl I have added to my wisdom to realize that, "what other people think of me is none of my business". His thoughts contaminate his own brain and cannot touch me if I don't allow them to.

It was almost three months between the time I made

the announcement and my last Sunday. This was the most excruciating difficult time of all. People were so anxious to look to the future it was as if I was already gone. But Buzz put the lag time to good use. The instant he knew that I was going he took it upon himself to find a way to not only provide a new parsonage for the incoming pastor, but to put up the money himself to raise the salary substantially. He by-passed all protocol and channels of communication by contacting the District Superintendent and making that offer to the Conference. The United Methodist Church is not one to turn down money for any reason, so the deal was accomplished. His reasoning was that a better salary would provide a better pastor; it is my belief that part of what that meant was, 'a male pastor'. Such a pastor would certainly not want to live in the current parsonage.

I don't know if he believed his generosity would make him a hero, or if he cared. I have no doubt that he felt very strongly that this was something that needed to be done for the good of the church and that he was called upon to do it because he could. There were other people in the congregation who were very moneyed also. But I do not believe any of them would have seen this kind of dramatic action to be something actually good for the church and it is a little surprising that the Conference would so quickly grasp such a scheme.

Sagely advice might have counseled him and the church against it if he had actually approached the church first, but in spite of that, wouldn't you know - God's hand was guiding the entire process. Buzz and a few other church leaders found a wonderful house high on a hill overlooking Weston to rent for the incoming pastor while a new parsonage was built on land they purchased with

Buzz's money. I had visited the house when the owner had died and some of us from the church had gone to visit the family. It was almost as grand as the house Buzz had built for himself. It was not recommended for a permanent parsonage because it was on such a steep incline that there was concern about getting up and down when the weather was icy.

Because of these arrangements Charmaine and I were allowed to remain and pay rent on the house on Blackhawk Street for the next year. Even though I did not know what I would do for a source of income I didn't think I would be able to come up with the full rent the house was actually worth so the church board agreed to rent it to me for less than an outside party might have paid. I still had more friends than enemies and I began to understand that God was in control and we were going to be alright.

The philosophy the Conference had tried to maintain about parsonages is that the value of the pastors residence should fall somewhere in the median range of those of the parishioners; with an equal number of their residences worth more and an equal number worth less. However, the parsonage that Buzz provided out on the highway, just outside of town was well beyond the median. It was far more house than most churches in the Conference could provide. Maybe Buzz and those who applauded him for his action believe that it will inspire a pastor to work very hard to feel worthy of such a residence. I am sure that every pastor who has ever lived in it has been overwhelmed by its richness, and surely intrigued by the story of how it came to be. I wonder how much of the story they have passed along to them.

At a farewell reception it was Tess's duty to present

me with gifts of appreciation. It almost seems that in this particular situation they could have arranged for someone else to do it, since it felt like to me that it was practically she alone, who was responsible for my leaving. We managed to be quite cordial to one another. The church gave me a large framed picture of the historic old building which had been signed around the border by most of the congregation, and a heavy leaded crystal bowl. The picture particularly is a treasured object which has always hung in a prominent place in the many houses that I have lived in since.

I was, and still am, sorry for the people who still regarded me as their pastor, who I had to leave. I am sorry I could not have stood up to the criticism. None of the persons who worked so hard to get me to leave had much of anything to say after that but I received tearful visits from several who were angry and hurt that I had been pushed out. One even vowed never to enter the church again. I don't know what Charmaine had to hear from school or people in town that last year. I hope it wasn't too hard; but she's pretty strong minded, much more than I am.

At a final meeting at the church with the DS to make arrangements for the new parsonage he remarked before the group that after my voluntary leave was up he was sure I would return to be appointed to a church somewhere in the Conference. I was grateful to him for making it clear that at that time I was in good standing with the Conference. Thus ended the five best and worst years as pastor in Weston. A part of me will always remain there.

MY LIFE AS AN EXPATRIATE

THE LAWYER'S OFFICE ACROSS the street from the church was most kind in allowing me to send faxes to places I was applying to for work. Who knows what the rest of the community thought about this strange United Methodist situation. I almost had the feeling that there was a certain amount of empathy from people I didn't even know. I applied everywhere I could think of whether they were advertising an opening or not.

My memory is a blur about when I received the career counseling, but there were two other times that the Conference provided that kind of assistance. I think this was one of those times. I went for several day long sessions with a career counselor and took tests that evaluated my values, beliefs, attitudes and skills. The tests revealed that I should have become a counselor and that if selling something was the last job on the planet, I would have to live under a bridge; or something like that.

During the summer I was able to do some temporary work for agencies in Kansas City. One of the placement counselors bristled when I mentioned that I would enjoy doing the work that she was doing. We managed to squeak through the summer on what I got from temporary work. I was beginning to find out that a woman over 55 was not going to find it easy to find any work anywhere. The only real qualifications I had were my seminary degree and fifteen years experience as a minister which didn't mean much to the business community.

When Charmaine started her senior year at West Platte I was still looking for work. I tried to talk myself into doing substitute teaching but remembering the horrors of my teaching years, I just couldn't bear the thought of it. The job counselor had told me that the best way for me to find anything was through networking. That is exactly how I was able to secure the position I finally found.

September 10, 2001 was an ordinary day. I went to St. Joseph that day and interviewed for a position at InterServ in St. Joseph. The director of InterServ was a man who had been on the HeadStart staff years ago at the time of David's death; he remembered me well. InterServ is a social services agency supported by churches and other community groups, including the United Way. It was one of the mission outreach organizations supported by United Methodists. I had always admired their work and the thought of working with them was exhilarating to me.

It was a job that intrigued me and I wanted to do it. I talked with Jeanne A, who was to become my supervisor. She described the Transitional Housing Specialist as one who would help women and children, displaced by domestic violence, to find a new place to live, employment, childcare, and all the other things that are needed to start a new life. I was to manage a program called 'Living Successfully'.

The next day, September 11, full of hope and apprehension about what I would do if I wasn't offered that position I so much wanted, I waited in silence. I did not turn on a TV or radio and no one called me. Little did I realize the turmoil that the world outside was experiencing. If I had still been a pastor I would have been in the midst of it, there at the prayer gatherings, and crowded around a television somewhere. Instead, I heard it first from Charmaine when she came bursting through the door after school. "Have you seen the TV? Do you know what's happened? Two airplanes crashed into the World Trade Center in New York. Thousands of people are killed. There's total destruction." The words came tumbling from her as she ripped through the house toward the TV. There with Charmaine I saw it and heard it for the first time, the same as everyone else had been all day.

All that evening we sat and watched with anguish, the images from New York along with the rest of America. In minutes I was caught up on the details and began to experience our collective anger and despair. For years I would hear people talk about where they were on 9/11 and I would remember too. On September 13 I started to work at InterServ in St. Joseph.

The staff at InterServ had cultivated a family sort of atmosphere which was cooperative in nature and easy to become a part of. There was a variety of duties and activities in addition to my main job, which included helping out in the food pantry especially during those times when donations were coming in and going out rapidly. It could get hectic, but I loved it.

To find clients for my program I went frequently to the Shelter for Battered and Abused Women and their children at the YWCA. The offerings of the Living Successfully program were a genuine bonus for the women who were lucky enough to get into it. There was only enough funding for a few participants so there was some competition for the slots. In addition to my assistance in helping them locate a place to live, the program paid much of the rent for the first six months. I would continue to make weekly visits during that time to monitor their progress. Often they needed moral support and someone to talk to about their struggles as much as anything.

The shelter staff was well acquainted with the guidelines of the program and helped me by keeping an eye out for the girls they believed could be responsible and live up to the expectations of becoming independent. I enjoyed going there to interview the women who wanted to talk to me about getting in the program. They all wanted so much to be out of the shelter and on their own. We often talked about a range of subjects so that I sometimes felt that I was in the position of a counselor. It was a great learning process for me to learn to discern those who would say anything to make a good impression. Most were very good at saying whatever they thought would help their case. I learned to rely on the reports from the staff regarding how hard working or dependable they were and how well they followed the shelter rules.

After a few months it was determined that there would not be enough funding to keep me at a full time position and my hours were cut. I had already been struggling tremendously and that was a hard blow. The first month my pay was slashed when I went to take the rent to Mary Edna, who was the church treasurer, I could only take her half of it. I was so distraught I even said, "I guess they'll have to put us out on the street." though I had complete faith that they would not. Mary Edna was reassuring and said not to worry about it. After the next board meeting she told me that it was arranged that the rent would be taken care of. I didn't know what exactly that meant and it was only after I left Weston that I learned that several friends were taking turns chipping in the rent for me when I could not. I am deeply humbled in the face of such caring and years later even as I write these words I am amazed at the incredible grace of God and grateful to these friends. There were those on that board who really would have put us out on the street. I believe they thought that I should move to the city or somewhere where I could get a better paying job because they were not sympathetic to my determination to remain there for Charmaine. They did not grasp or perhaps did not care, that the job market was not open to older women and that I was already in a very precarious situation.

The more I visited the shelter the more I was drawn to the women who had sought refuge there. I was also building a rapport with the staff, who I greatly admired for their compassion which often had to take the form of tough love. That is how the process of networking continued when a position opened up for facilitator of the support group at the shelter I was ready and eager to take over. It was also part time, but the shelter staff also took turns doing night duty in the shelter office once a week. With those part time hours I was getting a little financial relief as well as doing something I really felt was significant and rewarding.

Nothing I have ever done has touched me as deeply and profoundly as being with those women who had suffered abuse at the hands of someone they wanted to love and trust. I entered into their stories as I listened. The support group was required for the shelter residents to help them in processing the experiences that had brought them there. Often they did not want to come and when there did not wish to share because it was too painful. Sometimes they would say, "I don't want to talk about it, it only makes it worse". I explained that it was like cleaning a wound. It was necessary to purge the toxins or poison, and sometimes that hurts, but like tears, it is cleansing. The other reason for being together was that hearing one another's stories helped them each to heal. Often they bonded because of their common shared experiences.

After an hour or more of hearing their anger, hurts and despair we always ended our group meetings with prayer. I thought about collecting the stories I was hearing from them into a book and naming it 'Prayers From the Shelter'. But because so much of my attention was required to keep my own life afloat I did not even keep a journal of those conversations. Driving back home to Weston after group meetings I was overcome with a sense of great love toward them. Often I would laugh because these women could be very witty, and often I would cry because they were so tragic. I tried to hold out hope to them, but a great truth became evident: that it is impossible for a person who has never been shown love, to understand what it is. They were in various stages of crisis; some would recover and become strong and have much to give. Others were so deeply scarred that they had never experienced real healthy love from anyone and did not really believe it was possible.

There was an occasion during the year in which I was visiting with some other UM pastors. They wanted to hear about what I was doing. As I described the work and expressed my feeling that victims of domestic violence were a group that the church wasn't giving much thought to, one of my colleagues suggested that I inquire about being placed in a category the church calls extension ministry with my work being the ministry. That was intriguing to me because it would keep me in the connectional system and I thought it might be an opportunity to regain health insurance and pension which I did not get while on voluntary leave. But most of all it would simply be a recognition that the work I had found was valid ministry, recognized by the church.

I contacted the Conference office and dutifully filled out the required paperwork to apply for extension ministry. I due time I was given a time and place to meet with a committee to review the request. The committee was only two persons. One was the man who had been the DS when I first went to Weston and the other was a clergy woman who had entered the ministry after me and who I did not know. In our discussion the DS told me that this setting for ministry did not meet the requirements of extension ministry because the employer did not require a clergy person for the position. It did not matter that in fact, I was a clergy person doing ministry the same as I would whether it was required or not. He went on to say that in the new restructuring of ordination that the church had evolved only Deacons were in settings such as this.

Before I continue this I must make it clear that at the time of my ordination the Deacons orders were a preliminary to being an Elder. There was more status involved in being an Elder. I believe this is fairly well engrained in the very hierarchical system the Methodists have in place. Now they were trying to backpedal and say that Deacons and Elders are equal just doing different tasks. While I agree with that assessment so heartily that I wish they had come to it a century earlier, the fact still remains that for a person who has already been ordained to both orders the Elders was a greater one. It took more time, work and scrutiny to attain and it was a greater honor.

The next thing this DS said was, "There is a process in

place in which you could give up your Elders orders and be a Deacon so that you could do extension ministry." With a bit of sarcasm, I calmly remarked, "I bet there is!"

I finally got it that this man did not want to see me continue as an Elder and ever be appointed to a church again because I did not fit the corporate model of the UM Church. I was a round peg trying to fit into a square hole. The interview was over shortly after that. Neither of them had shown the slightest compassion toward victims of domestic violence or any indication that it was an area of mission the church should be concerned with. The very idea of saying that in order to do a certain kind of service a person must give up the recognition they have worked hard to attain is a little like saying that if the CEO of a company is found emptying his trash he must be demoted to custodian.

After that I began to feel even more disenfranchised from the UM Church. During the last year that we lived in Weston and I was not a pastor Charmaine and I drove to Good Shepherd UM Church in the north part of Kansas City. The pastor there was a friend who I had gone to seminary with. I'm going to call him Denny because I never knew anyone by that name. It is interesting that the professors in seminary who told me I would be a good minister and encouraged me, were critical of Denny. With those few exceptions, he was everyone's fair-haired boy. He was the corporate game player they were looking for. He was very successful in the system and had a large fast-growing urban church. He was one of the best preachers I ever knew and I was very grateful for his words after 9/11. I only visited with him briefly about my activities during that year. He seemed amazed when I told him about my experience of being invited to give up my Elders orders.

During the last few months of Charmaine's senior year the West Platte school board became nervous about the increase in school shootings across the country. In what I consider a zealous overreaction to it they made a ruling that students could no longer carry backpacks to class. They reason they gave was that it was cluttering up the aisles in the classrooms. Everyone knew the reason was that they thought it would reduce the risk of concealed weapons, but that isn't what they were saying. They also told students that it was a state ruling. Checking with her friends in the other schools she had attended, Charmaine verified that no other schools were enforcing such a rule. It made her quite angry. She had carried a backpack every day since kindergarten and now in the last few months of high school they were trying to take away what she considered a necessity. She steadfastly refused to comply. I agree that it was a stupid unjust rule. In retrospect there are several things I wish I had advised her to do, such as taking it up with the school board. I think the other students were intimidated and were being told by their parents, "It's a rule, just do it". Personally, I don't think stupid rules need to be obeyed, but one does need to make your position clear to those in charge with the goal of getting the rule changed. I'm not sure how she was able to get by with it as much as she did, except that most of the teachers just looked the other way; all except for the librarian. Charmaine started going far out of her way to avoid walking past the library because she always got called out for having the backpack. She, the class valedictorian, had to serve detention for it at least once. I was proud of her for taking a stand against an unnecessary rule that didn't make sense. I have to smile every time I see the sign, "Well-behaved women seldom make history".

The day of Charmaine's graduation from high school was one of the happiest, proud days of my life. She was, indeed the valedictorian and Matt's son was salutatorian. Every student from the UM Church was an honor student, in the top tenth of the class. The only cloud in an otherwise perfect day was the way the principal introduced Charmaine. It seemed that he must have held a grudge against her, I suppose as a result of the backpack situation. This was the sixth annual graduation I had attended, as pastor of the UM Church and also because Charmaine played in the band each year. Always the principal would give the valedictorian a nice introduction, saying what they had done, naming their accomplishments, and just a little personal note about them. However, when he introduced Charmaine all he said was, "This year's valedictorian is Charmaine Crabaugh". I was stunned.

She was really nervous about standing before the huge crowd to speak. I regret that I did not try harder to offer suggestions about the speech. She offered a very short, witty personal reflection about her classmates, which was unique to her.

The day was like a homecoming of sorts. My sister, Jan came, Kay H, from Wichita and Grandma and Grandpa Crabaugh from Kansas City. After we had found a seat on the bleachers for the ceremony Dixie and Mike came toward us looking for a seat. It was a wonderful surprise because I didn't even know they were coming. The other surprise was that her father, Les, came with his wife. I didn't see them but he spoke to Charmaine after the ceremony and gave her $350, which he said was for a down payment on a car. She had been admitted to Oberlin

College in Oberlin, Ohio and I didn't think it was enough of a down payment for a car that could be expected to make that trip safely so it went for other things.

After the graduation ceremony there was a big gathering at our house on Blackhawk Street. I had a cake specially made that said 'Congratulations Charmaine, #1'. The family and friends who had come for it were all there and also many church friends who dropped in. Sue from across the street brought some flowers from her garden to help decorate. It was a proud and happy occasion; a glowing crown to all our days in Weston as well as Charmaine's growing up years.

ST JOSEPH

THE WARM GLOW WAS not to last. Within days of graduation I received a curt letter from the UM Church board. It stated that I must vacate the premises by June 30 or a lawyer would be contacted to press charges. A simple friendly phone call to remind me of that agreement would have been more than enough. It was like killing an ant with a firing squad. It was the most hostile act I think I ever received. I was so hurt and angry that I took it to the new pastor to see if he could shed any light on the severely contentious tone of the letter. He said he didn't know anything about it, but it helped a little just to talk to him about the extreme vindictiveness some in his congregants were capable of.

I quickly found a little vintage bungalow type house on Pacific Street in St. Joseph that I could afford if I could hold on to both part time positions. It was much smaller than the house in Weston and I had to let go of several items, a process that was to continue each time I moved in the next few years. Even after giving away a few pieces of furniture the five room house was cramped and not quite comfortable. I did not even look at apartments because I was determined not to become an apartment dweller. My sister, Jan and her son Jody and son-in-law, Kevin and some of their friends helped me move with some trucks they had or borrowed. Jody is a meticulous truck packer but it was very late into the night when we arrived at the house in St. Joseph and had everything unloaded.

The house had a yard and this time there was no one to come to my rescue for the mowing. The old mower from Sedalia simply was too hard for me to start. After several attempts at mowing I finally hired a young man to do it and gave the mower to one of the girls in my program who I had got settled into her own place. In a space along one side of the house I planted zinnias. There was only one side yard because the other side was so close to the neighbors there was only a wall and no space to walk. There were some curious rock arrangements and old partly overgrown concrete work that seemed to indicate there had once been a garden with a fountain or maybe a fishpond. The house had a rickety back porch which was crammed to the gills with everything from Christmas decorations to gardening tools and boxes of other things. It was a little like mountain climbing whenever I had to go searching for something.

I was outnumbered by the animals; the three cats, Abby, DJ, and Ernie and the rabbit, Aretha. In the smaller quarters, the cats, who had never been good buddies, each staked out a room as their territory. Poor Aretha had to spend much of her time in her cage on the back porch, although I usually brought her in to watch TV with me like Charmaine used to do whenever I was home for an evening. I tried to keep her warm with an electric heater out by her cage. It was probably the stress of moving and being away from Charmaine's attention as much as anything, but the ten year old bunny died while Charmaine was home for Christmas break. We buried her in a grassy spot that in earlier times must have been full of flowers and beauty.

Early in the spring Ernie got tired of being cooped up all winter and got the urge to roam. He seemed to stay close to his new home and I got used to him being out for a few hours each day. One day he didn't show up for supper and for days after I was looking for him and putting up flyers about a lost cat. My friends at InterServ would inquire if he had come back yet. Almost two weeks later I had an unexplainable urge to go down the narrow dark steps to the basement. There on the floor under the window was the small black lifeless form of Ernie. He had apparently been struck by a car and managed to make it in through the window. He had been here all these days and I didn't know to look there. I was devastated. He was a good friend and Charmaine and I missed the little Arkansas Traveler often. I buried him next to Aretha in the old garden ruins in the back.

St. Joseph is an old historic town on the banks of the Missouri River. The magnificent old cathedrals and castle like homes near the downtown area speak volumes of the glorious hey day of its beginnings when it was a major route of commerce along the Missouri. In its beginnings it was more significant than Kansas City, a few miles to the south on the same river. Everyone knows the stories that possibly school children all over Missouri and maybe in other places learn about St. Joseph. The spirited statue of a pony express rider setting out on his brisk steed for the west is a landmark, as is Patee House and the house where Jesse James was shot. You can tell much about the character of a town by its nicknames; Joe Town doesn't have to try as hard as some places to retain its historic ambiance. Maybe they're working too hard to keep the unemployment and crime rates down to have much left over for a lot of touristy frills. In keeping with the spirit of this place, I would sometimes get the distinct feeling that

I was rubbing elbows with the descendents of Jesse James. It's a real place with not much pretense about it.

I liked St. Joe and I was comfortable in the blue collar neighborhood I lived in. I still have a picture of Calamity Jane and a copy of the original poster advertising for pony express riders, "WANTED: young, skinny wiry fellows not over eighteen. Must be expert riders, willing to risk death daily. Orphans preferred." I thought part of it could be an ad for Methodist ministers. It is not an easy place to be in, as the women who came to the shelter for refuge could attest to. The expectation was that they would find jobs, education if necessary, take good care of their children, and not get mixed up with another abusive man. None of these things came easily; here maybe less than in other places they could be.

All of the women I met in my work at the shelter made a great impression on me. I owe them a debt of gratitude for finally opening my eyes to the truth of just how exemplary my own family of origin truly was, after all these years of bemoaning our dysfunction. They came with all kinds of stories. Opal, who lived for years locked up, unable to escape or go out or even wear any clothes. Karen, whose husband poured an entire six-pack over her head one at a time because she brought home the wrong brand. Beautiful Lisa, who had started out with such promise as a cheerful, popular girl who married her high school sweetheart and had been pregnant almost constantly ever since. She had endured a life of poverty and depravity, living on welfare, raped by her own husband – yes, it is certainly possible, and in front of their children. I heard stories of men who have not progressed beyond the animal-man stage of evolution.

But there were also the women who were themselves

abusive. They spoke proudly of how "no one was going to treat me that way". Sometimes there was tension between those who were victims and those who were abusers. Tensions ran high in the shelter just as a general rule. One image still remains in my mind from a night when I was on duty; standing in the middle of the hallway with my arms outstretched, in a gesture of keeping two women at bay, who seemed out to hurt one another. I commanded each one to return to her room and not come out until morning, restoring calm for the time being. Life in the shelter was hard because it required cooperation and obeying the rules.

Being right there in the shelter with them for a few hours each evening was a much better vantage point to assess who would do well in the Living Successfully program that InterServ offered. One night Jeri, a white woman, appeared at the shelter with her two black skinned children. Tearfully she related how her husband was in prison for stealing and drugs and her mother, who had always been abusive, would not take them in. In the days that followed I grew to admire Jeri's spirit which I saw as a kind of plucky doggedness. Almost all the other staff and residents in the shelter saw her differently. They thought she was rude and sometimes caustic. I could certainly understand why they thought this, but I could also understand Jeri perfectly. I saw that she was hardworking and intelligent. Those things she did that the others didn't approve of were all for the purpose of survival and doing whatever she needed to for her children. Against all advice, I was eventually able to move her out of the shelter and into a three bedroom house. The day I decided to sign her into the program I spoke very seriously to her, telling her plainly that "I am sticking my neck out for you"; because no one else thought she was a good risk.

Jeri responded to my faith in her with complete determination. She had a job at McDonald's and she was an enthusiastic worker who the customers remembered and appreciated. She fixed up her house often with items she found discarded by others. The struggles were huge, as they were for all the women trying to make it on their own with no help from a family. She worried about their safety when her husband would be released from prison. She didn't have a phone and on days when one of her children was sick and she had to call in she had the dilemma of either taking them with her to a nearby telephone or leaving them alone for the minutes it would take to go call. It was excruciating for her. At times when she was detained at work or for any reason would be late picking up her children from daycare or school she had to find a way to get the message and hope everything worked out. As if that wasn't enough, her mother was always threatening to take her children away and have her declared incompetent. Even when the nine months that she was in the program was over, I kept in touch and visited her until I had to leave St. Joseph. It always seemed that we had a connection, a special bond. I think of her often and imagine that her spirit has triumphed over all the adversity.

The UM District Superintendent over the St. Joseph churches was the same one who was a friend of Buzz. He told me about two churches in the district that didn't have a pastor. I could go there on a weekly basis to preach for a certain amount per Sunday. They were in a charge together, one in Trenton and the other in the rural area nearby. So I began going to Crandall and Grundy UM

Churches to preach each Sunday. Grundy reminded me most of Conway and Crandall was different from anything I had ever seen.

In 1968 the Methodist Church had merged with the Evangelical United Brethren and the two denominations became known as United Methodist. In towns where there was one of each of them they had to decide whether to worship together and leave one of the buildings or continue meeting as two congregations. That is why there are some towns that have two UM churches very close together. In Trenton I would pass the First UM Church on my way to Crandall, just one block away. There were only about a dozen holdouts at Crandall, a large church which had originally been EUB. It had been built to accommodate a congregation of about two hundred. Over the years people had gradually moved over to First Church or somewhere else. The small number and their stubbornness was why they didn't have a pastor. The Conference was reluctant to close a church if the people were dead set against it. They were told that if they wished to continue to meet as a congregation they would have to find a lay speaker or someone else to fill the pulpit. The Crandall Church considered it to be a stroke of luck to have an ordained pastor rather than a lay speaker, but Grundy was a contentious group. They had a mindset against clergy women and never did give me a chance. I made friends with the people at Crandall and they even took my picture and put it on the wall with pictures of all the clergy who had served there over the years. But after a few months Grundy called the DS and told him they would find their own pastor. The DS had instructed them not to tell me that had been decided, but they either didn't get that message or disregarded it. One Sunday when I arrived I was caught totally off guard when they told me it would be my last Sunday. There were some very kind people there and a couple of them even apologized for the rest, saying they were ashamed to be part of such a group. But I found the majority of them to be rude and hostile for no discernible reason. The small group at Crandall accepted me as their pastor and that was the last church I ever pastored.

Crandall had an apartment on the second floor of the church building that was the living quarters for the pastor. It was over an hour drive to get there so I would drive in the evening after support group meeting at the shelter and sleep in a sleeping bag in the apartment so that I wouldn't have such a long drive on Sunday morning before church. It was a very pleasant apartment and I couldn't help imagining how it would be to live there. I thought about where my furniture would go and how it would be arranged. It would be a more comfortable place than the little house I was in. I think I would have liked it but it was just a pipe dream.

This district superintendent tried to appear supportive and I appreciated the conversations we had, but I began to realize how much damage Buzz had done to my reputation in the Conference. This DS didn't really have much regard for my pastoral abilities. He relayed to me that the people of the Grundy Church had said I was 'unfriendly'. They said that at a church dinner my daughter and I sat off by ourselves and didn't talk to anyone. I remember that dinner well. We were asked to go through the line first. We sat in a central location and no one came to sit with us. I wonder if they meant for us to get up and go sit somewhere else after we had sat down.

I began to get the distinct feeling that my

relationship with the Conference was very tenuous. My entire experience of pastoring churches in the Missouri Conference of the UM Church had been fraught with difficulty so I really did want to try to find some other niche to thrive in while waiting for the time when I could draw my retirement. That was one of the things on my mind in my conversations with this DS. The Conference seemed to have no sympathy for the fact that I didn't have enough in the pension fund to retire comfortably and that no more would go into it if I didn't return to an appointment. In addition, I had no health insurance while I was working part time jobs. It was as if I had brought it on myself and it was none of their concern. Perhaps they were right. I was relieved that Charmaine is so resourceful and independent that she was able to obtain scholarships and enough employment as a student that she was doing well.

After moving to St. Joseph I cracked the engine head on our bright 'seriously purple' Mercury Tracer. Charmaine was with me when we found the next purple car on the lot of Cecil Meyers, 'the dealer with a heart'. It was a Dodge Neon, exactly the color of redbuds in the spring, with a decal on the sides that looked a little like ocean waves, making it very distinctive. Again, I was not looking for a purple car, it was just there.

It was while I was in St. Joseph that I finally discovered The Course in Miracles. As long ago as Sweet Springs I had read an interview in The Sun Magazine with Kenneth and Gloria Wapnick about the Course. That was my introduction to it. I was intrigued by it because it sounded like a deep spiritual kind of work that would greatly expand a person's spiritual experience. At the time I was seriously searching for more substance to spirituality than I was finding in any material the church produced. I was actually afraid to look for the book and begin reading because it was controversial and I didn't want to be confused and led astray. On a trip to Kansas City I ventured into the bookstore in Unity on the Plaza and there was The Course In Miracles. Not only the book, but a little card announcing when classes met to discuss it. I bought the book and began going to the classes at Unity, which I continued until I left St. Joseph. Before I opened it up and began to read I prayed to be guided by the spirit of Truth, to show me whether it was Truth from God. I was open to receive the message that was there for me, but I did not want to be gullible either. In the next five years I read through the entire book, reading a page or two a day and doing the workbook exercises. The Spirit spoke strongly to me in the words of that book. No one who truly reads it with an open mind can deny the wisdom of it. The difficult part is that it certainly does challenge old established ways of thinking that I have been taught my entire life. But I knew that I had to get to a 'higher plane than I have found' and to do that I would have to leave the comfort of the status quo.

Another part time position as Court Advocate opened up with the YWCA at the Buchanan County Court House across the street. It was only funded for six months so for that time I went to the court house and sat outside the county clerks' office waiting for people to come to fill out orders of exparte, or restraining orders. It was important to write it in such a way that it was clear to the judge that the person was in physical danger and not to muddy it up with details which might be very important to the individual, but which wouldn't have much bearing on the case from the judge's perspective. Emotional distress, which in reality, is much more controlling and more abusive, was not enough to get a restraining order against someone. I listened to their stories and helped them get it down on paper. Other times I would meet one of them to go to the court room when their case came up. They often needed someone to be there with them just for emotional support. I was just getting used to the court house routine and getting recognized by some of the judges when the time was up. I would have liked more training in that area and to be able to continue, but it was not to be.

The Living Successfully program finally dried up because there was not funding to keep it going. It became impossible to help pay rent for six months for the amount of participants we needed to make it a viable program, with the amount of money available. So in the months before I knew I would be terminated as an employee I tried every way I could possibly imagine to find a job in St. Joseph. No one would hire me for any kind of social work without a degree in social work. I knew I didn't really want to do any kind of clerical work but it seemed the only option. I took the test for employment with the state and had to decide where I would like to be placed. Because I was desperate and also I was acclimated to the idea of moving around from my experience in the UM itinerancy, I said I would go anywhere in the state.

I made forays to about half a dozen towns in Missouri before being summoned to the state capitol in Jefferson City to apply at the state museum. Before I went for the interview I didn't realize the state museum was right in the capitol building. I thought I didn't do too badly in the interview and as I was leaving that day I sent out a prayer expressing my great desire to work in the capitol building. I thought if I had to be employed at work I didn't feel too enthusiastic about that being in a place as awesome as that would make up for it. In a few weeks I was offered the job and made arrangements to begin working at the capitol building in March of 2004.

JEFFERSON CITY

A FEW DAYS AFTER I accepted employment at the Capitol I drove over to Jefferson City and went straight to a real estate office. I explained to the agent what I needed and the first house they told me about was the one. The landlord was an old tall lanky cowboy from Wyoming. He drove me to St. Martins, a small town a few miles west of the city.

The house was a small cottage on a lot with a spacious amount of grass between me and my neighbors. There were peculiarities of its construction that made me think maybe it had originally been a drive up restaurant. It had a little arched window between the kitchen and the outside room that one could imagine might have been a place to hand food through and there was another arched doorway on the other side of the kitchen. It had recently been remodeled with new cabinets and tile in the kitchen, which made it a step up from the house I had been in. The front room was not much larger than a large foyer, but it had a nice French door that opened onto a front deck. There was a basement garage to put the car in and also the dining room table, chairs and buffet, which would not fit upstairs. When I sent my college daughter a picture of the modest little house she responded, "It's so you". I enjoyed living in the curious little house and made it quite cozy. Abby, DJ and the frogs were with me, along with several house plants that had traveled with me for years.

Part of this new experience was driving into Jeff

City every day and watching the capitol building from a distance, grow closer. St. Joseph and Jefferson City were as different as a western cowboy is from a polished Washington politician. It was astonishing that towns so different could both be in the same state. The City of Jefferson seemed polite and refined in contrast. Being the mutable water sign, I could adapt to any place, but Jeff City seemed a little stiff to me.

I went to visit a certain large Methodist Church very near the Capitol building a few times. The last time I went I thought I would try out a Sunday school class. There were about thirty people middle aged and younger seated in a circle around the room. It seemed obvious that I was the only stranger in the room, but instead of anyone coming over and introducing themselves, they went around the room all introducing themselves. It felt preposterous because I was the only one everyone else didn't know. It was not friendly and even the one or two who spoke seemed to be doing it out of a sense of duty, as if that is what they had been told they should do. Maybe it was because the dress I wore was a few seasons old.

Working in the Capitol is one of my life's experiences I treasure. From September to May there was great deal of activity. A different lobbying group would serve food in the rotunda at least two or three times a week. At Christmas high school students from all over the city comprising a full symphony orchestra and a large chorus, all elegantly attired, came and presented a musical program in the first floor rotunda. The beautiful sounds of Christmas echoed and reverberated off the marble and granite walls all through the building. In all seasons the grounds around the capitol were beautiful and I appreciated all the flowering plants immensely.

I worked closely with the tour guides and my tasks in the state museum included scheduling the tours for school groups in the spring months and recording and taking the money from the sale of souvenirs to the Truman Building across the street. I will always remember with gratitude, Connie, the patient, sweet clerk who tried to train me and help me in those early months. She had to be moved to a building just down the hill from the capitol before I was completely confident in my duties and occasionally I would have to ask her to come back and rescue me.

The first few months there was not a permanent museum director but everyone I worked with was very congenial and friendly. Things were never as pleasant again after the new director arrived. He was a young man who reminded me a little bit of a weasel. I will call him Dirk because I don't want to contaminate these pages with his real name. He took an immediate dislike to me for reasons known only to him and he found fault with everything I did. One of the earliest run-ins we had concerned my skills, or lack of them, with the computer. When I asked a question about some procedure he retorted that I should know things like that if I was to work as a clerk for the state. I was dumbfounded, too much to give a proper reply, a reaction which has been so common throughout my entire life. If I could have, I wish I had cleared it up by explaining to him that I had taken and passed, with flying colors, the test given for this position. If I had not, I would not have been placed in this position. What he wanted was a clerk a step or two above my ability. If he wanted someone with more computer expertise he would have to pay someone at a higher pay level. He was trying to get a grade A clerk for a grade C pay level.

His negative reaction had started almost the first day

he was there. Maybe I shouldn't have been so open about my past profession. It seemed he was prejudiced against religious institutions and maybe had preconceived ideas about clergy. Further, I began to learn that it really raised eyebrows when people found out I had been a minister. They thought it was suspicious, or curious that I would go from being a minister to a clerical position. And they were so right. I began to learn more and more to keep quiet about that. Dirk wanted to know what my 'career goals' were. How could I tell him that my career was over and I was trying to survive until I could draw my retirement. Yet, that is pretty much what I told him. So that was the beginning of the end of my clerical career.

When Charmaine came home for the summer she was hired as a tour guide for summer work. She added a spark to things around there and gave tours with a flourish. She was hired just before Dirk got there and he was always disturbed by her presence. She liked to wear the tie that was part of the uniform, tied loose with the knot several inches lower than the collar and she had to get new shoes because the ones she wore were shabby. While those criticisms were probably valid, it was his pretentious, judgmental manner that was hard to take. But it was certainly refreshing to me to have her around for those months and the tour guides and the rest of the staff enjoyed her, also.

It was the summer of 2004 and the presidential race between John Kerry and GW Bush was going full steam. Kerry had a rally at the capitol while Charmaine was home and we stood in line for hours to get a place to stand on the lawn. We couldn't see very well from the sea of people, but it was great to be there.

The Wesley United Methodist Church was quite a

lot closer to me than the one downtown so I began going there. It had a vastly different feeling to it and I found friends there and it became the most important part of my life while I was in Jeff City. I sang in the choir and attended a class of just women on Sunday mornings. I was even asked to be guest speaker for a worship service during Christmas while Charmaine and George were there. I had not known the pastor, Steve, before I started attending there but we became good friends. Steve wrote a play for the Lenten season and it was a great experience for me to have a part in it.

The pay scale that I was on for the state was one of the lowest, and in spite of the advantage of having health insurance and a retirement account, I just wasn't making enough to get by on. Charmaine desperately needed a car at school so I purchased a Dodge Intrepid, that had been a state vehicle and she took the Neon to school. I had been putting moving expenses on my credit cards and using it for other things and during this year my financial situation just bottomed out.

I found a part time job as an attendant at a Laundromat. The man I worked for there was as wonderful as the one at my other job was awful. I would go to the laundry immediately after leaving the capitol. I had to get special permission from Dirk to even have a second job and he was contrary about it, but as long as it didn't interfere with my duties there it was allowed.

We did drop off laundry for people and also took in dry cleaning to be sent to a dry cleaner and returned. The manager, Bill taught me how to fold everything "just like a Christmas present" for the drop off customers. I enjoyed the other workers there which made the work go fast for an hour or two. But most of the evening I was alone until closing time. The first night I was left alone there was a break in a pipe. I had been shown where all the turn off places were, but when the time came, I just couldn't find the right one. Water was running out and filling up the entire laundry. I called Bill, who came right over and with his help I had found how to turn it off by the time he got there. I was as calm as I have ever been in a crisis, but I had to really struggle to keep from being hysterical. Bill said I had done a great job, but I thought he was just being nice, and I felt bad because I couldn't just go and immediately find the right place to turn it off before so much water had run all over the floor. He was there for the rest of the evening running a pump and getting rid of all the water.

I have always been apprehensive about learning any kind of machine so I didn't like the cash register at all. I was slow in learning all about it and Bill remarked about how 'nervous' I was, but eventually I became familiar with it. Bill liked to keep his Laundromat sparkling clean so when there wasn't wash to put in or laundry to fold, or customers to wait on there was always something to wipe down. We wiped out all the washing machines and cleaned all the lint filters every evening. Before closing I had to mop the entire very large laundry and empty the trash. That is probably the most disgusting task I have ever had to do. It is amazing what people will throw into a trash can. Someone has to come along and carry it out. Sometimes late in the evening when there was only one customer finishing up laundry and I was mopping the floor, I would think about having once been a pastor of a church, as I swiped the mop from side to side. I thought about the people I could blame for causing me to be in such dire straits and I struggled then to keep bitterness at bay more than at any other time.

Abby was getting on in years and she seemed to be cold a lot. At least that was the explanation I came up with for why she wanted to be sitting on me constantly. In the evenings that I was home, watching TV, I would hold her and during commercial breaks I would go into the computer and play FreeCell, never even putting Abby down, I just carried her from one spot to another. One evening DJ became agitated and wanted out. I should have realized that was not a good idea, but I let her out and in a very few minutes I heard her scream. I raced out to find her dead on the street not far from the house. I think she had been chasing another cat she believed to be intruding on her territory. I found something to wrap around her and carried her to the house. Almost overcome with grief and guilt, I let Abby sniff of her so she would know, and then dug a grave not far from the house and laid her in it. It was awful to have to tell Charmaine that the little kitten she had wanted so much and had prepared a bed with her name on it when she was just a little girl in the second grade, was gone.

Things at work just kept getting worse. We had a computer software program that was used for scheduling the tours and either it had flaws in it or there was some procedure about using it that neither Connie nor I had realized. It kept making errors, which caused tours to be double booked. By the time the glitch was discovered many tours had been scheduled. It was not my fault, I was running it and doing everything exactly as Connie had showed me. I tried to fix it by reverting back to using paper and pencil, but by that time the damage was done and there was not even any way to discover how bad the damage was. When school groups began coming in during the spring of 2005 they would bring a letter, signed by me, saying the date and time of their tour. No more than three groups were ever to be in the building at one time, it was just too noisy and confusing. However when five and six groups began showing up, all with a letter, there was nothing to be done except crowd them in. Alternate tour guides had to be called in and none of them were getting many days off for those months. The tension was so great you could cut it with a knife. The tour guides were hardly speaking to me and I was so tense I was about to snap. I imagined that probably everybody in the building, from the Governor on down, was ready to string me up. Actually, good old Dirk was the one taking the flack for it. Connie came to my defense and we tried to explain that it was the confounded software. Perhaps if I had been a stellar clerk and this had been my first mistake, it would have been understandable, but this came on the heels of a year full of blunders.

Dirk was tight-lipped but one day I got a call from some Chief of Clerks who wanted to make an appointment to see me and Dirk in her office. When I began to imagine how that meeting would go, after all the hostility I had already experienced I believed I simply couldn't endure it. On the day of the last tour, when the last group had left the building, I left a note of resignation on Dirks door, took all my things, and cleared out. I did not say good-bye to anyone, although I tried to find LT Shelton, the museum curator, who I considered a good friend. I could not find him and I regret that I could not have said good-bye.

There is not any defense for the way I left. It is simply evidence of how stressed I had become. I didn't have anyone to confide in and made a very bad judgment based entirely on fear. Since then I have learned that "fear is imagining what might happen and reacting as if it has". That is exactly what I did.

Now I was desperately looking for a job again and just as in St. Joseph, there was nothing to be had. I found a part time position at RACS, the Rape and Abuse Crisis Shelter. It was very similar to what I had done in St. Joseph except the shelter was very different. It was a new, very nice facility and the way it was administered was very different, perhaps better. The biggest difference in my duties was that I wasn't support group facilitator here. I was only in the office to be there for calls and new arrivals and whatever needs came up during the night a few nights a week.

They gave me some very good training on answering hotline calls. I fielded a few of these calls while I was there, in which a woman in trouble or danger would call for help or just to have someone to talk to. I liked working there and would have liked to be full time, but it wasn't meant to be.

It was a certainty that I wasn't going to work for the state again, although I did apply and go for a few interviews. I realize that I had been justifiably black listed.

During this time I had to cash in the stocks I had bought for Charmaine, liquidate my IRA, borrow on life insurance, sell the dining room furniture that was in the basement, and borrow money from my sister, Jan. Even after all that I was still in debt and struggling with living expenses. Mom had always bailed us out all our lives and whenever things got hard we could always count on her and I don't think things had ever been this bad for me.

Now she was in a nursing home and Charlene was in charge of keeping her finances straight. It made me feel very ashamed to have to call Charlene to see if she could let go of any money to help me out. I had to have been at my wits end to do it, and I should have known it would do no good. Charlene was more careful with Mom's money than Mom had been. That is probably a good thing, but I cried into the phone, "What am I going to do?"

The thought of coming off leave and pastoring a church seemed appealing by this time but it was the wrong time of the year. Appointments had just been made and it would probably be a year before I could be appointed. Even if there was an opening somewhere it would take several weeks or months to go through all the processes necessary. This was positively the lowest ebb I arrived at in these years since leaving Weston.

I didn't really want to leave Jefferson City after only a year and a half. I liked the Wesley Church very much and my little house, and other things about it but I didn't have any really close connection to anyone, I couldn't find work, I felt all alone, and for the first time in many years being near my family seemed like it might be a good thing. My sister, Jan came through again and loaned me the money to move. Pastor Steve and some men from the Wesley Church came and helped load the U-Haul moving van in the searing August heat. One of them also drove the truck to my Aunt Martha's house in Blue Springs. She let me store everything in her large basement and I stayed with her for a few weeks.

At this point I was receiving help from every quarter. I couldn't help thinking how destitute I would be if I was one of the women in the shelter who have no family they can turn to. I would have had to sell or give away everything like one of the gossipy women in Maysville so long ago had predicted, but for the goodness of my family and the friends at church. They were the physical hands of God reaching out and assuring me I was not alone. I will be forever grateful.

HARRISONVILLE

NETWORKING IS ONCE AGAIN what saved me. A colleague in the ministry, who I had known when we were both pastors, offered me a job as church secretary. I tried to tell him that I really wasn't good at office things. He thought I was just being modest. Maybe I should take it as a compliment, that having known me as a pastor, he just couldn't believe I would have any difficulty carrying out the secretarial duties of the church. At least he can't say I didn't warn him.

So it came to be that I was hired as church secretary for the Harrisonville United Methodist Church. Harrisonville is probably as close to Kansas City as a small town can be without being called a suburb. I only stayed with my Aunt for a few weeks before moving to Jan's in Belton, which was much closer to Harrisonville.

While I was at my Aunts in Blue Springs our dear old Abby died. The old cat we had found at the shelter in Lebanon when Charmaine was in kindergarten had been my companion for as long as anybody had. At fifteen years, she was one of the few cats we had who died of old age, which was probably accelerated by the stress of moving yet again. Deeply saddened, I groped about for how to bury her in a way that would bring Charmaine and me some comfort; as I was virtually homeless at the time. Weston was the place we had lived where she felt most at home. She would often be on the steps of our house on Blackhawk to greet the mail carrier and others who came. I called Sue, our neighbor across the street and asked her if I could bring Abby to be buried somewhere at their house. Being the true soul sister that she is, Sue understood the need to have Abby somewhere special. She agreed, and I drove the many miles to Weston. She buried Abby near the herbs and flowering shrubs in her yard.

After I had been working in Harrisonville for about a month I was able to rent a small house from a couple at the church. It was a prefab building that had been built recently and it looked like it could have been used for a store or restaurant but it made a clean comfortable house. It was outside the city limits and I could see and hear the traffic on I-70 about a mile away, from the large front porch. There was a horse stable next to the property which boarded beautiful horses. In the spring some of them had colts and I was captivated by watching them cavort and frolic about with their mothers. The house was on farmland with several acres of fields. Behind the house there were cattle and a large milk barn with many cats roaming around. The people didn't want me to have a pet but they congenially pointed out the assortment of cats that were around the barn. It was lonely not to have any company at all in the house with me that whole year. I missed Charmaine and the house full of pets we used to have; though Pat and Morrison sometimes still would sing their little trilling tune.

It was the Thanksgiving weekend when I moved in, the same as it had been so many years ago when we had arrived on the St. Paul campus. I put up the Christmas tree even before I had unpacked many other things, in anticipation of Charmaine coming home for Christmas.

The secretary position was five hours short of being full time and was only minimum wage. It was certainly not intended for a person's sole source of income and it took almost all of it for rent. David and I used to live in poverty like this, but at least I had him to go through it with me. Instead of a phone line in the house I purchased a Tracphone because it doesn't have a monthly bill. That way if I couldn't afford a phone card at least I wouldn't be going further in debt. I couldn't even spare an extra few dollars for fast food and sometimes I wasn't sure I would have enough gas to get from the church and back until payday.

Almost everything I learned to do for the position was new to me. I learned to prepare the PowerPoint slides used for Sunday morning worship, to assemble the newsletter on desktop publisher, how to use specially perforated paper for the worship bulletins, just to name a few of the things I didn't have a clue about. I was extremely slow and was often there after time to go home. That of course, didn't set well with the church board, to have to pay extra hours to a secretary who was slow and made a lot of blunders.

The ways I excelled were things that have little relevance to being a church secretary and were virtually unknown to the people there, who wouldn't have cared if they did know. That was the way I responded to the public and church members who would occasionally wander in to the office. Sometimes they would need help and sometimes just someone to listen. One woman in particular, wanted to know if I could arrange a counseling session with her. I told her she would have to ask the pastor, which of course, put an end to that idea once she brought it up to him. Occasionally I was able to answer questions about church polity, scripture, and worship that no church secretary could be expected to know.

The pastor was a closed, uncommunicative person. I didn't know him any better after working there most of a year than I had to start with. The rest of the staff was a joy to work with. Jeri, the youth director, was a godsend. I don't know what I would have done without her help. She taught me everything the outgoing secretary wasn't able to in the two days she had to teach me.

In addition to Jeri, the other very dear person on the staff was Rev. George Moore. He was actually the pastor's father-in-law, a retired UM pastor, who was the visitation minister. Rev. Moore was a very caring, empathetic person. He seemed to understand what a difficult position I was in and was a good friend.

This church wasn't accustomed to their secretary being a part of the congregation, and seemed to think it was better if they weren't. I still find that very odd but probably their reasons for it went back to some past history they were still living in. So even though I attended church and visited a Sunday school class, I never found any niche there except in the office during the week. The last few months I was there I drove thirty miles into Kansas City to attend a church pastored by a clergy woman friend I had known since seminary days.

In the spring of 2006 Charmaine graduated from Oberlin College in Ohio. I stayed overnight on the campus to be there for as many of the weekend activities as I could. Dixie and her husband, Mike had moved to Ohio about the same time Charmaine went there. It was phenomenal that they were able to be there with us for that outstanding occasion. It made an already amazing day even more stupendous. I had already met Charmaine's boyfriend, George, but now I met his parents and we all had a very pleasant dinner together.

Charmaine stayed on in Oberlin for most of the summer and only came to my house in Harrisonville for a few days before she and George headed out to San Francisco. She had landed a job in the research laboratory of the San Francisco University Hospital and George was going to try his luck with the music business there. The similarities to my own experience were startling, remembering how David and I had set out for Los Angeles all those years ago so he could play in a rock band.

Eventually my precarious position as church secretary began to unravel. I had always been keeping an eye out for any opportunities, but finally the pastor told me I would need to look for something else as soon as possible. That was when I decided to come off leave and seek another appointment as pastor with the Conference. Thus began the last of my unpleasant experiences with the United Methodist Church.

I filled out the required paper work and went for the first interview with a committee of about four clergy peers. We discussed the reasons for my going on leave, the conditions now, and various things about coming back. They said they could find no reason for me not to come off leave and be appointed. In a few weeks I was again summoned for another interview. This was only a little unsettling because I thought there was nothing else to say about it. This group expressed some doubt about my being appointed again and I was dismayed because as far as I knew, there was no reason for it. I was brought before a final group whose instructions apparently had been to tell me that I could not be appointed because there were not enough churches for elders. There were only openings for 'local pastors'. It was almost as if I was overqualified.

The denomination, or at least this Conference, had

developed a policy that elders could not be appointed to serve below a certain salary level. I would have been happy to serve a part time position but they would not discuss it. Finally it was revealed that former district superintendents had reported that I was 'ineffective' as a pastor. This was a reference to the bad time I had while in Sweet Springs, before I went to Weston. It didn't seem to matter that more district superintendents had recommended me than had not, or that I had left my last position in Weston in good standing after a successful pastorate there. What carried weight was that one of those DS's was still alive and powerful in the Conference. I had made an enemy the day he suggested I give up my elders orders, or probably before that, and I believe he was the one giving instructions to these committees and there was nothing more I could do about it.

In the last interview in relating how impossible it was to find adequate employment, I reported some of the places I had applied. The questioner asked if I would want an appointment if I had been hired particularly for a social services position. I honestly don't know the answer to that question, then or now. If I had been asked about that further, I could have had the opportunity to elucidate that if the work provided a way to attend and watch over the needs of people in a way that I had as minister, I might have been content to stay in that position. We never got that far in the conversation because the committee wasn't interested in my ability or caring as a pastor. It was always only about the Conference.

They chose to ignore the fact that at ordination I was promised, as all those ordained are, that I would always have an appointment. When I brought it up one of the clergy on the committee tried lamely to suggest that I was not willing to go where I would be sent. That was pure fabrication and I soon filled him in on the facts; that I was to be reappointed to Weston, but decided to go on leave for personal reasons. The reality is that if I had stayed on in Weston one last horrible year, dragging the church through a lot of negativity, undoubtedly harming my own health in the process, I would still be up for appointment. But because I had the integrity to quit when it was in the best interest of all concerned, I was being punished as if I had done some awful moral wrong. I was hurt and dismayed to find that the United Methodist Church did not keep its part of the covenant agreement, made at ordination, even though I had kept mine, and no one ever did address that with me.

Since I was not to be placed in an appointment I had the choice of being on 'involuntary leave' or 'honorable location', which would mean that I was not ever seeking an appointment again but was in good standing. You have to be a Methodist clergy for any of these things to make sense to you. Because 'honorable location' had a little nicer ring to it, I chose that. I asked the Harrisonville pastor if I could be placed there because it was the only church I had any relationship to at that time. It didn't mean anything except that my name would be on the roll and they would report at charge conference time if I had performed any weddings, funerals, or any other clergy activity during the year.

I was fifty nine years old and could not draw what little pension I might be getting or social security until I was sixty two so I had no choice but to plunder ahead, and try to find employment once again. After many dismal attempts in which I discovered that age discrimination is alive and well, though virtually impossible to prove,

I discovered an ad in a newspaper for manager of a residential care facility. The ad promised to provide all the training necessary in two days so I took the bait.

The Last Resort Manor was administered out of Sedalia with facilities in several Missouri towns. I had visited residents there in Sedalia and in Weston so I was familiar with them. I met with a sweet personable young woman who was to become my supervisor. She was impressed with my letter of application and resume. The position was as a live-in manager of a care facility. I would have a nice salary and not have any housing or even food expenses. It wasn't something I had ever envisioned doing, but I thought it seemed like a good opportunity to pay off my debts while doing something meaningful. She gave me the choice of a facility in Aurora or one in Pleasant Hill. Aurora is near Springfield and I was feeling the pull to go back home, so I chose Aurora.

A week before I moved I went to Sedalia for the training provided for new managers. While Charmaine and I lived there I never dreamed that I would ever have an opportunity to stay at the historic Bothwell Hotel, but that is where the corporation put us up for our stay. It was a nostalgic trip back for me and I enjoyed visiting with my old friend, Carol, for dinner one evening.

In the training we were taught how to give medications, including insulin injections and blood testing for diabetic patients. I was impressed with our trainer, who received an injection of water from every one of us for our final exam. That was probably over a dozen injections; her arm had to have been sore the next day. I was very nervous about sticking a needle in someone's arm, but so was everyone else in the class and we all managed to do it. We learned really basic things, like taking pulse, temperature and blood pressure, and all the rules and regulations of the medical and legal ends of the business. After two full days of this I was issued a card that declared I had completed level 1 Medication Aide Training. Armed with that and what I am sure my employers hoped was a large amount of common sense and a loving heart, I was good to go.

Once again, it was Thanksgiving weekend when some friends from the church including Rev. George, helped me load a truck and move out of the little house. I had been using the same boxes for about twenty plus years, but somehow a few of them had got away from me. So at the last minute we had to send scouts to local grocery stores for more boxes while stashing things in paper bags and anything we could find.

I could always count on my nephew, Jody, who was there again with a couple of his children to help load and drive the truck. Charmaine had left the purple Neon with me but she wanted me to keep it for her, which I promised to try to do. So it was loaded onto a trailer and pulled behind the truck. In November of 2006 this caravan set out for my new adventure in Aurora.

AURORA

THE MANOR OF LAST Resort was a facility made to accommodate twelve residents, but with only three there were nine empty rooms. I was allowed to store my household furnishings in two of the empty rooms and live in the one which was the manager's quarters. I put as many of my own things in the room I was to live in as I could, making it quite cozy. My plants were distributed in the building except for the ones crowded into the window sill of my quarters. The piano was placed in the main common room and a small desk found a resting place in a quiet corner. I used many of my own cooking pans in the sparsely furnished kitchen, as one of my main duties was preparing meals.

My responsibilities were to plan and prepare meals, grocery shopping, laundry, clean rooms, administer and record medications, do safety checks on doors and alarms. Last but not least, I was the only public relations/marketing agent for the facility. I was expected to recruit more residents to fill up the empty rooms. This was the only part of the job that I really did not make much effort to do even though I was badgered about it constantly. With only three residents this left me a lot of free time during the day but I could not leave the building unless a relief manager came. I was also expected to locate and employ the relief manager. Management was not much help with hiring a relief manager and that was finally the reason I could not continue working there any longer than the year I did.

The three residents, all in their eighties, were wonderful and I loved them all. But I was glad at times to be able to go into my room and shut the door. Living there required that a person be able to bathe and clothe themselves and ambulatory enough to get to the table without assistance. One woman had dementia, the male resident had diabetes, and the other woman was just frail. I soon learned their particular characteristics and we got along well and settled into a routine.

The first week I was there the one who was most frail fell in her room early in the morning. She was not able to get to the call button to summon me. She might not have had the presence of mind to do it even if she had been able to. I had no way to know she had fallen until I got up at 6:00 a.m. and heard her calling faintly from the floor in her room. She had hit her head on the end of the bed and was lying in a pool of blood. I called the ambulance and her family. It was that very morning that my friend, Rev. Moore, from Harrisonville called to see how I was doing. I didn't know about synchronicity at the time, but it was a very well timed call. It was so reassuring to hear a friendly voice after that trauma was over. Her family moved her to a facility where she would be more closely monitored during the night. After that there was only Don and Bonnie for a long time. I thought often that I wouldn't mind having my own roomy house to take care of just them without having to deal with the management which was constantly badgering me to get more residents. It was strange to be knocking around in the large building with so many empty rooms.

I was able to hire a good relief manager for the first

several months. It was only part time and she needed to work more hours than the corporation would allow so that is why she eventually quit. After that I never had good luck finding one. There were a few weeks when I didn't get to leave at all. It was okay to take them places and that is often the only way I was able to leave for even awhile. I once mused that they got to leave with their families more often than I did.

Sometimes when Don went somewhere with his family I would take Bonnie with me to the store. She loved these outings. Once she stopped at the produce aisle and breathed, "Isn't it beautiful" and it was. The fruits and vegetables in such vibrant colors displayed like a lovely, well-ordered garden. Even though she had lived in Aurora her entire life she would frequently ask, "What town are we in?" When I would try to reassure her that it was Aurora she would say in a surprised voice, "Why that's the name of my town!". I would drive her around so that she could recognize a few things and I learned many things about the town's past from her. She had worked at the bank and declared that she had taught a prominent financier in town everything he knew about banking and I do not doubt it. We went by the house she used to live in and other places she remembered. She was always amazed and sometimes seemed to think there were two Auroras because the town had changed a lot from the time that she was remembering. At this point in my life I can agree with her; there are two of every place I have ever been, the one in the past and the one in the present.

Almost every day after breakfast Bonnie would get her coat, purse, and a book or some papers and go sit by the front door to wait for her parents to come and get her. She seemed to think that she was in a hotel of some sort and that they would be back to get her any time. I had never been around anyone with dementia or even discussed it very much with anyone. So I was really finding my own way in how to relate to her. At first I thought I should try to get her up to date on things in the present, but it didn't take me long to realize that it was actually cruel to tell her that her parents were dead. She would go through a period of grieving until she forgot about it again. It soon became apparent that there was no point in putting her through that over and over. One day she was genuinely upset that they hadn't come for her. Tearfully she mourned, "I guess they just don't care about me". I put my arm around her and reassured her that it wasn't that they didn't care, they just couldn't come right now.

Sometimes I would get very impatient with Bonnie's forgetfulness. I would think that if I had to tell her one more time that she was at The Last Resort Manor, what street it was on, what town we were in, when dinner would be, that she didn't have to pay for it, and all the other things she was constantly asking, that I would scream. I think that if I only saw her for a few hours five days a week I could have been more consistently patient, but on a 24/7 basis it was a strain.

The male resident, Don was like an unruly little boy. He had serious diabetes and had to have insulin shots twice a day and more if his blood sugar was high at one of the four times it was checked during the day. He had no respect at all for all the shots and numerous medications the medical profession thought he needed. At times he would lamely try to talk me out of giving him his pills or shots, saying they did no good, or that it wouldn't hurt to skip just one. His family brought him snacks that he really shouldn't have had and it was always a struggle to keep his blood sugar down. One day he took off walking to a restaurant four or five blocks away just to get a Snickers candy bar. He was quite a kidder and on a few occasions we got into quarrels, but neither of us would bear a grudge indefinitely. His wife would take him to stay overnight about once a week and he always went to church with her. I envied him for getting away from the building on these occasions and he looked forward to them with great anticipation.

On the weekends when it was just Bonnie and me I would go to church and take her with me. Sometimes we went to the Methodist Church where her brother went and a few times we went to the Presbyterian Church where she had gone with her husband when he was alive. I knew I would never be anything other than a visitor in either place and everyone there seemed to feel that way also. We went most often to the Methodist Church in Republic, about thirty miles away. Steve, who had been the pastor in Jefferson City was now there, so it seemed our paths were destined to cross once again. When I had a relief manager I could go without Bonnie and visit in a Sunday school class.

The first time I realized how cut off from the world I was because of the relief manager problem was Christmas when I had only been there for a month. I planned to go visit Charmaine in San Francisco but the person I had arranged to stay while I was gone backed out just a few days before I was going to leave. I was very upset and took the problem to my supervisor. I wanted to drop the problem on her because I had made the arrangements and it seemed to me that the relief manager going back on her promise was a problem for the facility, not me personally. I told my supervisor that I was leaving in a few days and they needed to get someone to stay for that week. She informed me that if I left I would be liable for a lawsuit for leaving elderly people unattended. I argued that I was telling her now so she would have time to remedy that; I was not abandoning them without letting anyone know. It would be interesting to know how that might have actually played out in a court. It probably would depend on who had the best lawyer.

I had a shouting match with the supervisor over that after being there only a month. I was extremely upset when I called Charmaine to tell her the problem. She was able to book a flight and come to Missouri for Christmas. Her cousin, Jody, met her at the airport in Kansas City and drove her to Aurora on Christmas Day. So we celebrated her twenty third birthday at The Last Resort in Aurora. I still think Christmas in San Francisco would have been more fun but she got to meet the residents and see what my life was like. As it turned out, there were terrible storms in Denver, where almost all the connections are made. People were stranded and unable to get out for days. I wouldn't have been able to get to California anyway and probably would have spent Christmas in an airport. So once again, what seemed to be a disaster turned out for the best.

In January of 2007 the Mother of all Ice Storms hit southwest Missouri. After three days of wind and freezing rain enormous crusts of ice, some as much as one and a half inches in diameter, weighed down every tree and broke thousands of branches in several counties. Power lines were broken and disabled all over eight counties so that 200,000 were without electricity for two or more weeks. Churches and other public buildings were being used as shelters. Electrical workers from other states, even as far away as New Jersey, came to assist in the aftermath. This part of the state was declared a disaster area and it was a very dismal time for a lot of people. At that time I felt such gratitude to be where I was because hospitals and places that take care of the elderly are put in an emergency system that practically guarantees they will always have power. We continued to have electricity at The Last Resort even when thousands around us were without. At one point I thought they were going to use the building as an emergency shelter and I went around getting all the beds ready, but other arrangements were made, or the power began to come back, so that didn't happen.

Once I had been a little girl who cried because the cedar trees were bent over with ice. I discovered that little child was still inside me, and she felt like crying again when I drove around Aurora or Springfield or anywhere in the area for many weeks. Huge branches of trees were fallen and piled in every yard and roadway. When the debris began to be cleared there were literally walls of branches lining every street waiting to be hauled off. Many beautiful trees were disfigured and hundreds of workers and homeowners spent many hours of labor clearing it all away. There has been a big market for generators in this part of Missouri ever since; people get edgy when they hear 'ice storm'.

Once in a fit of boredom or curiosity, I'm not sure which, I looked up Springfield on Wikipedia. It is said to have the most diverse climate in the country. When we have sub zero temperatures or heat waves they don't last more than two or three weeks, but while they are here they can be almost as severe as they are anywhere. We get a little taste of everything here, it just doesn't last as long as it does in some places.

Now, three years later, most of the landscape has greatly recovered, but there are still scars. Sometimes we might look at a strangely shaped tree or one with a large trunk and small branches and remark sagely, "ice storm".

One of Charlene's daughters got married and I sold her and her husband the Intrepid because I certainly didn't need two cars sitting out in front of the building. We also made another curious exchange. My niece brought me a cat which she was very fond of but couldn't keep any more. She is a tortoise shell a lot like DJ had been. Sofie was shy and fearful so she stayed away from everyone else in the building so that they hardly knew she was there. I was just so glad to have a little companion to keep me company.

During the year I was able to pay off the debts I had incurred in the past few years and then begin saving. For most of the year I was able to go into Springfield once a week. On those occasions I would often visit with my sister, Charlene, and my Mother in the nursing home where she was. There were many times that I would have liked to come for some special occasion but could not because it seemed that most of the time I could not pick what day I would get someone to relieve me; rather it was at their convenience.

I was very cut off from the world during that year. I kept in touch with Dixie and Charmaine and a few others by phone and e-mail. One of the few places in town I got acquainted with was the library and I did a lot of reading. I read classics I had never had time for before such as Don Quixote and Steinbeck and some others. I kept reading The Course in Miracles and wished often that I had a group to discuss it with again. I had worked through the lessons twice by this time. I wanted very much to be able to retire and didn't think a lot about what I would do with my time then because there were so many little projects I wanted to work on if I had my own house and garden.

Sometime during the year I received in the United Methodist mailings, a flyer they print occasionally about women clergy. In it was featured a piece about a young clergy woman. I suppose the idea of it was to relate how capable a minister she was in the face of her challenges. However, this particular woman had every thing in the world that one could imagine in her favor. Her parents were strong Methodists who had even moved to the town she served so that they could support her. Her husband was part of her ministry team and there to share in the caring for their infant child. From my perspective it was a fairy tale dream of how fortunate some people can be. I felt the urge to write a response asking them why they don't spotlight a clergy woman who has overcome adversity, as most have, instead of this one. In my opinion there was no way someone in her place could not succeed gloriously.

Dixie sent me a book, <u>Beyond Positive Thinking</u>, which began to get me thinking in a more purposeful way. What I remember is getting clear that I needed to decide what my intention for life is or I would continue to drift without purpose.

Realizing that I needed companionship with like minded people, the first intention I set was to find a Course In Miracles group. Recalling that the first group I went to in Kansas City was held in the Unity Church, I looked in the Springfield phone book for the Unity Church. I called and learned that the Course group met there on Monday evenings. I was able to arrange with the relief manager to come so that I could go to the group on Monday evenings. There I met Mickey, who facilitated the class, and later John C. and Ruthann, all of whom became very important friends and remain so even yet. The group and the wisdom of The Course became an anchor for me and helped me find my way for the next unfolding of my life. That was something I had not had before when I was faced with transitions and decisions.

Eventually the struggle to find a competent relief manager drove me to a bad choice which caused the unraveling of my precarious position there. I hired a girl for relief work who was not certified to give insulin shots, though she was trying to find a way to get that certification as soon as possible. She was the only help available and I reasoned that if Don needed a shot while I was gone she could call me and I could get back quickly enough. Also, if he was going to be with his wife she could give him the shots. Except for not being qualified, she was good help. Don had been going for a long stretch without needing the extra shot in the afternoon and that caused me to get relaxed about staying around close because I didn't expect him to need one. I no longer remember how it happened, either she couldn't get me on my phone or maybe forgot that she was supposed to. She gave him the extra shot because his blood sugar was high, and she gave him more than the dose allowed. When I got back and discovered it I was terrified that he would go into insulin shock. However, he seemed fine without any detectable signs. It seemed that God was with us and tragedy was averted. It would have been except that she recorded the amount she gave him and when the supervisor came and inspected the records it was discovered and all hell broke loose. This was when I realized that there was no way I could get fired from this job.

Don's children had always been surly and disapproving of me for no reason and now they had one. They called the Sedalia office and demanded I be relieved of duty. The boss at the corporate office was the most contentious person I have ever met in all the pages of this book and beyond. She had been combative and hostile beyond all reason from the very beginning and now that I had actually done something unforgivable there was no holding back her wrath. I have a theory that the only reason employers don't fire an employee is because they will have to pay into the unemployment for them. Or maybe even having someone there who scares you to death is better than having no one. Or maybe, just maybe, they really knew I was a good manager who had made one bad error and they wanted to be sure I would never do it again.

My supervisor came with a manager from one of the other facilities and they went over my records with a fine tooth comb. When they found another error in medications she started in on how people's lives were in danger and this was unacceptable. I said I would leave immediately, and I meant it but this was one time when I was able to be convinced that I might land in jail if I left. I could not leave until they were able to hire a new manager. That was to be a few more weeks.

During the oppressive days that followed before I could leave events became more and more unbearable. Without any warning one day the manager who had come with her to go over my books came and began scouring my kitchen and the carpets. No one had ever even hinted that my place wasn't clean enough. In fact, that was one area in which I got high marks and no one had ever requested that I move out the kitchen range and clean behind it or any of the other things she began doing. So it was particularly insulting and annoying when this began to happen.

When confronted with what to do next when I was ejected from the Manor I knew that this was going to be the best opportunity I had ever had to finally realize my life long dream of having my own house. At the time I applied for a FHA loan I was employed so I was accepted. I made an appointment with a realtor in Springfield to look at houses but on the day when I was to go the relief manager who was to come couldn't make it. So rather than miss the appointment, I piled the three residents I had by then into the purple Neon and we all took a field trip to Springfield. They enjoyed the ride and stayed in the car as we stopped to look at each house. It would be hard to say if the realtor was more amazed or amused.

I might not have had the courage or hope to think that I could finally buy my own house and live somewhere permanently except for the encouragement I received from more than one source. The Course in Miracles, the book Dixie sent me, and Unity Principles were all helping me to realize that we create our own reality. I am not a victim, but a creator. All it takes is to visualize the life you want and open your heart and mind to receive it. I have thanked God every day since for the people and the energy of the Universe that enable me to know this and for the faith to act on it.

It wasn't an ideal way to come to a decision about a house since I had those distractions and not a lot of time to mull it over. However I felt drawn to the little bungalow on Fort Ave. When I had a chance to get away again I came back and walked around it and got a feel for it and a few of the other places. The only thing I really didn't like was that there was so much traffic on the street. There is a large elm tree in the front yard that hadn't suffered too much in the ice storm and a magnificent sycamore in the back yard. It is a little two bedroom house built in the 1940's with original wood floors and a cozy feel to it and a deck that has been added on to the back.

It takes awhile for all the checks to be made to enable a loan to go through and all the paperwork that is necessary, so during the month that all that was happening I lived with Charlene and her husband. In one notable act of mercy, The Last Resort management allowed me to leave my furniture in the two rooms where they were stored until I was able to move them into my house. It was a roller coaster month because a few times I thought it wasn't going to go through but we made it. For a liberal Democrat to be living in the same house with conservative Republicans while the 2008 election was heating up and to remain friends is an example of a miracle in itself. Yes, there can be peace on earth.

Charmaine came home for Christmas and we still hadn't had a closing on the house. We were at Charlene's for Christmas and on December 28, 2007 we were able to move into our first little house.

HOME AGAIN

I WAS GLAD CHARMAINE was home when we finally moved into the first house that is really ours. In every town we lived in over the years we would walk or drive around and point out the houses we would feel at home in and that we hoped to have one day. This one is similar to some of those, but we always thought it would be a two story one. It was a long time in coming and Charmaine will probably never live here, still it is a place to come home to and a place to leave all those college books and other memorabilia from youth and childhood. I gave her a mug with the reminder on it that "home is where your Mom is".

It was one last trip back to Aurora to get all my household furnishings from The Last Resort. Two Men and A Truck were the most excellent movers I ever had. Considering all the moves I have made that is no small endorsement. They carefully removed the furniture from the rooms they were stored in and wrapped them in padding covered with plastic. Maybe I wouldn't have scratches and dents to remember every move I have ever made if that had been done before. I have marks on furniture that I can point to and say, "That happened when we went from Kansas City to Conway", "we got that one moving to Sedalia", and so on.

Since moving into my own house the joyous part of my life has begun. As we say at Unity, 'my life is good and just keeps getting better'. I continued to go to the

UM church in Republic for several months but it became more and more clear to me that what I was learning about Christ consciousness, the nature of creation, and our purpose in it was so vastly different from my old way of thinking that I could no longer be comfortable with their beliefs and values. They were sometimes critical of things that I value greatly; from Oprah to evolution. I had visited Christ Church Unity while I was staying with Charlene, while waiting to get into my house. The first time I ever experienced the warmth and open acceptance there I felt that I had come home. But it took awhile for me to wean away from certain aspects of the Methodist worship that I continued to feel were essential. Even in the new UM contemporary style I had missed the hymns. But the more my theology has changed the less I miss them because my understanding of what the words mean has grown and changed. For awhile I would leave the Unity service thinking, "Well, that was fun, but it doesn't seem like worship". But the more I began to understand the message the more meaningful it became to me.

Now the words of some of the songs of new thought singers and writers that we sing at Unity carry me through my days. When I am starting to feel a cloud form I will begin to sing, "I'm choosing heaven today". When I sing "Gratitude before me, gratitude behind me," I am overcome and tears of gratitude almost always accompany that song. One of the most empowering is Sue Riley's "I am the thinker who thinks the thoughts that have the power to change my life". Just in case I ever begin to think I don't have a choice about the kind of day or the kind of life, including health, wealth, love and joy, I am going to have.

Coming home to Springfield after forty years was like, as John Denver said, "Coming home to a place I've never been before". I had visited family here many times over the years as Charmaine was growing up so it wasn't a total shock but there were parts of town that just didn't exist when I last lived here. Sense of place is important to me. That is probably why I never left Missouri for very long. It is good to be in a place where I encounter a memory of childhood almost every day. I have the constant expectation that I could encounter an old half forgotten acquaintance at any turn and that it would be a joyful surprise. In the southwest part of town where I live I travel streets daily that were only corn or hay fields then. But most streets have names I remember and many places that, if they have survived, look even better than they used to. The nature of the physical is change so we must never expect earthly things to remain the same. Just as trees are reconfigured by storms, buildings, streets, people and human institutions are transfigured by time.

For the first year back in Springfield I still had to find a source of income. Some of my friends had suggestions which seemed very hopeful but none of those worked out. I had received an e-mail about a Crime Victims Advocacy Council that that was trying to get a start in the area. It was a United Methodist based effort. What was needed was a grant to get started as a chaplain for the group. It sounded like work that I could become very passionate about. I even took the online training that was required. It was suggested that I contact church leaders in the area for support in the grant writing and other suggestions they might offer.

The friend from seminary days who I had mentioned in my 'expatriate' days, who I called Denny, was now the

D.S. in Springfield. I thought it was fortunate to have someone who knows me to talk to about this project. How wrong I was. It became one of the greatest disillusionments of my life the day I went to talk to him. He was cold and unsympathetic to all I had gone through since leaving the ministry. He asked with some annoyance why I was bringing this project to him; what was he supposed to do about it?

The hurt and anger I felt when leaving that meeting was as much about being turned on by one I had considered a friend as it was discouragement in getting help with grant writing. Just like Charlie, many years earlier, this one was also placing his status in the UM church before friendship. I was beginning to believe that this church has a definite poison streak in it.

The soul, that part of us that is who we are, is eternal. We will one day shed this body, this personality, this particular human life story, but that which is really who we are will go on for eternity in another form. But even the soul grows and learns from this earthly experience and is surely altered by it.

As I drew near to the end of this story that tells the tale of the first two thirds of my sojourn this time around I became uneasy. I thought, "This isn't really a very pretty picture. I don't have a lot to be proud of. I don't know if I even want anyone to know how much I have failed". But just as quickly the lessons I have learned returned to me. I have not failed. I have been learning soul lessons which I will take with me forever. There is no failure except the failure to learn.

If I had already known these lessons it would have been an easier, and a different journey. If I had already known what I came here to learn, my purpose would have been different. Maybe my purpose would have been only to help others to learn the lessons they came here to learn. But as it turns out, we have helped one another. I have deep gratitude for every soul I have encountered in this life. If our relationship was a harmonious one of friendship you helped me with love and acceptance which no one can get far without. It may be that I owe the greatest thanksgiving to those persons who pushed me to a point of pain and discomfort. At times I fled and thought you were the enemy; at times I tried to reconcile, but always I learned. I wonder if it is possible that before we entered this life we made a pact. You promised, out of great love, to help me learn that lesson I needed no matter how painful it would become and no matter how hard I resisted and believed that I hated you for it.

David was possibly the single most important person in the experiences that have led to my soul growth. It was as if we recognized one another from another time and place as soon as we met. Many times I have thought I would have been happier if I had shared my life with someone else, but considering all the lessons I needed to learn, that is probably not true. In that powerful position in my life he pushed me to learn the first, most difficult lessons which caused me to let go of fears and limited ways of thinking that enabled the permanent learnings I have gained since.

I have great gratitude to many in this life who seemed to be enemies at the time. To all those who made it seem that I was in the wrong place doing the wrong thing at the wrong time. Thank you. I might still be stuck in the wrong way of thinking if you had not done what you needed to do. I might add that some need to learn a bit of gentleness and compassion; still, you got the job done, and maybe the manner in which it was done was part of the lesson. No physical place is ever the wrong place, and no task the wrong task. It is only the place we are in our conscious awareness that can be wrong.

Most of all I have great gratitude to the United Methodist Church in Missouri. You believed in me at a time when I needed a star to steer by, an anchor, and a ship to climb aboard. You gave me a home to raise my daughter in, the best life we could have possibly asked for and more than I dared imagine when I faced the prospect of being a single mother. Most of all, I thank you for throwing me out, which is what it felt like you did, and I am truly grateful. My time with you was finished and if you had honored the misguided promise made at my ordination I might still be stuck and not have advanced to the higher ground I have found. Those persons who carried out the deed did what they felt they needed to do and because the Universe is benevolent, it truly was for the best. My thanks is sincere. The apostle Paul was speaking a Universal Truth when he said, "We know that in everything God works for good with those who love him". (Romans 8:28)

After coming back to Springfield my life began to revolve around the many classes and activities at Christ Church Unity. I have made many friends there and my understanding and experience of God has grown enormously. Because of Unity's close parallel with the School of Metaphysics that became the next step on my journey. In 2010 I began classes there and I have made strides in spiritual and conscious awareness.

All my life I have tried to find a deeper and more meaningful understanding of God and the meaning of life than I was finding in church. In the study of metaphysics

I have found what I was looking for all those years. I have found a more complete understanding of God, the Ultimate Reality, the Source. Scripture speaks of 'seeing in part' and 'through a glass darkly' in 1 Corinthians 13. Now I feel that I can see a bit more of that 'in part' and that some of the glass has been rubbed a bit more clear. Through the study of the Universal Language of Mind dream interpretation has been opened up and the meaning of all Holy Works is illuminated as never before. Those I worship and study with have a true understanding that we are really spiritual beings having a physical experience. We don't just give lip service to those words. We live in that understanding, which eliminates the prejudice and judgments that come when people believe their physical bodies are the real self.

I look forward with hope and joy to the day when all religions will share the wisdom and truth in their holy works with all other faiths and read with open understanding from all others. I am learning through my classes at the School of Metaphysics to "become a whole functioning Self, not dependent on any person, place or thing, for peace, contentment and security". Everything I do from now on will be with the intention of helping to "accelerate the evolution of humanity, by ushering in Intuitive Spiritual Man", which is the ideal and purpose of the School of Metaphysics.

This is the "higher plane than I had found" and I live in gratitude to God for the journey that has brought me to this place.

End Part II